TEACHING SOCIAL WORK

Teaching Social Work

Reflections on Pedagogy and Practice

EDITED BY RICK CSIERNIK AND
SUSAN HILLOCK

UNIVERSITY OF TORONTO PRESS
Toronto Buffalo London

Toronto Buffalo London
utorontopress.com
Printed in Canada

ISBN 978-1-4875-0382-6 (cloth)
ISBN 978-1-4875-1886-8 (PDF)
ISBN 978-1-4875-1887-5 (EPUB)

Library and Archives Canada Cataloguing in Publication

Title: Teaching social work : reflections on pedagogy and practice / edited by Rick Csiernik and Susan Hillock.
Names: Csiernik, Rick, editor. | Hillock, Susan, 1963– editor.
Description: Includes bibliographical references.
Identifiers: Canadiana (print) 20200310208 | Canadiana (ebook) 20200310259 | ISBN 9781487503826 (cloth) | ISBN 9781487518868 (PDF) | ISBN 9781487518875 (EPUB)
Subjects: LCSH: Social work education.
Classification: LCC HV11 .T43 2021 | DDC 361.0071—dc23

University of Toronto Press acknowledges the financial assistance to its publishing program of the Canada Council for the Arts and the Ontario Arts Council, an agency of the Government of Ontario.

Canada Council for the Arts
Conseil des Arts du Canada

ONTARIO ARTS COUNCIL
CONSEIL DES ARTS DE L'ONTARIO
an Ontario government agency
un organisme du gouvernement de l'Ontario

Funded by the Government of Canada
Financé par le gouvernement du Canada
Canada

FSC www.fsc.org
MIX
Paper from responsible sources
FSC® C016245

Contents

Preface

By three methods we may learn wisdom: first, by reflection, which is noblest; second, by imitation, which is easiest; and third by experience, which is the bitterest.
– Confucius (as cited in Anzalone, 2010, p. 87)

The twentieth century witnessed the global emergence of doctoral social work education to guide the newly emerging profession of social work. In the United States, a social research program first emerged in 1915 at Bryn Mawr College in Pennsylvania, with the University of Chicago beginning a social administration program in 1920 (Dzuback, 1993; University of Chicago, 2018). Presently, in the United States, over 760 social work programs are accredited by the Council on Social Work Education (CSWE). Of these, 80 have doctoral (PhD) programs with enrolment exceeding 2000 students (CSWE, 2017). In the United Kingdom, there are 181 nationally accredited programs, with 25 offering PhD degrees related to social work (British Association of Social Workers, 2018). Australia has 32 universities where social work is taught, with four granting a PhD (Australian Association of Social Workers, 2018), and in New Zealand, two of the country's 12 universities offering social work programs provide the opportunity to earn a doctor of philosophy degree in this practice-oriented discipline (Aotearoa: New Zealand Association of Social Workers, 2018).

Social work education at the university level has existed in Canada since 1914, when the Department of Social Service was first established at the University of Toronto (Shier & Graham, 2014). There are 96 universities in Canada, 81 publicly funded and 15 private institutions. Of these, 41 (42.7 per cent) offer degrees in social work: 40 at the bachelor's level (28 English speaking, 11 French speaking, and 1 in both official languages) and 31 at the master's level (21 English speaking, 9 French speaking, and 1 in both official languages). As well, 14 universities offer a PhD program in social work (11 English speaking and 3 French speaking). There are now also three distinct social work programs with a primary focus on Indigenous issues (at First Nations University of Canada, Laurentian University, and Wilfrid Laurier University), and ten Canadian universities offer full social work degrees through alternative delivery formats, including online and distance education. Social work education at the university level is available in nine out of ten Canadian provinces but in none of the territories. As well, nearly 100 community colleges offer diplomas in social services and related fields. Based upon the 2018–2019 annual report of the CASWE-ACFTS (Canadian Association for Social Work Education – L'Association canadienne pour la formation en travail social, 2019), nearly 15,000 students were studying social work either full-time or part-time in Canada. Of these, just over 11,000 were bachelor of social work (BSW) students, with the remainder being graduate students. As well, the CASWE-ACFTS annual report indicated that within the various schools and faculties of social work, there were 614 full-time faculty teaching, although programs rely heavily on part-time instructors, most of whom are either doctoral candidates or experienced field practitioners.

Historically, Canadian social work educators have had limited, if any, prescribed training in teaching and likewise limited, if any, formal exposure to educational theory and methods. Indeed, for most, little time is devoted to learning how to teach social work in schools and faculties of social work, although it can be argued that this critique applies across many disciplines. Most instructors and professors learn to teach by observing their own professors during their undergraduate and graduate educations, often through trial and error, bringing their own style, experiences, and preferences to the endeavour, rather than having a formal program of education and instruction on how to best educate and instruct. What social work educators have in common with the contributing authors of this edited book is that we all learned to become educators in the field of social work without a dedicated book written for our profession by members of our profession. This gap in social work training is more glaring when one considers that social work tends to have more rigorous standards than many other programs, as it is not only an academic discipline but also a regulated profession that has been tasked with serving vulnerable populations. This entails not only internal academic, university-wide, and government reviews but also examination by formal professional accreditation bodies with many provinces, states, and countries requiring individual social workers to join registered accrediting bodies if they are to practise and use the title "social worker."

In attempting to fill this gap and address the complex and uncertain field that is social work, we have brought together 30 experienced professors and practitioners who teach at both undergraduate and graduate levels and created the first Canadian book that provides a framework for educators to reflect on how they teach, why they teach in specific ways, and what works best for teaching in our discipline. While the book's contributors focused on classroom teaching issues, many of the topics explored apply equally to those engaged in providing online education. After the introductory chapter, which entails an overview of current issues in teaching social work, the manuscript is divided into three sections that explore major social work education themes: pedagogy, practice, and additional issues in teaching.

Different skill sets are required for teaching in BSW, MSW, and PhD programs, and few faculty teach across all three domains. Most BSW programs in Canada take a generalist focus, MSW programs provide advanced training, and doctoral programs prepare us for teaching, research, and leadership in the field. Thus, one edited book of 19 chapters cannot hope to discuss all the complex issues arising on how to best educate at both the undergraduate and the graduate levels. As a result, we do not explore the expansive area of practicum education; curriculum design, including the role of distance education; or student suitability for practice. As well, page constraints did not allow us to explore the issues of work-life balance that faculty face, particularly new faculty, in attempting to balance their teaching with their research and service. However, we do bring forth myriad voices, ideas, and recommendations from those who, it could be argued, are ideally situated to explore, evaluate, and challenge what and how we teach social work. This, in turn, will hopefully allow readers to think about their own teaching pedagogy and practice in a more in-depth, comprehensive, and evidence-informed manner. Our hope is that this reflection and exploration will have long-lasting influence not only on the students we are now teaching, but also on the thousands of service users that these students will reach over the course of their professional practice lives.

Rick Csiernik
Hamilton, Ontario
August 2020

Susan Hillock
Peterborough, Ontario

REFERENCES

Anzalone, F. A. (2010). Education for the law: Reflective education for the law. In N. Lyons (Ed.), *Handbook of reflection and reflective inquiry*. Springer.

Aotearoa: New Zealand Association of Social Workers. (2018). *Social work education*. https://anzasw.nz/social-work-education/

Australian Association of Social Workers. (2018). *Studying social work.* https://www.aasw.asn.au/careers-study/studying-social-work

British Association of Social Workers. (2018). *How to become a social worker.* https://www.basw.co.uk/resources/become-social-worker/how-become-social-worker

Canadian Association for Social Work Education – L'Association canadienne pour la formation en travail social. (2019). *2018–2019 annual report.* https://caswe-acfts.ca/wp-content/uploads/2019/06/Rapport-annuel-Annual-Report-2.pdf

Council of Social Work Education. (2017). *2017 statistics on social work education in the United States.* https://cswe.org/CMSPages/GetFile.aspx?guid=44f2c1de-65bc-41fb-be38-f05a5abae96d

Dzuback, M. A. (1993). Women and social research at Bryn Mawr College, 1915–1940. *History and Education Quarterly, 33*(4), 579–608. https://doi.org/10.2307/369614

Shier, M., & Graham, J. (2014). Social policy in Canada. In C. Franklin (Ed.), *Encyclopedia of social work* (pp. 1–13). Oxford University Press; National Association of Social Workers Press.

University of Chicago. (2018). *History.* School of Social Service Administration. https://www.ssa.uchicago.edu/history

TEACHING SOCIAL WORK

1 Issues in Teaching Social Work

RICK CSIERNIK AND SUSAN HILLOCK

Introduction

The opportunity and obligation to develop new knowledge, ways of thinking, and approaches to challenging issues, and then to teach and debate these, are the foundations of academic life. They strike to the heart of what a university is meant to be, that is, a place to develop critical thinking skills and exercise the right to academic freedom. However, perhaps the most important fundamental question in this process, how to best teach, is often given short shrift given the nature of modern universities and the never-ending struggles related to funding, budget cuts, recruitment, and retention priorities. Social work education has the potential to be about transformation, consciousness-raising, social change, justice, and liberation, and to manifest the hope in students that we can create more just systems. An understanding of oppression, its diverse manifestations, and its differential impact on vulnerable individuals and groups is also essential to contemporary social work education. To that, Freire (1996) stated that oppressed people see themselves as ignorant and, thus, view professors as the ones who have the knowledge and to whom they must listen. What then, in an anti-oppressive context, is the best manner in which to prepare educators for this immensely important, complex, and multidimensional role as teachers of social work?

The academy of the twenty-first century has not been immune to the global neo-liberal shift that is reflected in the regression in social rights and government support for social services, the growing disparities between different groups of the population, and the fragmentation of social solidarity (Cwikel et al., 2010; Reisch, 2013). Trends in higher education include rising enrolments but falling revenues and more non-classroom-based teaching. There has also been a shift towards the commoditization of education and a move away from progressive enlightenment such that the employability of graduates is becoming the priority, rather than traditional liberal arts principles such as the free exchange of ideas and the creation of wisdom. This change has led to increasing emphasis on accountability through the standardized assessment of teaching and learning, which we also see in the push towards competency testing in social work (Regehr, 2013).

Kreber (2002) argued that a focus on competencies has contributed to teaching being undervalued, particularly at research-intensive universities and where students, and their parents, want and expect a return on their educational investment, while employers' primary desire becomes readily employable workers (Craig, 2015). Thinking, critical reflection, and debating are not deemed desirable outcomes or useful products when education becomes a corporate enterprise. In this scenario, students become consumers demanding that the employee, the professor, give them what they paid for: high marks and a degree that gives them a job. Added to this is an increasing emphasis on technologically focused online and distance teaching that comes at a cost for how we engage in the educational process as universities become more corporatized. This is occurring in an environment where educators are competing for student attention in a world of sound bites and texting, which contribute to short attention spans and have created a new expectation: educatainment.

Given the breadth and scope of social work, teaching within this discipline, at both the undergraduate and graduate levels, requires a diverse set of knowledge and skill in practice, policy, and research. Good teaching is extremely time-consuming and requires scholarly activity, sound comprehension of one's discipline, and a complex understanding of how to help students grow and progress within and, in optimal environments, beyond the discipline (Kreber, 2002). Social work educators are responsible for identifying what is essential to teach and then communicating that specialized knowledge (Devlin & Samarawickrema, 2010). Unfortunately, many doctoral programs do not fully prepare their candidates adequately for this task (Ishiyama et al., 2010; Rinfrette et al., 2015). Shulman (2005a, 2005b) states that social work education involves the integration of knowledge and skills coupled with a depth of understanding about what it means to perform. As increasing attention is being focused on the student as consumer, there is increasing pressure to ensure effective teaching by professors. However, the term *effective* remains nebulous, especially in an area where those being educated do not yet know what they do not know. Thus, professors are asked to demonstrate that they are competent, technologically adept, and able to apply theory to real-life situations. Is this enough in a practice-based profession such as social work?

New faculty members, teaching at both undergraduate and graduate levels, have reported spending extensive time preparing for courses and addressing student concerns regarding their grades, as opposed to their learning, during the teaching process. This is also a gendered experience, with female professors experiencing more student demands and spending more work hours doing what has been labelled "emotional labour": dealing with student issues (Flaherty, 2018). This time and energy can deflect faculty members' attention from pursuing their research goals, which directly impacts tenure (Rinfrette et al., 2015). One can argue that, from the students and institution's point of view, this is a necessary use of time as it has been well documented that the quality of students' educational experience is greatly influenced by teacher expertise in the classroom (Hill et al., 2003; Yair, 2008). Yet, as Darling-Hammond (2000) reported, it takes from five to eight years to fully appreciate and acquire the art, science, and techniques of teaching. Less clear is whether this expertise impacts recruitment and retention with regards to funding and budgetary bottom lines. Moreover, what happens if the profession's expertise, such as social work's traditional and long-standing ethical commitment to work towards social change, is not valued or desired in the current neo-liberal, educatainment climate?

Reflections on What Effective Teaching Entails in Postsecondary Institutions

> effective [ih-**fek**-tiv]
> adjective
> 1. adequate to accomplish a purpose; producing the intended or expected result (Dictionary.com).
> synonyms: effectual, efficient, good, helpful, successful, useful, valuable

We assume that most professors aspire to be effective, if not excellent, in their teaching endeavours. So then, what does this term imply? What is needed to be *effective*? Teaching entails two distinct but intertwined activities: instruction and class management (Bocquillon et al., 2015; Duţă et al., 2014). Instruction includes the selection and structuring of content, the teaching approach used, and the clarity of the actual presentation. Class management includes how the classroom environment is structured, from seating to the use of technology; the nature of assignments; how students are engaged in the learning process; and how knowledge acquisition is evaluated. Also vital is the instructor's comfort with and use of authority in the classroom and, of course, the professor's teaching approaches (Bocquillon et al., 2015; Duţă et al., 2014). In the university environment, despite much educational theory and research that proves its ineffectiveness, the primary tool of instruction still remains the lecture, with its main purpose being to provide a framework for knowledge interaction and transfer (Ghazali et al., 2012). This style retains a reliance on what Freire (1996) called *banking education*, teaching from the perspective that students are empty vessels in which we deposit knowledge, rather than providing transformational education (Hillock, 2011). This conservative ideology views educational institutions primarily as places where students seek occupational and technical skills to successfully gain employment upon graduation.

Devlin and Samarawickrema (2010) state that effective teaching is oriented to and focused on students and their learning and requires a set of particular skills and practices, as identified by research, that meet the requirements of the context in which they occur. The development of collaborative and relational processes within the teacher-learner environment are likewise crucial. How we engage and what we do as educators, through genuineness, spontaneity, and congruency, mirrors how emerging social workers transfer theoretical knowledge and understanding to their own practice (Earls Larrison & Korr, 2013).

Hativa et al. (2001) propose four dimensions of teaching effectiveness: interest, clarity, organization, and a positive classroom climate. Similarly, the Australian Universities Teaching Committee developed five key guiding criteria for determining excellence in university teaching (Devlin & Samarawickrema, 2010):

1 approaches to teaching that influence, motivate, and inspire students to learn;
2 development of curricula and resources that reflect a command of the field;
3 approaches to assessment and feedback that foster independent learning;
4 respect and support for the development of students as individuals; and
5 scholarly activities that have influenced and enhanced learning and teaching. (p. 115)

Furthermore, Harvey et al. (2003) state that effective teachers are transformational leaders. Effective educators motivate respect and pride and inspire students to practise in a similar manner. Transformational leaders communicate values, purpose, and the importance of the social work profession's mission. This approach to teaching exhibits optimism and excitement about what it means to be a social worker and to work with service users. Transformational teachers act as mentors, helping students to solve problems and complete tasks from new perspectives while developing ideas new to themselves, for there is a positive relationship between enthusiasm, creativity, flexibility, and adaptability, and the academic success of students (Eagly et al., 2003). This push towards effectiveness has led to what some educators consider to be a narrower perspective on teaching but one that many aspire to: competency.

The Emergence of Competency-Based Education and the Implications for Teaching Social Work

In 2012, the auditor general of Ontario released a report examining university undergraduate teaching quality. Among the recommendations was that tenure and promotion decisions reflect a professor's teaching ability and that there be an increased emphasis on teaching as a core element of a professor's ongoing professional development. Social work learning outcomes have increasingly been framed as competencies (Birnbaum & Silver, 2011), which are the "minimum requirements for entry into the profession" (Canadian Council of Social Work Regulators, 2012, p. 4). While the Canadian Council of Social Work Regulators actively promotes competency-based evaluation of social workers in Canada as critical for both self-regulation of the profession and public protection (Birnbaum & Silver, 2011), there is no consensus that teaching competencies relate to quality teaching. For some, the use of competencies is viewed as a market-driven enterprise linked to the rise of neo-liberalism in the academy, as undermining anti-oppressive social work practice, and as a viciously reductionist technicist approach to education that entails ticking off simplistic and reductionist boxes, rather than creating wisdom (Csiernik et al., 2000). In addition, one could argue that the drive to competencies as a measure of social work value comes not from Canadian social workers but from movements in the United States and the United Kingdom that privilege conventional approaches to social work practice (Campbell, 2011).

University education in the United States has been transitioning to a competency-based model of education since the end of the last century. It is argued that competency-based education prepares a student to perform a work role that meets a clearly defined standard. Under this type of model, the educational program identifies competencies, focuses its efforts on the student's performance, and evaluates students on their ability to consistently perform the specific competency, with its necessary knowledge and values. For social work, this implies that educators need to be able to teach specific skill sets within the broader multidisciplinary knowledge base as students must now acquire extensive comprehension of human behaviour, exhibit an understanding of practice theories and modalities, apply detailed knowledge of current social policies and programs and how these are developed, demonstrate and apply knowledge of research methods, and be able to interpret research findings for practice (Colby, 2009).

Duţă et al. (2014) argued teachers should be competent in their respective fields of practice in eight areas:

1 scientific competence – to have specialized field-specific knowledge;
2 teaching competence – to know how to teach and to perform effectively and didactically;
3 transversal competencies – to have abilities not specific to one discipline but that have interdisciplinary utility such as teamwork skills and language skills;
4 relational competencies – to be able to talk with students;
5 vocation and dedication competencies – to be motivated to teach and to have an interest in the stimulation of students' learning;
6 experience in educational institutions – to have knowledge about the reality of educational institutions and of the teaching role within them;
7 self-assessment and professional development – to have the capacity for self-critique in order to improve one's teaching ability; and
8 research – to conduct research both in relation to education and in relation to one's own subject, in order to improve teaching (p. 392).

In a practice-based profession, to be a successful educator in social work entails offering more than just competency. The practice of social work teaching requires the provision of useful, valuable, meaningful, and beneficial knowledge and skills that allow new practitioners to successfully engage with service users and systems across micro, mezzo, and macro levels of practice. However, the current generation of social workers must now also consider and incorporate the appropriate and professional use of technology.

Technology and Teaching

Technology is ideology (Nolan & Lenski, 1996; Saravanamuthu, 2002; Schwartz, 1997); that is, it is a tool that supports and privileges the production of specific types of knowledge and the development of skills that may benefit some, at the expense of others (Cwikel & Cnaan, 1991; Kreuger & Stretch, 2000). The reality of the twenty-first-century social work educator is that our students live in a world of technology that makes information, if not knowledge or wisdom, readily accessible. Technology is part of current teaching processes but should not be confused with innovative or competent teaching. Using technology to enhance participation in lecture-type class environments, to simulate service-user encounters in social work practice, and to offer quality online learning opportunities has become an accepted and even expected component of social work teaching (Regehr, 2013). Ayala (2009) discusses how technological learning has allowed for the increased expansion of distance education, as well as hybrid blended-learning environments, integrating face-to-face classroom time with online components. However, a natural tension arises given the direct nature of social work practice and our knowledge that for isolated and alienated service users, technology, while producing connections, does not necessarily create intimacy or trust (Csiernik et al., 2006). Along with this tension, online teaching formats and delivery methods can lead to increased educational costs, as well as more faculty time and labour spent developing courses, grading assignments, and providing student feedback and support (Cavanaugh, 2005; DiBiase, 2000).

Nonetheless, contemporary social work students rely heavily upon social media to stay informed and to connect with peers. Thus, the use of technology and social media must be considered as part of the teaching repertoire, for despite its limits, social media has the potential to enrich students' academic experience, to increase student engagement and interest in reviewing and rehearsing practical skills, to promote analytical and reflexive learning experiences, and to deepen overall learning. Furthermore, social media can promote a more participatory learning process than traditional classroom experiences (Fang et al., 2014).

Technology is ever present in contemporary social workers' lives and, thus, teaching that introduces appropriate and ethical use of online group work, e-counselling, and e-therapy have merit as these are developing trends in the profession. The increasingly prominent information technology has a dark side, though, one that requires caution and prudence. Just as industrialization brought great benefits, it also brought great disparities, inequalities, social injustices, and oppression, including child labour and environmental degradation. Indeed, these social problems gradually led to the development of the social work profession. So, too, with technology. As stated by one BSW student in a qualitative study examining the virtue and limits of technology in the classroom (Csiernik et al., 2006):

> We are losing interpersonal skills. There is something to be said for coming to class, coming to campus. Interactions with … classmates, learning new perspectives, new ideas and hearing other people's history and actually having one-on-one time with professors, [as] opposed to sitting in your room on a computer. It doesn't add (to interpersonal skills), it takes away. (p. 21)

What Do University Students Want from Their Professors?

A variety of studies have been conducted in various nations directly asking university students how they define quality educators. A qualitative study of students in Trinidad discovered nine prominent themes that lead to the development of the CARE-RESPECTED approach to postsecondary teaching (please see Table 1.1 below). In an online study conducted in

Table 1.1. Components of the CARE-RESPECTED Approach to Postsecondary Teaching

RESPECTED: Attributes students desire in their professors	
Responsive person	Provides frequent, timely, and meaningful feedback to students
Enthusiast	Exhibits passion in delivery of curricula, in particular, and represents the field, in general
Student-centred teacher	Places students in the centre of the learning process, prioritizes instruction in response to student diversity and interests, possesses strong interpersonal skills
Professional	Displays behaviours and dispositions deemed exemplary for the instructor's discipline
Expert	Demonstrates relevant and current content, connects students' prior knowledge and experience with key components of curricula
Connector	Provides multiple opportunities for student and professor interactions within and outside of class
Transmitter	Imparts critical information clearly and accurately, provides relevant examples, integrates varied communication techniques to foster knowledge acquisition
Ethical person	Demonstrates consistency in enforcing classroom policies, responds to students' concerns and behaviours, provides equitable opportunities for student interaction
Director	Organizes instructional time efficiently, optimizes resources to create a safe and orderly learning environment
CARE: Meta-themes	
Communicator	Serves as a reliable resource for students; effectively guides students' acquisition of knowledge, skills, and dispositions; engages students in the curriculum; and monitors their progress by providing formative and summative evaluations
Advocate	Demonstrates behaviours and dispositions that are deemed exemplary for representing the teaching profession, promotes active learning, exhibits sensitivity to students
Responsible person	Seeks to conform to the highest levels of ethical standards associated with the college teaching profession and optimizes the learning experiences of students
Empowerer	Stimulates students to acquire the knowledge, skills, and dispositions associated with an academic discipline or field and stimulates students to attain maximally all instructional goals and objectives

Source: Bissessar, 2014, pp. 14, 22.

2010 at Memorial University of Newfoundland, 330 respondents taking both distance and on-site classes were asked what attributes their proficient teachers had. Nine characteristics were identified that also intersect with the themes from the Trinidad study: respectful, knowledgeable, approachable, engaging, clearly communicative, organized, responsive, professional, and humorous (Delaney et al., 2010).

Similarly, content analysis drawing from a sample of 550 comments obtained during educational surveys conducted at the University of Mons, France, in 2010–2011, reported two prominent themes: teachers' actions (49.2 per cent) and teacher's characteristics (24.7 per cent). Bocquillon and her colleagues (2015) noted that students commented twice as often on what their teacher did as on personal characteristics, such as simply knowing the first names of their students. They concluded that the evaluation of teaching by students is not merely a popularity contest in which the most favoured instructor is the friendliest or gives the highest grades; students attached greater importance to instruction and class management as characteristics of quality teaching. Much earlier, Gorham (1988) had likewise reported that smiling, moving about the classroom, using student names, and having a relaxed body position produced increased cognitive and affective learning.

New Social Work Instructor Concerns

We recognize that today, more than ever, there are extreme pressures on new faculty members, as well as on part-time faculty juggling either professional careers and teaching or completing their doctoral program while gaining experience in the classroom. For new faculty there is demand not only to provide excellent education in the classroom but also to produce research and fulfil service requirements that maintain the integrity of faculties and schools of social work. As discussed by both Hillock in chapter 3 and Yorke and Shute in the closing chapter, this balancing act is also intersectional and impacts gendered and racialized faculty more than those belonging to dominant groups.

A series of teaching workshops for faculty and doctoral students at the State University of New York – Buffalo School of Social Work was conducted, in part, to examine the concerns of new instructors (Rinfrette et al., 2015). The prominent underlying theme that ran through the sessions was the anxiety and apprehension of how to be a successful educator. To extrapolate this to the standpoint of social work students: the imposter syndrome[1] many new students face in entering the field is analogous to that of new instructors teaching them.

1 Imposter syndrome refers to individuals' feelings of not being as capable or adequate as others perceive or evaluate them to be (Clance, 1985, as cited in Brems et al., 1994, pp. 183–4).

Not surprisingly, an initial concern expressed by new instructors was how to begin the first class well. New instructors discussed several issues including how to engage a passive group and teach "less interesting" social work topics, such as macro-level courses or research to direct practice-oriented students. Questions were raised regarding what icebreakers work well, especially if students have already been in class together for one or more terms. The importance of attending to students was discussed, particularly in courses such as policy and research that new social work students did not yet find relevant to their long-term professional needs. Thus, active listening on the part of the professor is just as important in a research course as it is in an applied practice class, and there is a need for engaged activities, experiential exercises, and connections made between research and practice throughout the curriculum. The notion of doing "with" students, rather than "to" them, was discussed as being just as important in the classroom as it is in a practice setting.

Another theme discussed was the use of authority and the balance between attempting to create a safe and egalitarian environment, respecting differing opinions, and discussing controversial topics vital to the course's objectives. Other issues raised were simpler but still perplexing for some, such as how should students address the instructor: Susan or Rick? Dr. Hillock? Professor Csiernik? Then there is the sensitive matter of how to address time burglary: students who continually raise self-serving arguments and issues of excessive self-disclosure, particularly in classes dealing with substantive issues, such as interpersonal violence, addiction, and mental health. The need to balance sharing, particularly by more introverted, vulnerable, and/or marginalized students, with the risk of turning a classroom into a counselling session is another ongoing challenge for all teachers of social work.

New instructors also discussed their discomfort when they could not answer a question. In the workshops, participants were constantly reminded that they were, in fact, human and that not being perfect and not knowing everything was not a weakness in the eyes of students; rather, it was a comfort, as students themselves grappled with not knowing and with imposter syndrome. Honesty, spontaneity, and humour are among the best ways to connect with a class (Huss & Eastep, 2016), and making mistakes does not diminish teachers in their role. There are appropriate responses, such as not ignoring errors and not pretending to know an answer. As instructors we should not gloss over questions we cannot answer or deny when we make an error. We need to take ownership of what we do not know and why we do not know it, and address it earnestly (Rinfrette et al., 2015).

Conclusion

Successful university teachers develop their excellence through formal research, collaborative inquiry, the use of literature, and, of particular importance to social workers, practice and experience (Kreber, 2002). Shulman (2005b) states that professional education involves socializing students into the ways, practices, and habits of a discipline. In doing so, professional pedagogies help shape the emerging practitioner's future actions and behaviours, as well as facilitate understanding about ethics, values, and constructs within the profession. In addition, the educational process is not neutral. Who we are as faculty, students, and social workers, and our intersecting social locations, identities, privileges, awareness, and experiences complement or hinder teaching-learning processes and the dynamics in the classroom (Hillock & Mulé, 2016). Thus, awareness of intersectionality and reflection on the self are also essential to the teaching process.

As social work educators, we embrace and endorse a set of knowledge content, practice areas, and competencies that are vital to counselling preparation as prescribed by our educational accreditation bodies. According to the Canadian Association for Social Work Education – Association canadienne pour la formation en travail social (2014), students must be trained in basic interpersonal skills, core social work theories that pertain to practice, group processes, issues of diversity, social justice, inclusivity, anti-oppressive practice, and ethics. Increasingly, there is recognition that social workers also require theoretical and practical knowledge about trauma and its symptoms, intervention, and recovery (Didham et al., 2011; Wilkin & Hillock, 2015). In addition, students must also know how to read and evaluate research. Moreover, to be meaningful practitioners, they must undertake study in areas relevant to their preferred specializations, such as addiction, community work, marriage and family counselling, mental health, and social action/justice. Education for counselling professionals is partially about passing on our legacies of knowledge and skills and partially about passing on the ability to do what every good counsellor and researcher does well: gather information, assess, hypothesize about relational patterns, think outside the box, and develop creative approaches to problem solving (Nelson & Neufeldt, 1998).

Faculty members face many challenges. These challenges are greatest for new faculty as they attempt to determine how best to provide meaningful education, including transitioning from being a field practitioner to an educator; learning how to teach various groups of students; finding the balance between teaching, research, and service obligations;

and seeking tenure and promotion. Of course, learning to teach social work involves handling all the pragmatics of educating students: evaluating them in a constructive manner, teaching them how to practise social work, and managing the pressure and expectation of obtaining positive teaching evaluations. On top of this, faculty must meet the requirements of academic accommodations for individual students and support student creativity and research while developing their own research agenda. To meet all these expectations and become a successful educator, faculty must also find ways to motivate and inspire students, convey new and complex concepts, assist students to overcome difficulty in their learning, and, in social work, help them become aware of their positions of privilege and power, as well as address imposter syndrome, if they experience it. New faculty and sessional instructors have the added burden of balancing full-time work with part-time teaching or doctoral studies with educating others.

Added to the challenges described, reduced government financial support of postsecondary education while aiming to increase the proportion of individuals with postsecondary degrees, particularly graduate degrees, has forced universities to expand enrolment to offset increasing costs. This increase in numbers has not been accompanied by an equivalent increase in faculty complements. In turn, this has led to greater student-faculty teaching and supervision ratios and increased strain on the teaching component of a professor's academic life. For both new and seasoned social work educators, these realities increase the relevance of the chapters of this book, as we continue to explore how to do more than just pass along practice skills and technical knowledge as we seek to create wisdom in our complex and uncertain field, and work together to create conditions for social change. The next 18 chapters contain the reflections, insights, and practice wisdom of 30 Canadian social work educators pertaining to all three levels of social work education: BSW, MSW, and PhD. These contributions will assist readers to better understand social work education, become better teachers of social work, and better prepare the next generation of practitioners for quality social work practice.

REFERENCES

Auditor General of Ontario. (2012). *Undergraduate teaching quality: Annual report 2012.* Queen's Printer for Ontario.

Ayala, J. S. (2009). Blended learning as a new approach to social work education. *Journal of Social Work Education, 45*(2), 277–88. https://doi.org/10.5175/jswe.2009.200700112

Birnbaum, R., & Silver, R. (2011). Social work competencies in Canada: The time has come. *Canadian Social Work Review/Revue canadienne de service social, 28*(2), 299–303.

Bissessar, C. (2014). Students' perceptions of effective teacher characteristics in higher education. *International Journal of Teacher Educational Research, 3*(6), 10–22.

Bocquillon, M., Derobertmasure, A., Artus, F., & Demeuse, M. (2015). Students' comments about university teaching: Which links with effectiveness models? *@tic revista d'innovació educativa,* 15. https://doi.org/10.7203/attic.15.3931

Brems, C., Baldwin, M., Davis, L., & Namyniuk, L. (1994). The imposter syndrome as related to teaching evaluations and advising relationships of university faculty members. *The Journal of Higher Education, 65*(2), 183–93. https://doi.org/10.2307/2943923

Campbell, C. (2011). Competency-based social work. *Canadian Social Work Review, 28*(2), 311–15.

Canadian Council of Social Work Regulators. (2012). *Entry level competency profile for the social work profession in Canada.* http://www.ccswr-ccorts.ca/wp-content/uploads/2017/03/Competency-Profile-Executive-Summary-ENG.pdf

Canadian Association for Social Work Education – Association canadienne pour la formation en travail social. (2014). *Standards for accreditation.*

Cavanaugh, J. (2005). Teaching online – A time comparison. *Online Journal of Distance Learning Administration Content, 8*(1). https://www.westga.edu/~distance/ojdla/spring81/cavanaugh81.htm

Colby, I. (2009). An overview of social work education in the United States: New directions and new opportunities. *China Journal of Social Work, 2*(2), 119–30. https://doi.org/10.1080/17525090902992339

Craig, R. (2015). *College disrupted: The great unbundling of higher education.* Palgrave and MacMillan.

Csiernik, R., Furze, P., Dromgole, L., & Rishchynski, G. M. (2006). Information technology and social work –The dark side or light side? *Journal of Evidence-Based Social Work, 3*(3–4), 9–25. https://doi.org/10.1300/j394v03n03_02

Csiernik, R., Vitali, S., & Gordon, K. (2000). Competency-based education in child welfare: An exploratory examination. *Canadian Social Work, 2*(2), 53–64.

Cwikel, J., & Cnaan, R. (1991). Ethical dilemmas in applying second-wave information technology to social work practice. *Social Work, 36*(1), 114–20. https://doi.org/10.1093/sw/36.2.114

Cwikel, J., Savaya, R., Munford, R., & Desai, M. (2010). Innovation in schools of social work: An international exploration. *International Social Work, 53*(2), 187–201. https://doi.org/10.1177/0020872809355393

Darling-Hammond, L. (2000). How teacher education matters. *Journal of teacher education, 51*(3), 166–73. https://doi.org/10.1177/0022487100051003002

Delaney, J., Johnson, A. N., Johnson, T. D., & Treslan, D. L. (2010). *Students' perceptions of effective teaching in higher education.* Memorial University of Newfoundland, Distance Education and Learning Technologies. http://www.mun.ca/educ/faculty/mwatch/laura_treslan_SPETHE_Paper.pdf

DiBiase, D. (2000). Is distance teaching more work or less work? *The American Journal of Distance Education, 14*(3), 6–20. https://doi.org/10.1080/08923640009527061

Devlin, M., & Samarawickrema, G. (2010). The criteria of effective teaching in a changing higher education context. *Higher Education Research & Development, 29*(2), 111–24. https://doi.org/10.1080/07294360903244398

Didham, S., Dromgole, L., Csiernik, R., Karley, M. L., & Hurley, D. (2011). Trauma exposure and the social work practicum. *Journal of Teaching in Social Work, 31*(5), 523–37. https://doi.org/10.1080/08841233.2011.615261

Duţă, N., Pânişoară, G., & Pânişoară, I. O. (2014). The profile of the teaching profession–empirical reflections on the development of the competences of university teachers. *Procedia-Social and Behavioral Sciences, 140,* 390–5. https://doi.org/10.1016/j.sbspro.2014.04.440

Eagly, A., Johannesen-Schmidt, M., & Van Engen, M. (2003). Transformational, transactional, and laissez-faire leadership styles: A meta-analysis comparing women and men. *Psychological Bulletin, 129*(4), 569–91. https://doi.org/10.1037/0033-2909.129.4.569

Earls Larrison, T., & Korr, W. (2013). Does social work have a signature pedagogy? *Journal of Social Work Education, 49*(2), 194–206. https://doi.org/10.1080/10437797.2013.768102

Fang, L., Mishna, F., Zhang, V. F., Van Wert, M., & Bogo, M. (2014). Social media and social work education: Understanding and dealing with the new digital world. *Social Work in Health Care, 53*(9), 800–14. https://doi.org/10.1080/00981389.2014.943455

Flaherty, C. (2018, January 10). *Dancing backward with high heels.* Inside Higher Education. https://www.insidehighered.com/news/2018/01/10/study-finds-female-professors-experience-more-work-demands-and-special-favor

Freire, P. (1996). *Pedagogy of the oppressed* (Rev. ed.). Continuum.

Ghazali, A. R., Ishak, I., Saat, N. Z. M., Arifin, R. A. Z., Hamid, A., Rosli, Y., Mohammed, Z., Firdaus, M. S. O., & Kamarulzaman, F. (2012). Students' perception on lecture delivery effectiveness among the Faculty of Health Sciences lecturers. *Procedia-Social and Behavioral Sciences, 60,* 67–72. https://doi.org/10.1016/j.sbspro.2012.09.348

Gorham, J. (1988). The relationship between verbal teacher immediacy behaviors and student learning. *Communication Education, 1*(1), 40–53. https://doi.org/10.1080/03634528809378702

Harvey, S., Royal, M., & Stout, D. (2003). Instructor's transformational leadership: University student attitudes and ratings. *Psychological Reports, 92*(2), 395–402. https://doi.org/10.2466/pr0.2003.92.2.395

Hativa, N., Barak, R., & Simhi, E. (2001). Exemplary university teachers: Knowledge and beliefs regarding effective teaching dimensions and strategies. *Journal of Higher Education, 72*(6), 699–729. https://doi.org/10.1080/00221546.2001.11777122

Hill, Y., Lomas, L., & MacGregor, J. (2003). Students' perceptions of quality in higher education. *Quality Assurance in Education, 11*(1), 15–20. https://doi.org/10.1108/09684880310462047

Hillock, S. (2011). *Conceptualizing oppression: Resistance narratives for social work* [Unpublished doctoral dissertation]. Memorial University of Newfoundland.

Hillock, S., & Mulé, N. J. (2016). *Queering social work education.* UBC Press.

Huss, J., & Eastep, S. (2016). The attitudes of university faculty toward humor as a pedagogical tool: Can we take a joke? *Journal of Inquiry and Action in Education, 8*(1), 3.

Ishiyama, J., Miles, T., & Balarezo, C. (2010). Teaching the next generation of teaching professors: A comparative study of Ph.D. programs in political science. *PS: Political Science and Politics, 43*(3), 515–22. https://doi.org/10.1017/s1049096510000752

Kreber, C. (2002). Teaching excellence, teaching expertise and the scholarship of teaching. *Innovative Higher Education, 27*(1), 5–23.

Kreuger, L., & Stretch, J. (2000). How hypermodern technology in social work education bites back. *Journal of Social Work Education, 36*(1), 103–14. https://doi.org/10.1080/10437797.2000.10778993

Nelson, M., & Neufeldt, S. (1998). The pedagogy of counseling: A critical examination. *Counselor Education and Supervision, 38*(2), 70–88. https://doi.org/10.1002/j.1556-6978.1998.tb00560.x

Nolan, P., & Lenski, G. (1996). Technology, ideology and social development. *Sociological Perspectives, 39*(1), 23–38. https://doi.org/10.2307/1389341

Regehr, C. (2013). Trends in higher education in Canada and implications for social work education. *Social Work Education, 32*(6), 700–14. https://doi.org/10.1080/02615479.2013.785798

Reisch, M. (2013). Social work education and the neo-liberal challenge: The U.S. response to increasing global inequality. *Social Work Education, 32*(6), 715–33. https://doi.org/10.1080/02615479.2013.809200

Rinfrette, E., Maccio, E., Coyle, J., Jackson, K., Hartinger-Saunders, R., Rine, C., & Shulman, L. (2015). Content and process in a teaching workshop for faculty and doctoral students. *Journal of Teaching in Social Work, 35*(1–2), 65–81. https://doi.org/10.1080/08841233.2014.990077

Saravanamuthu, K. (2002). Information technology and ideology. *Journal of Information Technology, 17*(2), 79–87. https://doi.org/10.1080/02683960210145977

Schwartz, B. (1997). Psychology, idea technology and ideology. *Psychological Science, 8*(1), 21–7. https://doi.org/10.1111/j.1467-9280.1997.tb00539.x

Shulman, L. (2005a). Pedagogies of uncertainty. *Liberal Education, 91*(2), 18–25.

Shulman, L. (2005b). Signature pedagogies in the professions. *Daedalus, 134*(3), 52–9. https://doi.org/10.1162/0011526054622015

Wilkin, L., & Hillock, S. (2015). Enhancing MSW students' efficacy in working with trauma, violence, and oppression: An integrated feminist-trauma framework for social work education. *Feminist Teacher, 24*(3), 184–206. https://doi.org/10.5406/femteacher.24.3.0184

Yair, G. (2008). Can we administer the scholarship of teaching? Lessons from outstanding professors in higher education. *Higher Education, 55*(4), 447–59. https://doi.org/10.1007/s10734-007-9066-4

PART ONE

Pedagogical Perspectives

In their article, Earls Larrison and Korr (2013) asked if social work has a signature pedagogy. They argued that a signature pedagogy would be one that enabled students to "think and perform like social workers" (p. 194) and allowed for the integration of practitioner knowledge, performative action, and awareness that emphasized the development of the professional self. In the United States, the Council on Social Work Education has made field education the signature pedagogy; however, knowledge and skill acquisition often occurs outside the classroom and, for the most part, outside the control of faculty. While there is no arguing that field work is integral to social work education and professional practice, the field of social work is too diverse, too rich, and simply too heterogeneous to subscribe to any one pedagogy. Supported by this belief, this section presents seven distinct intersecting and disparate pedagogical orientations to highlight the ranges of approaches to teaching social work.

In the opening chapter, Csiernik challenges social work educators to undo the traditional education approach in which students have been indoctrinated throughout their entire academic lives. Trained as a group worker and an occupational social worker, Csiernik views the origins of the social work profession as arising as a response to industrialization. This shift in human culture substantively altered education, moving teaching from a personalized, engaging process, to an industrial pillar-and-column model that promotes competition and individual learning over cooperation and meaningful group interaction. Csiernik argues the obvious: that to be successful in facilitating service-user and societal change, social workers need to be cooperative in their practice, working together and not at cross purposes. However, this is in direct contrast to how the majority of students have been educated and how they are taught to succeed in traditional learning environments before entering social work programs – and sometimes even within social work programs.

Thus, he believes that the place to begin to teach the "radical" idea that social work students should not be pitting themselves against each other, is in the social work classroom. Csiernik states that this is a radical concept because for social work students to earn a place in a limited enrolment social work program, they must compete and succeed as individuals, not work collectively towards mutual beneficial outcomes. This opening chapter of the pedagogy section reviews the literature on how group interaction, when properly facilitated, produces more positive outcomes in knowledge and skill acquisition, and demonstrates how to fully incorporate group activities into the classroom. Csiernik's closing discussion, providing examples of how he brings his pedagogy to life in his classroom, serves as a bridge to the next section of the book that examines practice issues in teaching social work.

Susan Hillock follows by introducing us to a new educational approach in her contribution "Femagogy: Centring Feminist Knowledge and Methods in Social Work Teaching." She begins her chapter by defining feminism as a way of thinking, approaching, and analysing women's and other marginalized groups' socio-economic-political status and situated experiences of oppression within patriarchy, racism, and capitalism. Hillock then briefly reviews feminist theory, values, concepts, principles, and goals. She argues that popular culture has portrayed feminism in negative and stereotypic ways. These stereotypes function within patriarchy to keep people in the dark about what feminism actually is, perpetuating misogyny, violence, and homophobia, to decrease the likelihood of individuals identifying themselves as feminist and speaking out against social injustice. Similarly, traditional social work education and conventional teaching and learning theories, methods, and models have been criticized for maintaining patriarchy, classism, racism, and the status quo. Historically, traditional notions of education have been dominated by masculine constructions of knowledge production, science, research, teaching theories and methods, and scholarship. To counteract this, and resist dominant cultural narratives, Hillock recommends femagogy. Hillock then defines the concept of femagogy and explains its relevance and significance. She explains that femagogy is a way for education to offer reflexive intersectional critical analyses and uncover, explore, value, and emphasize women's, and other marginalized groups', ways of knowing, doing, relating, and being. To assist readers in further understanding this new perspective, Hillock also briefly explains how the white, bourgeois, heterosexual, Christian male became socially constructed as superior in modern Western society. She closes by providing a comparison of femagogy to traditional education, and discusses recommendations for instructors, on how to apply femagogy to social work education.

June Ying Yee and Anne Wagner, in their chapter "Tackling Whiteness in the Classroom and Challenging/Shattering the Skills-Based Curriculum through Anti-oppression Teaching in Social Work," begin by acknowledging the substantive impact that neo-liberalism has had on academia. They write that, in the contemporary audit culture of higher education, even critical scholars are unable to inure themselves to neo-liberal political rationality that emphasizes the supreme importance of job readiness. They further state that in the field of social work, competency-based initiatives increasingly undermine theoretically informed approaches. In adopting hierarchical relationships, competency approaches position workers as experts and devalue the wisdom of those with whom they work, with technical and procedural solutions being adopted in response to complex problems.[1] To support their perspective, Yee and Wagner explore the *whiteness* of the social work profession in Canada. They discuss how that pedagogy produces practices, systems, and values aimed at producing good social workers who help others. However, this same pedagogy fails to deliver a critical stance that prepares students to enter a profession where experiences of oppression and marginalization are essential to the goal of social work: creating and being agents of change.

When one of the editors of this book was completing his undergraduate (McMaster University, 1979–1983) and graduate (University of Toronto, 1983–1984) social work education, and the other was completing her BSW studies at Saint Thomas University (1984–1987), there was no discussion of "Indian" issues in Canada. There was no discussion of Aboriginal residential or day schools and no acknowledgement of First Nations, Inuit, Innu, or Métis peoples as part of the Canadian or social work landscape. Respectful and inclusive language was not considered. As social work education and the language we use in teaching social work have changed over the decades, we have likewise greatly broadened the pedagogy used to inform students' learning. Cyndy Baskin and Cassandra Cornacchia provide vital insights to us through their contribution, "Classrooms as Circles: The Pedagogy of Sharing Indigenous Worldviews." Their timely chapter takes up the recommendations of the Truth and Reconciliation Commission (2015), emphasizing how Indigenous worldviews and knowledges are of value to all peoples of the world and, of course, also to the teaching of social work. Baskin and Cornacchia share their insights arising from their teaching and learning in classroom circles within a Canadian school of social work. They explore how, as

1 We have invited other contributors to this book to counter this claim, and their writings will argue in favour of competency-based approaches for social work education.

Indigenous educators, alongside both Indigenous and non-Indigenous learners, their pedagogy has evolved and been shared. In their classroom environments, learners speak to the importance of (w)holistic learning whereby they explore and use all aspects of themselves, not only the psychological and intellectual but also the physical, emotional, and spiritual. Baskin and Cornacchia conclude by sharing with other educators how this classroom process has transformed how they see learning and teaching, as well as their understandings of the world around them.

Daphne Jeyapal and Liz Grigg next offer another pedagogically challenging chapter in their contribution, "The Crying White Woman and the Politics of Emotion in Anti-oppressive Social Work Education." For Jeyapal and Grigg, Indigenous, postcolonial, and feminist educators have long espoused the embodiment of being and learning. In their understanding and teaching of social work, emotion is the missing piece in rationalist, positivist, Eurocentric approaches that privilege the mind over the body. For them, emotion is a critical component in the creation of anti-oppressive social work classrooms invested in challenging and deconstructing social and racial relations. The pair write that emotion is encountered as we learn, unsettle, and disrupt our positions of power and marginalization. Yet the potentials, limitations, and politics of emotion in anti-oppressive social work education remain under-theorized. Drawing from their own student and teaching experiences, along with critical race scholarship on the politics of emotion, they explore the conditions of what "we" construct as "good/bad" emotion, who is socially sanctioned to be "emotional," and when and how the expression of emotion may challenge and contradict anti-racist classrooms.

Carolyn Campbell and Gail Baikie follow by discussing "The Practice of Critically Reflective Analysis." The authors have co-taught a course on social justice to BSW students for almost a decade. Based in an experientially, critically transformative pedagogy, their course supports students in learning fundamental principles of social justice and social work. In their chapter, Campbell and Baikie review the theoretical foundations they employ while also providing a description and examples of experiential exercises that they have used in this workshop-based course. The exercises they discuss are designed to teach concepts relevant to social work's social justice mandate and to help students to develop skills of critical reflection and analysis.

Laura Béres is a recognized global expert on narrative therapy and uses this knowledge in discussing "Teaching and Learning Critical Reflection of Practice: Why Was It So Engaging?" In this closing chapter of the pedagogy section, Béres discusses the findings of a research project regarding the process of teaching and learning critical reflection of practice (CRoP), as a required course in a graduate-level program. CRoP is a form of accountability and practice-based research that fills a gap in professional development at a time when economic stress and heavy workloads often result in lack of supervision in many social work agencies. The chapter is based upon research Béres undertook involving weekly feedback from 44 students, using a critical incident questionnaire and pre and post written comments regarding what the course participants previously knew about critical reflection, what they learned, and whether it was useful for their ongoing field education and practice. In addition, as the facilitator of the course, Béres discusses how she also used the CRoP framework to critically reflect on two significant incidents that occurred during her teaching of the course.

REFERENCES

Earls Larrison, T., & Korr, W. (2013). Does social work have a signature pedagogy? *Journal of Social Work Education, 49*(2), 194–206. https://doi.org/10.1080/10437797.2013.768102

Truth and Reconciliation Commission of Canada. (2015). *Calls to action, education.* http://trc.ca/assets/pdf/Calls_to_Action_English2.pdf

2 Undoing Traditional Education

RICK CSIERNIK

Introduction

The New World Encyclopedia (2019) states that the word *university* is derived from the Latin *universitas magistrorum et scholarium*, meaning "a community of teachers and scholars." The university is a medieval institution whose origins can be traced back to the twelfth and thirteenth centuries to the University of Paris, the University of Bologna, and Oxford. Universities gained prominence as guild-like institutions that grew with the emergence of urban life. As guilds, these collections of teachers with their students moved away from Papal and royal stewardship, becoming self-regulating bodies, determining who was fit and qualified to belong to these specialized, insular groups (Malden, 1835). Over the centuries, universities have evolved and grown in numbers: more exist now than at any time in history, with new institutions continually being established and proposed (Government of Ontario, 2004; Katawazi, 2017). Despite increasing numbers, universities have not lost all their medieval practices, which are most readily evident during convocation ceremonies. Convocation is a fete bestowing recognition on a limited number of the populace who competed to gain entry and continued to compete for four or up to as many as ten years to maintain their position within the university. Finally, after years of study, these students are graduated into the broader world with a designation – bachelor, master, or doctor – that establishes their relative competitiveness, and thus their relative worth, in the marketplace.

The historic system of knowledge transfer was dramatically changed with the onset of the industrial revolution. Mass education was now needed to fuel the increasingly complicated world of work, with literacy and numeracy becoming of value to the tens of thousands being educated for employment in the industrial world. With mass education came a different model, one that resembled the factory. While lecturing remained the prominent means of knowledge transmission, despite the continued lack of empirical support for its utility (Freeman et al., 2014), the new educational assembly line took on a new form, with military-like pillar-and-column aligned rows of desks in classrooms becoming the norm, not only at the grade-school level but extending to the university. There is no valid argument against the value of universal education, which has been enshrined as a human right in documents such as the United Nations Declaration of Human Rights (1948), International Covenant on Economic and Social Cultural Rights (1966), and Convention on the Rights of the Child (1990). There is also no valid argument against the fact that knowledge is power, but this should not prevent us from asking why competition within educational systems remains the dominant model, especially as people move from grade school to high school to postsecondary institutions. Who is served by this? What epistemology supports and replicates this approach to education? What alternatives exist?

Traditional Academic Learning

To succeed in the traditional postsecondary academic system, one must be competitive, one must be an egoist, and so on. Students tend to work against each other to achieve a goal for a limited resource: the highest grade possible. This has led students to believe, and to be taught that, for one person to succeed, others with whom that person is competitively linked need to fail, or at least be less successful. Academic success depends upon beating, defeating, and obtaining more than other students within a bell-curve system (To, 2018). Competition and consumerism have become key driving forces within the academy for both students and professors (Lewis, 2006; Pollio & Beck, 2000). Rather than achieving excellence, competition values winning, which can lead to cheating, obstructing, sabotaging, and using performance-enhancing psychoactive drugs such as Adderall, Concerta, and Ritalin (Hosny & Fatima, 2014; Jones, 2011; Neville, 2012; Schermer, 2008; Shillington et al., 2006).

Other students are not seen as colleagues in a competitive environment; rather, they are viewed as obstacles to success. In this context, the failure of others is as valued as one's own success. When teaching is structured with only the individual student in mind, there is no need for students to consider anyone other than themselves. In the traditional individualistic learning environment, individuals are rewarded for seeking outcomes that are personally beneficial without concern for the effects on others. The values that individualistic experiences teach are commitment to self-interest and reliance only on one's own efforts. It is an isolating and ultimately alienating process (Johnson & Johnson, 2000).

This behaviour is learned early and reinforced regularly within the industrial model of education, with children being separated into gifted and special education programs or remedial, college, and university educational tracks. From the onset of their education, children are taught a hierarchical system of value, based upon the grading by their instructors and increasingly standardized testing. This is further emphasized in classes where assignments are returned with the highest score handed out first to create a sense of rank and competitive viability within the classroom environment. This practice, of course, does not end in public school with the traditional education system teaching students to work independently, to not look at or copy anyone else's work, and to remain focused on demonstrating their individual merit. However, individual thinking has never been the best way to achieve successful process or task outcomes; that is the domain of the group (Blinder & Morgan, 2000; Hill, 1982; Podsakoff et al., 1997).

While individually focused teaching is the prominent method of education and evaluation, group work is also a type of learning and engagement that occurs from an early age in the education system. Yet when group work is introduced, students are not taught the principles of group activity or interaction, let alone group work theory. There appears to be a general assumption that the ability to successfully work in a group is an innate skill (Kagan, 1985). What historically results is that a group becomes five or six individuals working on a project as five or six individuals, rather than as a collective. They remain a collection of I's rather than a We. Thus, even when students are placed in a group, competitive goals remain, leading to some overachieving while others simply step back and do little to nothing, allowing the dominant members to spearhead the group, creating yet again a competitive hierarchy (Toseland & Rivas, 2016). This then further supports the traditional academic competitive approach, and the potential of bringing students together, of valuing the power of collaborative work, is lost. Whether goals are competitive or cooperative greatly influences the activities that work towards the objectives of the group and the relationships between group members. In school, it has been about winners and losers, grades determining how successful a person is, and competition following us through life (Furman et al., 2014; Napier & Gershenfeld, 2004; Palmer, 2017).

How does this pertain to social work that is viewed, in theory, as a profession that is egalitarian? Simply put, virtually all social work programs from the bachelor's to the doctoral level have limited enrolment. Thus, obtaining the best mark and the highest grade demonstrates that certain students are better than those around them from program entry until graduation. The question is how to turn competitive goals that place one social work student ahead of another to cooperative goals so that the entire group succeeds, to coordinate efforts and share resources rather than battle over them. Cooperation is a productive conduit through which knowledge production may occur (Knottnerus, 2005); it reduces stress (Kikusui et al., 2006) and is beneficial to all parties (Luco, 2014) while teaching values necessary for social workers to possess in challenging and changing oppressing systems (Deutsch, 2006).

Preparing for Cooperative Learning

Working as a group is the foundation of our society; it is a universal activity. When you look at the establishment of human cultures, it has involved circles where no one is excluded so that everyone has equal access to the primary life-maintaining resource: the fire (Brownbill & Etienne, 2017). If in our digital era, the primary resource has become knowledge, then to ensure success, the functionality of the group, group processes, and equitable learning again become essential (Hill et al., 2011; Toseland & Rivas, 2016).

The education industry is populated with students who are not and have not been taught to be self-regulated learners. In most cases, teachers are still steering and guiding the learning process, a situation that does not invite students to use or develop their cognitive or motivational self-regulatory skills nor be altruistic. Usually, students are expected to reproduce and apply the new information that the teacher has presented or made available (Boekaerts, 1997; Palmer, 2017). A major pedagogical shift towards the end of the twentieth century in universities was for active learning, which refers to course-related activity that all students in a class session are called upon to do, rather than simply being lectured at and taking notes. This may range from asking questions of students arising from a theme in the lecture to flipping the classroom and using the entire time for interactive class activities (Blatchford et al., 2003; Faust, & Paulson, 1998; Meyers & Jones, 1993; Niemi, 2002). Active learning can also involve engaging and supporting students in working together in groups for their collective benefit and for a common grade. However, while cooperation may evolve, it is not a primary intent of active learning (Roehl et al., 2013). Unfortunately, most students who have successfully competed to earn seats in limited enrolment programs have had to become exclusively self-focused rather than being parts of a collective that has the capacity for greater problem solving, knowledge acquisition, and skill development. So what can be done to undo 12 to 16 years of early education that has taught individuals that group work is a competitive endeavour?

Cooperative Learning

Cooperative learning entails any instructional method that encourages students to work together to pursue common goals as they apply course material to answer questions, solve problems, or create outcomes that increase their understanding of content, provide them with distinct insights into the process, and build transferable skills (Colbeck et al., 2000; Johnson et al., 2008). Cooperative learning is characterized by positive, mutual interdependence, where students perceive that better performance by individuals produces better performance by the entire group (Johnson et al., 2014). It can be formal or informal but often involves specific instructor intervention to maximize student interaction and learning. Central to this process is the small-group experience and the pursuit of a common goal. Other than mutual interdependence, the core tenets involved in cooperative learning are the following:

- individual accountability
- face-to-face interaction (note: not electronic or digital)
- appropriate practice of interpersonal, social, and small-group skills, most importantly by an instructor
- regular assessment of the group's development and action (Johnson & Johnson, 2013; Johnson et al., 2008; Kagan, 1985; Prince, 2004)

What is essential for the social work educator is to reinforce the focus on cooperative incentives, rather than competition or merely collaboration, to promote learning, a major paradigm shift from traditional education approaches.

While working in groups is not foreign to students, the hoped for outcomes often are. What is typically lacking when attempting cooperative learning is providing students with a core understanding of how a group develops, the dynamics of that group development, the roles played within a group, and the dual pulls of cohesion and conflict, approach and avoidance, leading and being led, and giving up the I to become the We. These core principles are taught in some social work programs, particularly in group work courses, but need to be reinforced in other learning situations outside of one or two social work classes.

At its core, cooperative learning is based on the premise that cooperation is more beneficial than competition, allowing students to better acquire knowledge and master skills. The use of cooperative learning groups in instruction is based on the principle of constructivism and the sociocultural theory of development. Constructivism is premised on the idea that individuals learn through building their own knowledge and connecting new ideas and experiences to existing knowledge and experiences to form new or enhanced understanding (Bransford et al., 1999); the sociocultural theory of development argues that learning takes place when students solve problems beyond their current developmental level with the support of their instructor or their peers (Davidson & Major, 2014; Johnson et al., 2014). In cooperative learning, the group works together to learn and to problem solve, rather than relying solely on the professor's thoughts and ideas. Cooperative learning uses both goal and resource interdependence to ensure interaction and communication among group members. This also entails professors changing their role from that of instructor to that of facilitator, fostering an environment that allows students to interact, developing cohesion, and assuring students that conflict is inevitable in group process but that resolving conflict builds cohesion and enhances the creative process and positive outcomes (Johnson & Johnson, 2013; Toseland & Rivas, 2016).

A range of studies have found that cooperation consistently improves learning outcomes relative to individual work and academic achievement, regardless of the discipline (Blumenfeld et al., 1996; Ebert-May et al., 1997; O'Donnell, 2006; Pai et al., 2015). In a meta-analysis Springer et al. (1999) found that students who participated in various types of small-group learning, ranging from brief to extended formal interactions, had greater academic achievement, exhibited more favourable attitudes towards learning, and had increased persistence. Working cooperatively creates positive relationships, diminishing demographic differences such as sex, race, sexual identification, ability, and class, and produces increases in social skills and academic competence. Cooperative learning also promotes interpersonal relationships, improves social support, and fosters self-esteem while generally resulting in higher grades, *if* it is properly facilitated. Cooperative learning environments have also been shown to enhance academic achievement, student attitudes, and student retention (Johnson & Johnson, 2000; Napier & Gershenfeld, 2004; Prince, 2004).

Activities to Develop Cooperative Group Learning

By definition, cooperative learning entails social interdependency, allowing outcomes to be dictated by the actions of others. In developing a healthy functioning social work group, we need to turn six or seven I's into a We. This is no different in the classroom, except, of course, for the pervasive presence of the grading scheme. The ongoing pursuit of a "good" mark limits cooperative learning, particularly in undergraduate programs, where the goal is increasingly not as much about learning as it is about being accepted into a graduate school program or maintaining a grade point average (GPA) to preserve scholarship money. Following are a series of activities that I have used to foster cooperative learning in the classroom.

The Kevin Bacon Game: We Are All Connected

Movie star Kevin Bacon became the centrepiece of the internet version of the game six degrees of separation. In the game, the goal was to find how any actor was connected to Kevin Bacon in six steps or less (https://www.sixdegrees.org). While I am not an actor, I can play the game: my cousin Jackie (one degree) was an extra in a movie filming in Hamilton, Ontario, featuring Kyra Sedgwick (second degree) and was actually in a scene with her. Kyra Sedgwick is, of course, married to none other than Kevin Bacon (three degrees of separation).

In the classroom, I use this as my opening ice breaker. I randomly assign the class into groups of six and ask them to find ways they are connected to each other through different people. For example, Student A: I worked at Canadian Mental Health in the summer and my supervisor was Susan. Student B: Susan's younger sister Violet was on my hockey team for two years. Student C: Violet went to the same school as my cousin, Debbie. Groups then draw a diagram (blackboard or flipchart paper) outlining the connections. Upon completion, each group member indicates how they are connected to each other. While presenting, the people who are connected stand up, introduce themselves to the class, and indicate how Student A is connected to B to C through Susan, Violet, and Debbie. Other members of the class are encouraged to jump in if they also know Susan, Violet, or Debbie. This is a simple way to find connections but also allows an instructor to quickly learn which students are not connected and, thus, have the greatest differences from their peers. This is important as the foundation of cooperative learning is cohesion.

Twenty Questions: Building Class Cohesion by Creating an Impossible Task to Solve

Twenty questions is the simple camp game based on creating a riddle and then allowing each person to ask a yes or no question until the answer is identified or 20 questions have been asked. In the cooperative learning version, an open-ended question is posed that cannot be solved by simply asking yes and no questions unless the class works together, and rather than individuals, an entire group has to agree upon what questions to ask.

In my group work course, there are either three or four groups depending upon the size of the class. Each group has a specific topic to present on at the end of term, also for a grade (20 per cent). Each week before having time to work on their group activity in class, each group is allowed to ask one question per week for the seven weeks of the course, which all other members of the class also hear. Some open-ended questions I have posed in the past have included these:

- Why and how is Henry Young of significance to this program and to this course?
- Why is Bill Lee the key to understanding the true meaning of this course?
- What is the "Original" Spider-Man's contribution to the course?

The order of asking is rotated each week. Frustration builds over the term, after the initial burst of enthusiasm, because the answer to the question posed cannot be obtained through a simple yes or no question. The insight necessary to be successful is that the groups need to work together, rather than as individual teams, and that process is the correct answer. This assignment is weighted at 2.5 per cent of the final grade, but the mark is not assigned for obtaining the correct answer. To succeed, the individual groups need to work together to coordinate their questions; if rather than three or four answers, they submit one, they have actually come to the correct solution. Each member of the class receives 100 per cent if they all submit the same answer. After the answers are submitted, the class is debriefed on the meaning of the exercise and why the answer provides insight into the true meaning of the course, which is, of course, that to succeed, they need to cooperate and not compete.

Using Group Development to Study Group Development: Journal the Process

In teaching my group work course, the central assignment is a group presentation. However, students have been completing group presentations throughout their academic careers, so how can we undo the damage that has been done by years of exclusively task-driven group exercises? For me, the first step has been to help students gain insights into the process of group activity so that they can begin to appreciate the advantages that cooperative learning can bring. Appreciating that education, especially undergraduate education, is motivated through assigning grades, I make the process of understanding the group twice as valuable as the group presentation. I ask each student to submit a descriptive record of their group's process that examines what occurred in the group's development, from initial formation to presentation, considering who, when, where, why, what, and how. Students are expected to journal after every group meeting, providing the following:

- a description of the group process and task
- a discussion of the effect of the group process and task on them
- an explanation that integrates the specific theory from class that explains what has occurred in the group and why

As most are likely thinking about group process for the first time, the surface goal of the activity is to have students appreciate what goes on in a group and why to gain insights into the process, as well as their own actions and reactions. The ultimate goal is for them to take that knowledge and actively change their behaviour within the group and, in turn, change the group process. Success in this assignment requires a balance between task and process. The activity cannot be solely task driven. Actively engaging in the stages of group development and being cognizant and reflective of that process becomes more important, thus moving the activity and the members' actions from being purely competitive to more cooperative. To foster this, students need to be assured that all journals are confidential and will be read by the professor alone.

Debrief the Group

The major disservice professors who assign group activities do to students, which builds competition and negates cooperation, is neglecting to debrief groups after their class presentations. While students certainly seek good grades, what is hopefully retained after a group presentation is completed is more the effect than the product: how the group worked together rather than just the presentation. I build time into group presentations such that immediately upon completion, I meet with each group to discuss how they felt about the presentation. We discuss how the presentation came together, the struggles they faced, and how they overcame them. We also explore, gingerly, the conflicts that arose and the cohesion that did or did not occur; then at the end, we discuss the actual product. During the debriefing period, there are degrees of honesty as students still want to be perceived as able and competent, and of course receive an A-range grade, but by focusing on the process and how they did or did not work together first and the actual product second, the importance of cooperation rather than competition is further reinforced.

Conclusion

The conditions for group learning in university rarely meet the standards advocated by cooperative learning scholars (Colbeck et al., 2000; Furman et al., 2014). Cooperative learning is premised on having group work skills, but even this is often a false principle as even in learning settings where group work is encouraged, students are not taught how to work cooperatively as they continue to compete for a perceived limited resource: the final grade. Successful cooperative learning involves understanding the process of group development and the inherent approach-avoidance conflict of joining any new group that reflects our inherent fight-flight response. Should I venture to risk to join this new initiative or should I keep my personal boundaries and ensure my social persona remains intact? How do I give up or share the I to become the We?

What is fundamental in creating an environment where cooperative learning is possible is shared responsibility. This is a simple concept that by the time a student reaches university has become a myth for most. Students in limited enrolment programs have been academically more successful than the majority of their peers, which in turn means they have traditionally learned, through experience, that a group project means they need to do more to earn the grade that the academic system uses to denote their competency. Thus, in preparing students to be successful cooperative learners, they need to unlearn what they have experienced over their past 12 to 16 years of pillar-and-column education. Along with gaining insights into why they have been forged into competitive learners and the utility of that, they need to be taught fundamental group work skills that it has been assumed they know. The first step should be simple as the essence of group work is enhanced communication skills. This of course is a core component of any social work program. It is vital that students have an appreciation for how to successfully send and receive information, and to assess communication at multiple levels. Becoming a cooperative learner is a trust experience, not much different from the first time you are asked to stand up on a table, close your eyes, and fall backwards into the crossed arms of a group of people you met 30 minutes ago. When this activity is videotaped, you are able to witness degrees of trust. Did you fall straight back, or did you knees buckle in anticipation of crashing to the ground, which is what we typically experience when we fall. Cooperative learning is the academic version of experiencing falling backwards into the arms of others without buckling our knees … too much.

REFERENCES

Blatchford, P., Kutnick, P., Baines, E., & Galton, M. (2003). Toward a social pedagogy of classroom group work. *International Journal of Educational Research, 39*(1), 153–72. https://doi.org/10.1016/s0883-0355(03)00078-8

Blinder, A., & Morgan, J. (2000). *Are two heads better than one? An experimental analysis of group versus individual decision making* (No. w7909). National Bureau of Economic Research. https://www.nber.org/papers/w7909.pdf

Blumenfeld, P., Marx, R., Soloway, E., & Krajcik, J. (1996). Learning with peers: From small group cooperation to collaborative communities. *Educational Researcher, 25*(8), 37–40. https://doi.org/10.3102/0013189x025008037

Boekaerts, M. (1997). Self-regulated learning: A new concept embraced by researchers, policy makers, educators, teachers, and students. *Learning and Instruction,* 7(2), 161–86. https://doi.org/10.1016/s0959-4752(96)00015-1

Bransford, J., Brown, A., & Cocking, R. (Eds.). (1999). *How people learn: Brain,* mind, experience, and school. National Academy Press.

Brownbill, K., & Etienne, M. (2017). Understanding the ultimate oppression: Alcohol and drug addiction in Native land. In R. Csiernik & W. Rowe (Eds.), *Responding to the oppression of addiction* (3rd ed., pp. 295–315).Canadian Scholars Press.

Colbeck, C., Campbell, S., & Bjorklund, S. (2000). Grouping in the dark: What college students learn from group projects. *The Journal of Higher Education, 71*(1), 60–83. https://doi.org/10.1080/00221546.2000.11780816

Davidson, N., & Major, C. (2014). Boundary crossing: Cooperative learning, collaborative learning, and problem-based learning. *Journal on Excellence in College Teaching,* 25 (3&4), 7–55.

Deutsch, M. (2006). A framework for thinking about oppression and its change. *Social Justice Research, 19*(1), 7–41. https://doi.org/10.1007/s11211-006-9998-3

Ebert-May, D., Brewer, C., & Allred, S. (1997). Innovation in large lectures: Teaching for active learning. *Bioscience, 47*(9), 601–7. https://doi.org /10.2307/1313166

Faust, J., & Paulson, D. (1998). Active learning in the college classroom. *Journal on Excellence in College Teaching, 9*(2), 3–24.

Freeman, S., Eddy, S., McDonough, M., Smith, M., Okoroafor, N., Jordt, H., & Wenderoth, M. P. (2014). Active learning increases student performance in science, engineering, and mathematics. *Proceedings of the National Academy of Sciences, 111*(23), 8410–15. https://doi.org/10.1073/pnas.1319030111

Furman, R., Bender, K., & Rowan, D. (2014). *An experiential approach to group work* (2nd ed.). Oxford University Press.

Government of Ontario. (2004). *University of Ontario Institute of Technology Act, 2002,* SO 2002, c 8, Schedule O. https://www.ontario.ca/laws/statute/02u08/v1

Hill, G. (1982). Group versus individual performance: Are N+ 1 heads better than one? *Psychological Bulletin, 91*(3), 517–39. https://doi.org/10.1037/0033-2909.91.3.517

Hill, K., Walker, R., Božičević, M., Eder, J., Headland, T., Hewlett, B., Hurtado, A., Marlowe, F., Wiessner, P., & Wood, B. (2011). Co-residence patterns in hunter-gatherer societies show unique human social structure. *Science, 331*(6022), 1286–9. https://doi.org/10.1126/science.1199071

Hosny, M., & Fatima, S. (2014). Attitude of students towards cheating and plagiarism: University case study. *Journal of Applied Sciences, 14*(8), 748–57. https://doi.org/10.3923/jas.2014.748.757

Johnson, D., & Johnson, R. (2000). Cooperative learning, values, and culturally plural classrooms. In M. Leicester, C. Modgil, & S. Modgil (Eds.), *Classroom issues: Practice, pedagogy and curriculum* (pp. 15–28). Falmer Press.

Johnson, D. W., & Johnson, R. (2013). *Joining together: Group theory and group skills* (11th ed.). Pearson.

Johnson, D. W., Johnson, R., & Holubec, E. (2008). *Cooperation in the classroom* (8th ed.). Interaction.

Johnson, D. W., Johnson, R., & Smith, K. (2014). Cooperative learning: Improving university instruction by basing practice on validated theory. *Journal on Excellence in College Teaching, 25*(1), 85–118.

Jones, D. L. (2011). Academic dishonesty: Are more students cheating? *Business Communication Quarterly, 74*(2), 141–50. https://doi.org/10.1177/1080569911404059

Kagan, S. (1985). Dimensions of cooperative classroom structures. In R. Slavin, S. Sharan, S. Kagan, R. Lararowtiz, C. Webb, & R. Schmuck (Eds.), *Learning to cooperate, cooperating to learn* (pp. 67–95). Springer Science + Business Media.

Katawazi, M. (2017, August 28). Ontario proposes French-language university in Toronto. *The Globe and Mail.* https://www.theglobeandmail.com/news/national/ontario-proposes-french-language-university-in-toronto/article36110367/

Kikusui, T., Winslow, J., & Mori, Y. (2006). Social buffering: Relief from stress and anxiety. *Philosophical Transactions of the Royal Society B: Biological Sciences, 361*(1476), 2215–28. https://doi.org/10.1098/rstb.2006.1941

Knottnerus, J. (2005). The need for theory and the value of cooperation: Disruption and deritualization. *Sociological Spectrum, 25*(1), 5–19. https://doi.org/10.1080/027321790500130

Lewis, H. (2006). *Excellence without a soul: How a great university forgot education.* Public Affairs.

Luco, A. (2014). The definition of morality: Threading the needle. *Social Theory and Practice, 40*(3), 361–87. https://doi.org/10.5840/soctheorpract201440324

Malden, H. (1835). *On the origin of universities and academical degrees.* https://books.google.ca/books?id=9N5BAAAAcAAJ&printsec=frontcover

Meyers, C., & Jones, T. (1993). *Promoting active learning strategies for the college classroom.* Jossey-Bass.

Napier, R., & Gershenfeld, M. (2004). *Groups: Theory and experience.* Houghton Mifflin.

Neville, L. (2012). Do economic equality and generalized trust inhibit academic dishonesty? Evidence from state-level search-engine queries. *Psychological Science, 23*(4), 339–45. https://doi.org/10.1177/0956797611435980

Niemi, H. (2002). Active learning—a cultural change needed in teacher education and schools. *Teaching and Teacher Education, 18*(7), 763–80. https://doi.org/10.1016/s0742-051x(02)00042-2

New World Encyclopedia. (2019). University. Retrieved March 2, 2020, from https://www.newworldencyclopedia.org/entry/University

O'Donnell, A. (2006). The role of peers and group learning. In P. A. Alexander & P. H. Winne (Eds.), *Handbook of educational psychology* (pp. 781–802). Lawrence Erlbaum Associates Publishers.

Pai, H., Sears, D., & Maeda, Y. (2015). Effects of small-group learning on transfer: A meta-analysis. *Educational Psychology Review, 27*(1), 79–102. https://doi.org/10.1007/s10648-014-9260-8

Palmer, P. (2017). *Successful group work: 13 activities to teach teamwork skills.* Alphabet Publishing.

Podsakoff, P., Ahearne, M., & MacKenzie, S. (1997). Organizational citizenship behavior and the quantity and quality of work group performance. *Journal of Applied Psychology, 82*(2), 262–9. https://doi.org/10.1037/0021-9010.82.2.262

Pollio, H., & Beck, H. (2000). When the tail wags the dog: Perceptions of learning and grade orientation in, and by, contemporary college students and faculty. *The Journal of Higher Education, 71*(1), 84–102. https://doi.org/10.1080/00221546.2000.11780817

Prince, M. (2004). Does active learning work? A review of the research. *Journal of engineering education, 93*(3), 223–31. https://doi.org/10.1002/j.2168-9830.2004.tb00809.x

Roehl, A., Reddy, S. L., & Shannon, G. J. (2013). The flipped classroom: An opportunity to engage millennial students through active learning. *Journal of Family and Consumer Sciences, 105*(2), 44–9. https://doi.org/10.14307/jfcs105.2.12

Schermer, M. (2008). On the argument that enhancement is "cheating." *Journal of Medical Ethics, 34*(2), 85–8. https://doi.org/10.1136/jme.2006.019646

Shillington, A., Reed, M., Lange, J., Clapp, J., & Henry, S. (2006). College undergraduate Ritalin abusers in southwestern California: Protective and risk factors. *Journal of Drug Issues, 36*(4), 999–1014. https://doi.org/10.1177/002204260603600411

Springer, L., Stanne, M. E., & Donovan, S. S. (1999). Effects of small-group learning on undergraduates in science, mathematics, engineering, and technology: A meta-analysis. *Review of Educational Research, 69*(1), 21–51. https://doi.org/10.3102/00346543069001021

To, G. (2018, January 13). Ahead of the curve: Uncovering Western's academic policies. *The Gazette.* https://www.westerngazette.ca/news/ahead-of-the-curve-uncovering-western-s-academic-policies/article_c33b6ffa-cb0a-11e7-a145-27b9bda503cf.html

Toseland, R., & Rivas, R. (2016). *An introduction to group work practice* (8th ed.). Pearson.

3 Femagogy: Centring Feminist Knowledge and Methods in Social Work Teaching

SUSAN HILLOCK

Introduction

Feminism is a way of thinking, approaching, and analysing women's and other marginalized groups' socio-economic-political status and situated experiences of oppression within patriarchy, racism, heterosexism, cisgenderism, and capitalism (Hillock, 2011). Popular culture has portrayed feminism in negative and stereotypic ways. If people close their eyes and think about feminism, many would imagine a man-hating woman who refuses to shave or wear makeup, who exhibits characteristics usually associated with men, and who spends her leisure time burning bras. This stereotype has a purpose. Within patriarchy, it functions to keep the populace ignorant regarding the intents of feminism while intimidating people from exploring feminism's ideals or identifying themselves as feminists.

In contrast, feminism interrogates these stereotypes and seeks to uncover, explore, and emphasize women's ways of knowing, doing, relating, and being. In this chapter, when I refer to the concept of *women's ways*, I am including all "othered" voices, knowledges, and identities that have been historically ignored. Furthermore, traditional social work education and conventional teaching and learning have been criticized for maintaining patriarchy, classism, homo/trans phobia, racism, ableism, and the "status quo" (Dominelli, 2002a; Hillock, 2011; Razack, 2002). Historically, education, including traditional notions of pedagogy and andragogy, has aided and perpetuated the construction of the White, bourgeois, heterosexual, Christian male as superior in modern Western society (Kirby et al., 2006). Thus, education has tended to be almost exclusively dominated by masculine, as well as White, cisgendered, and heterosexist, constructions of knowledge production, science, research, and teaching theories and methods (Hillock, 2011).

To challenge these Western norms, this chapter begins by briefly summarizing feminism and its key concepts and overall goals. It introduces and explores a new construct in education that I call *femagogy*. Similar to feminist social work and counselling theories and skills, femagogy applies specific teaching principles and methods that attempt to disrupt/decentre mainstream approaches. This chapter deepens understandings of this new educational perspective by defining femagogy, describing its fit with social work, comparing it to traditional education, suggesting specific teaching skills and methods to help transform social work education, and briefly exploring the challenges that arise when teaching from a critical feminist framework.

Feminism

Over the last century, an analytical and conceptual framework has emerged that can be labelled as distinctly feminist. Van Den Bergh (1995) defined feminism as a

> conceptual framework and mode of analysis that has analysed the status of women (and other disempowered groups) cross-culturally and historically to explain dynamics and conditions undergirding disparities in sociocultural status and power between majority and minority populations. (p. xii)

Additionally, feminist theory seeks to decode and dismantle patriarchy (Dominelli, 2002b; Enge, 2013), racism, and heterosexism/homophobia and assesses how these forces, which can be viewed as a politic of domination (hooks, 1989), oppress marginalized groups (Cohee, 2004). Although united in terms of looking at gender inequality, feminism is not monolithic in terms of its beliefs and recommendations. There are many variations of feminism including Black (Collins, 2000; hooks, 1994, 2000), green/eco-feminism (Mellor, 1997), liberal (Enge, 2013), Marxist (Bannerji, 1995), queer (Hillock & Mulé, 2016), radical (Enge, 2013; Nes & Iadicola, 1989), and socialist (Dominelli, 2002b; Hillock, 2011).

Despite the variations, most feminist perspectives emphasize two key concepts: oppression and the notion that the personal is political.

Oppression

Briskin (1992) proposed that feminism is the "basis of a coherent analytical and strategic approach to women's oppression" (p. 266). Indeed, feminism, along with radical/structural, anti-racist, and critical postmodernism theories, has been called a critical or anti-oppressive theory

(Hillock, 2011; Mullaly, 2010). As well, Van Den Bergh (1995) stated that "both social work and the women's movement have historically sought to remediate oppressive conditions for marginalized groups" (p. xxviii). Much of feminist theory and analysis has evolved in response to the damaging consequences and manifestations of various intersecting oppressions, such as patriarchy, racism, and classism, and their differential impacts on vulnerable populations. In addition, feminists deconstruct the binary notion of oppressor and oppressed, the faulty assumption that a person has to be one or the other, not both, and analyse how various oppressions are interrelated (hooks, 2000). To this end, Ellsworth (1989) called for an intersectional analysis, the explicit identification/awareness that people simultaneously inhabit sites of both oppression and privilege. Knowledge, as well as how it is produced and shared within systems of socialization and education, must also be understood and contextualized within these networks of oppression (Carniol, 2005; hooks, 1994; Sisneros et al., 2008).

The Personal Is Political

An essential concept within feminism is the notion that the personal is political (Hanisch, 2009; Levine, 1982). Linking the personal to the political helps facilitate consciousness-raising and critical thinking about how social structures contribute to the problems subordinate individuals and groups experience. Furthermore, feminist analysis addresses the "private/public split" in people's lives, thus changing the emphasis in social work, and other disciplines, from intra-psychic blaming of the victim to externalizing the problem, to identify and decode how a matrix of oppression subjugates women and other marginalized groups. Consequently, Nash (1989) and Briskin (1990) suggest that feminist theory and its principles can be viewed as strategies to help women challenge oppression and patriarchy, and handle everyday life situations and experiences.

Overall Goals

In terms of overall goals, most feminists support dismantling systems of dominance and working towards building a society free from violence, exploitation, discrimination, and inequality (Hillock, 2011). Feminists also emphasize the importance of using feminist theory in education and research to explain how social, political, and economic factors influence people's lives (Enge, 2013; Flynn Saulnier, 2008). To do this, feminists critique the way societies choose to organize and distribute power, status, privilege, and wealth, analysing how these choices privilege dominant groups and oppress marginalized groups. Seeking allies and joining with others to build feminist organizations and participate in social action are also seen as essential to the feminist movement.

Traditional Education: Privileging the White Male

Feminists argue that, along with other social institutions, like religion, policing, economics, and politics, traditional educational systems are implicated in perpetuating harm to marginalized individuals, groups, and communities. Additionally, as discussed in the opening chapter of this book, the reliance on education as banking, the notion that students are empty vessels in which to deposit knowledge (Campbell, 2002; Freire, 1970; Weiler, 1991), perpetuates and maintains hierarchical systems of inequality. How does this happen?

Traditional Education

Much of traditional education has focused on two approaches: pedagogy – the teaching of children, typically in kindergarten to grade 12 systems; and andragogy – the teaching of adults, typically in postsecondary settings. As mentioned previously, both approaches have been dominated, as well as constructed, by Western, White, male, able, and androcentric writers, academics, and researchers. Traditional approaches to social work teaching and research have also reified and entrenched White, Western, Christian, heterosexist, cisgendered, able-bodied, and masculine ways of knowing (Strega & Brown, 2015). Although there have been many attempts within social work to integrate feminist and anti-racist approaches, many of these efforts represent a hodgepodge of "add-on techniques such as multiculturalism, cultural sensitivity/competence, and diversity" (Schiele, 1996, as cited in Mullings, 2016, p. 208). This has clearly not been beneficial as social work education continues to be criticized for privileging White males and maintaining the status quo (Campbell, 2002; Dominelli, 2002b; Razack, 1999; Yee, 2005). How did this White male bias come about?

Privileging the White Male

Feminists have detailed how the White, bourgeois, heterosexual, Christian male became socially constructed as superior and the standard for normalcy within modern Western society. Haney (1989) and Weedon (1997) make the case that this phenomenon evolved from fourteenth-century to early-twentieth-century political, economic, and scientific schools of thought, production of knowledge, and discourse that legitimated and supported (1) the idea of man in charge of and controlling nature, (2) colonialization, (3) the commodification of land (the enclosure movement) and subordinate peoples (the slave trade), and (4) the entrenchment of modern man as "king of his castle" and family (patriarchy). This thinking and these formative events can be viewed as establishing normative standards of the White, Western, Christian male as superior to all others and, therefore, entitled to his dominant place and privilege in society (Hillock, 2011). From this history, one can easily argue that the bulk of conventional research and knowledge production within education, including social work, has continued this tradition. Indeed, social work, along with many other caregiving professions, is "still grounded in Eurocentric philosophical foundations: theories taught in social work education are derived from and based on white people's understandings of behaviour, growth and development, aging, child rearing, adaptation, and grief" (Mullings, 2016, p. 207).

The result of maintaining the status quo is that the voices and experiences of women and other marginalized groups have been denied and underrepresented in education. Indeed, Lorber (2005) states, "The viewpoints of marginalized 'others' ... do not enter the production of most knowledge" (p. 183). Consequently, feminists have analysed and critiqued examples of how female, queer, racialized, and all othered voices have been ignored, left out, or silenced in most education and research. Classic examples include medical research that focuses exclusively on males and then is generalized to women (Westervelt, 2015), Erikson's (1994) and Kohlberg and Hersh's (1977) developmental work with boys, which has been severely critiqued as not being universal or generalizable to girls and women (Gilligan, 1988), social group work premised on male patterns of collaboration and conflict (Schiller, 1997), and the historic gender, racist, and heterosexist bias and diagnoses in the *Diagnostic and Statistical Manual of Mental Disorders* (Hillock & Mulé, 2016; Jane et al., 2007; Wilkin & Hillock, 2016). Thus, from a feminist viewpoint, knowledge from primary to postsecondary education is seen as benefiting White males more than other groups and denying, ignoring, neglecting, and silencing the narratives of marginalized groups.

Femagogy: Centring Feminist Knowledge and Methods

Over the last ten years of my academic career, I developed the term *femagogy* as a way to describe the more collaborative, caring, learner-centred, intersectional, reciprocal, adult-based, and inclusive approaches that I have been experimenting with in class and in response to what I saw as weaknesses of traditional approaches to social work education. Frankly, I was tired of teaching male-centred and male-authored social work history, research, theories, books, and articles to my mostly female students. In addition, *pedagogy* and *andragogy* were not terms that accurately described how I was teaching; what was happening in my mostly female classrooms; the stories that I was hearing and sharing; the impact of emotion, relationship, and experience on learning processes; and the democratic mean-making process that I was hoping to achieve. Although I first believed that I had invented the term on my own, I found two other mentions of femagogy in recent online literature (Accardi, 2016; Pentney, 2006). While writing this chapter, I contacted the authors connected to these references. Neither could recall how that specific term had ended up in their online work. My best guess is that, as like-minded feminists and academics, we were synchronistically struggling for new ways of describing the unique types of learning we were seeing and the teaching that we were doing, and each of us landed on the same term: *femagogy*.

Femagogy Defined

I define femagogy as an approach to teaching and education that centres feminist-centred teaching theory, knowledges, methods, and practice. Essentially, femagogy offers educators a theoretical and practical educational framework for active resistance to social and cultural manifestations of misogyny, racism, and other manifestations of oppression. To achieve these ends, femagogy offers an intersectional analysis that uncovers, and centres on, all that is *not* White, male, able-bodied, cisgendered, and straight. It deliberately seeks to disrupt and unsettle traditional education by introducing and exploring approaches to teaching and learning that value and emphasize women's ways of knowing, doing, relating, and being (Belenky et al., 1997), as well as feminist-centred theories, methods, and research.

I acknowledge that the phrase "women's ways of knowing," with its underlying modernist assumptions related to the notion that people share common experiences and that there are monolithic structural forces at the root of people's suffering, may be problematic for some. This phrase originated in the late 1980s and early 1990s in the era of identity politics, long before postmodernism, queer theory, and intersectional analysis became the standard, if not in social work practice, then at least in academia. In turn, there is still debate within queer theory on the pros and cons of completely abandoning identity politics (Hillock & Mulé, 2016), and there are valid critiques of postmodernism, its relativist stance, and its negative impact on collectivism, mobilizing for social action, and community organizing (Hillock, 2011).

I also want to be careful here to acknowledge the subject category of "woman" as highly contested, as well as socially constructed, dynamic, diverse, and highly individual. Woman is not a homogenous classification. I do recognize that I run the very real risk here of essentializing or claiming some universal truth about that which is "female" or "woman." That is not my intent. Although I was brought up in a working-class family in rural New Brunswick, I recognize that presently, as a White, cisgendered, upper-class academic, I come from many layers of privilege and belong, in many ways, to the dominant culture in Canadian society. Thus, I recognize that I cannot speak for all women, nor can I represent all variations and diversity within the category of "woman" in our society. As a queer educator, it is also my intent to strike down binary notions of he/she and to deconstruct the limiting social scripts of gender and sexual orientation that exist in our stratified and unequal society. It seems obvious to me that under ideal social conditions, no response need to be assigned a gender; they simply represent diverse aspects of being human.

Conversely, as a woman who lives in an unequal society and who has experienced oppression and sexual violence solely because I present and identify as a cisgendered female, I am not willing to throw the baby out with the bathwater. As we try to avoid essentializing notions of what it means to be male or female, both, or neither, I stand with feminist educators who strive to balance social constructionist notions of subjectivity and fluidity with modernist assumptions about identity, social location, and organizing for social change while offering a nuanced understanding of voices, stories, methods, and ways of being that survive at the margins. In other words, all postmodern nuances aside, the reality is that my personal and professional experiences of oppression (which are further examined in chapter 18) are based on the fact that I am viewed as a cisgendered female. And, more importantly, I share this gendered oppression with millions of other girls and women.

Femagogy and Social Work Education: A Good Fit

I propose that femagogy is a good fit for social work education because it builds upon its philosophical base, shares its anti-oppressive values, advocates for the transformation of harmful societal structures, supports ethical practice (Barnoff & Coleman, 2007; Barnoff & Moffat, 2007; Marsiglia & Kulis, 2009; Osmond & O'Connor, 2004), and is congruent with progressive social work values (Briskin, 1990; Hillock, 2011, Nash, 1989). However, I also argue that the primary reason that femagogy is essential for social work education is that the majority of social workers, social service providers, social work students, and service users are women, many of whom share similar experiences of gender-based violence, inequality, poverty, racism, and other manifestations of oppression. It is also important to acknowledge that the concept of femagogy rests on the shoulders and work of our feminist foremothers who have enriched the fields of social work practice, research, and education. In particular, Jane Addams, who can arguably be called the founder of nascent feminist, queer, and community social work, stands out as she developed innovative approaches that emphasized women-centred and delivered models of practice (Hillock & Mulé, 2016). These models featured women living and working collectively with other women to ameliorate personal suffering and improve social conditions for all. In addition, many feminist scholars have been integral in the development of social work education (Collins, 1991, 2000; Dominelli, 2002a, 2002b; Ellsworth, 1989; hooks, 1989, 1994, 2000; Levine, 1982; Razack, 1999, 2002, 2009; Strega & Brown, 2015).

Social Work Education as Transformation

Key to applying femagogy to social work education is the notion of transformation. The goals of feminist social and political transformation include disrupting, decentring, overturning, and reconstructing oppressive educational beliefs, values, language, institutions, policies, and relationships. Mathieson (2002) also emphasizes the importance of recognizing, identifying, naming, and teaching about dominant-subordinate relations and oppressive structures:

> If we can't recognize it in our everyday lives, we won't be able to recognize it when it emerges in the classroom, in the conversations of our students, in the films we view and in the textbooks we use. If we can't identify it, then we can't confront it, and it will continue to perpetuate in our classrooms. Not only do we, as teachers, need to decolonize our thinking, we need to teach our students to decolonize theirs. (p. 166)

From this perspective, the social work classroom, field instruction, and practice are viewed as political acts of social and cultural resistance (Fook, 1999, 2004; Ife, 1997; Mullaly, 2010; Razack, 2002, 2009; Sisneros et al., 2008; Weedon, 1997) and potential sites of activism and transformation.

As acts of resistance to traditional White, cisgendered, heterosexist, and male-dominated views and theories, we can choose instead to celebrate and include alternative narratives and discourses in our teaching as they are untapped sources upon which we can draw to enrich social work, create the conditions necessary for social change, and meet our social justice ethical responsibilities as social workers (Canadian Association of Social Workers, 2005). To accomplish this, we need to pay closer attention to subordinate cultures and peoples, and diverse cultural, gendered, queer, and racialized ways of being and knowing. As a result of surviving generations of oppression, these populations have had to become experts on the subjects of effective resistance. In this way, femagogy seeks to purposefully broaden and transform education to include women's and "othered" voices, bringing diverse knowledge from the margins into the mainstream (Kirby & McKenna, 1989).

Social Work Education and Femagogy: Application

Femagogy and Traditional Education

It is true that both femagogy and traditional education attempt to produce and share knowledge. However, one of the primary differences between applying the two approaches is that when one centres feminist analysis and methods in the classroom, one seeks "not only to produce knowledge but also to examine, unsettle and shift power relations" (Potts & Brown, 2005, p. 255), as well as transform social structures and societies. To examine this further, Table 3.1 highlights the main differences between traditional education and femagogy.

Femagogy and Social Work: Teaching Recommendations

One of the keys to applying femagogy to social work education is for instructors to consciously attempt to incorporate teaching methods and approaches that support the principles from the right side of Table 3.1. This chapter has already discussed how femagogy is different from pedagogy and andragogy and emphasizes the inclusion and exploration of women's voices through multiple ways of knowing. Additionally, femagogy also validates and normalizes "othered" people's experiences as "normal" responses to trauma and oppressive conditions (Wilkin & Hillock, 2016).

Correspondingly, a critical analysis of how power operates in modern society, as well as in our educational systems and classrooms, has implications for social work. Furthermore, students, groups, organizations, and systems with whom and in which we work are implicated in how power is constructed and maintained in our society. Bishop's (2002, 2005), Darlington and Mulvaney's (2003), Leonard's (1996), Rebick's (2009), Rossiter's (1993), and Starhawk's (1987, 2002) work on power are all useful

Table 3.1. Comparison between Traditional Education and Femagogy

Traditional Education	Femagogy
Pedagogy/andragogy	Femagogy
Male, cisgendered, White, Western, and heterosexist-centred research, authorship, teaching, and voices	Alternative, women's, and marginalized perspectives including Indigenous, queer, and anti-racist
Power-over	Power-within/sharing
Competition/hierarchy	Cooperation/collaboration
Maintaining the existing balance of power/status quo	Revolutionary
Teacher-/institution-centred	Student-/learning-centred
Expert	De-experting
Banking education	Transformation/liberation
Products	Person/process

Sources: Adapted from Campbell, 1999, 2002; Enge, 2013; Fook, 1999, 2004; Freire, 1970; Hillock, 2011; Hillock & Mulé, 2016; hooks, 1989, 1994, 2000; Sinclair et al., 2009; Starhawk, 1987, 2002; Weaver, 2009.

in exploring how power operates in educational settings. A feminist analysis of power is important as it moves us away from a simplistic binary categorizing of people into either "powerful" or "powerless" and helps deepen our understanding of the concept. Starhawk (1987, 1988, 2002) explores multiple types of power. In particular, she compares two forms of power that are most relevant for this chapter's discussion. She argues that within colonialist and capitalist societies, the most predominant form is "power-over," which she defines as "domination or force" (Starhawk, 1987, as cited in Bishop, 2002, p. 51). Under this form of power, competition, hierarchy, and inequality are the norm. She then compares and contrasts this with the concept of "power within," or power sharing, which she describes as "power exercised cooperatively among equals" (Starhawk, 1987, as cited in Bishop, 2002, p. 61). This form of power encourages cooperation and collaboration, as well as self-conscious criticism related to one's own bias and privilege.

Similarly, Darlington and Mulvaney (2003) enrich the definition of power by defining it not merely as object but as process, commenting that power is not a commodity available only to the elite, but "rather a process we all engage in" (p. 7). Healy and Leonard (2000) add that one must always consider "who is exercising the power, in whose interest, and who had defined the interest" (p. 27). Feminists agree that continual analysis and assessment are required to understand how power constrains or enables differently located individuals and groups. Table 3.2 summarizes

Table 3.2. Femagogy: Power Analysis Strategies

Identify and analyse the uses of power in the classroom, education, and research.	Use only the forms of power we want to see in our new society.
Attend to power imbalances and inequality between dominant and subordinate groups.	Create safe spaces in which questioning of the use of power is encouraged.
Reconceptualize power.	Increase power sharing/minimize power-over.

Sources: Adapted from Campbell, 2002; Hillock, 2011; Mathieson, 2002; Pentney, 2006; Preston-Shoot, 1995; Rebick, 2009; Strega & Brown, 2015; Starhawk, 2002.

how applying femagogy and its related power analysis strategies can help identify and challenge forms of power in the social work classroom.

Additionally, transforming our classrooms into sites of resistance, as discussed earlier, means changing our traditional lecture style, product-based, and teacher-centred methods to ones that open up disruptive and revolutionary possibilities, that is, to centre the margins. Femagogy is an approach that can help instructors move in this direction. While the following list is not exhaustive, here are some recommendations on how to apply femagogy to social work teaching:

1. Reject teaching as a site of certainty (Rossiter, 1993).
2. Accept that knowledge is not politically neutral and the knowledge of marginalized groups is underrepresented (Wilkin & Hillock, 2016).
3. Analyse power, overtly naming types of power, and explaining specific uses of authority (Table 3.2).
4. Reflexively disentangle internalized oppression and personal bias (Preston-Shoot, 1995) and examine where one fits as part of systems of oppression and inequality (Hillock, 2011).
5. Examine major theories as stories that privilege some and oppress/silence others (Rossiter, 1993) while developing alternative discourses, voices from the margins, to address these (Collins, 2000).
6. Always ask who benefits and what voices are missing (Hillock, 2011).
7. Encourage active democratic student participation and a non-hierarchical classroom, namely, transformational versus banking education (Pentney, 2006).
8. Value and reflect upon how emotion, affect, relationship, and experience enrich the learning process, that is, an ethic of caring (Held, 1995; also Jeyapal & Grigg, chapter 6).
9. Bring "gender justice to the classroom" (hooks, 2000, p. 23) by explicitly discussing gender-based violence and providing trauma analyses and intervention (Wilkin & Hillock, 2016).

10 Engage in timeouts in the classroom to ask students to notice what is happening in the classroom and the group (Cohee, 2004).
11 Be open to alternative assignments (Campbell, 1999, 2002), rewarding creativity and innovation, and collaboratively developing self-directed learning, assessment, and evaluation, and innovative learning contracts (Lemieux, 2001).
12 Network with colleagues, students, unions/associations, and community partners to work together to build alternative power structures and create the conditions necessary for social change (Baines, 2003, 2007; Hillock, 2011; Mathieson, 2002).

Femagogy: Application Challenges

Despite our best intentions, teaching from a femagogy stance is not always easy for instructors or students. Academia is not immune from discriminatory practices. In addition, not all students agree with progressive approaches or desire transformational teaching and learning experiences (Bannerji, 1995; Hillock, 2011; Jeffery, 2007; Overall, 1998; Schick, 2005; The Chilly Collectives, 1995; Weaver, 2009). Moreover, research shows that educators who try to use progressive teaching approaches are more likely to face backlash (Hillock, 2011; Overall, 1998; The Chilly Collective, 1995). Backlash can manifest in many ways, including classroom disruption, poor course evaluations, and student complaints.[1] How we perceive and handle backlash, and the support we receive and give colleagues, are important considerations in terms of implementing alternative approaches.

Conclusion

This chapter has attempted to make clear that as social work educators, we have choices regarding how we identify and name what is happening around us and to us; the types of teaching and learning opportunities we want to provide to social work students; and how we act and respond, or not, to resist oppressive forces and structures. Social work educators also have an ethical obligation to educate future practitioners so that they are properly equipped to work with vulnerable populations and promote social justice. I suggested the use of a new perspective called femagogy to assist social work educators to apply feminist teaching-learning

1 See chapters 18 and 19 for a further exploration of the challenges and recommendations on how to transform social work education from a femagogical perspective.

approaches. I hope that by providing a brief summary of feminism, defining femagogy, describing its fit with social work, exploring its transformational possibilities, and comparing this innovative approach to traditional education, readers will reflect upon how we are all implicated in oppressive processes and structures and how we can work towards transforming social work education.

REFERENCES

Accardi, M. T. (2016, December 21). Feminist pedagogy: Changing lives, libraries, and the world. *The Open Stacks.* https://www.choice360.org/blog/feminist-pedagogy-changing-lives-libraries-and-the-world

Baines, D. (2003). Race, class, and gender in the everyday talk of social workers: The ways we limit the possibilities for radical practice. In W. Shera (Ed.), *Emerging perspectives in anti-oppressive practice* (pp. 43–64). Canadian Scholars Press.

Baines, D. (2007). Bridging the practice-activism divide in mainstream social work: Advocacy, organizing, and social movements. In D. Baines (Ed.), *Doing anti-oppressive practice* (pp. 50–66). Fernwood Publishing.

Bannerji, H. (1995). *Thinking through: Essays on feminism, Marxism, and anti-racism.* Women's Press.

Barnoff, L., & Coleman, B. (2007). Strategies for integrating anti-oppressive principles: Perspectives from feminist agencies. In D. Baines (Ed.), *Doing anti-oppressive practice* (pp. 31–49). Fernwood Publishing.

Barnoff, L., & Moffat, K. (2007). Contradictory tensions in anti-oppression practice in feminist social services. *Afflia: Journal of Women and Social Work, 22*(1), 56–70. https://doi.org/10.1177/0886109906295772

Belenky, M. F., McVicker, C. B., Goldberger, N. R., & Tarule, M. J. (1997). *Women's ways of knowing: The development of self, voice, and mind, 10th anniversary edition.* Basic Books.

Bishop, A. (2002). *Becoming an ally: Breaking the cycle of oppression in people* (2nd ed.). Fernwood Publishing.

Bishop, A. (2005). *Beyond token change: Breaking the cycle of oppression in institutions.* Fernwood Publishing.

Briskin, L. (1990). *Feminist pedagogy: Teaching and learning liberation.* York University, Social Science Division.

Briskin, L. (1992). Socialist feminism. In M. P. Connelly & P. Armstrong (Eds.), *Feminism in action* (pp. 263–93). Canadian Scholars Press.

Campbell, C. (1999). Empowering pedagogy: Experiential education in the social work classroom. *Canadian Social Work Review,* 16 (1), 35–48.

Campbell, C. (2002). The search for congruency: Developing strategies for anti-oppressive social work pedagogy. *Canadian Social Work Review,* 19(1), 25–42.

Canadian Association of Social Workers. (2005). *Code of ethics.*

Carniol, B. (2005). Analysis of social location and change: Practice implications. In S. Hick, J. Fook, & R. Pozzuto (Eds.), *Social work: A critical turn* (pp. 153–66). Thompson Educational Publishing, Inc.

Collins, P. H. (1991). *Black feminist thought.* Routledge.

Collins, P. H. (2000). *Black feminist thought: Knowledge, consciousness, and the politics of empowerment* (2nd ed.). Routledge.

Cohee, G. (2004). Feminist pedagogy. *The Teaching Exchange, 9*(1), 1–4.

Darlington, P., & Mulvaney B. (2003). *Women, power, and ethnicity.* Haworth Press.

Dominelli, L. (2002a). *Anti-oppressive social work theory and practice.* Palgrave MacMillan.

Dominelli, L. (2002b). *Feminist theory and social work practice.* Palgrave MacMillan.

Ellsworth, E. (1989). Why doesn't this feel empowering? Working through the repressive myths of critical pedagogy. *Harvard Educational Review,* 59(3), 297–324. https://doi.org/10.17763/haer.59.3.058342114k266250

Enge, J. (2013). *Social workers' feminist perspectives: Implications for practice.* (MSW paper 174) [Master's thesis, St. Catherine University]. Sophia Repository. http://sophia.stkate.edu/msw_papers/174

Erikson, E. H. (1994). *Identity and the life cycle.* W.W. Norton & Company.

Flynn Saulnier, C. (2008). Incorporating feminist theory into social work practice: Group work examples, *Social Work with Groups, 23*(1), 5–29.

Fook, J. (1999). Critical reflectivity in education and practice. In B. Pease & J. Fook (Eds.), *Transforming social work practice: Postmodern critical perspectives* (pp. 195–210). Routledge.

Fook, J. (2004). Critical reflection and transformative possibilities. In L. Davies & P. Leonard (Eds.), *Social work in a corporate era: Practices of power and resistance* (pp. 16–31). Ashgate.

Freire, P. (1970). *Pedagogy of the oppressed.* Continuum.

Gilligan, C. (1988). Theory of sex differences in the development of moral reasoning during adolescence. *Adolescence, 23*(89), 229–43. https://doi.org/10.4135/9781473984592

Haney, Eleanor H. (1989). *Vision and struggle: Meditations on feminist spirituality and politics.* Shell Press.

Hanisch, C. (2009). *The personal is political: The women's liberation movement classic with a new explanatory chapter.* CarolHanisch.org. http://www.carolhanisch.org/CHwritings/PIP.html

Healy, K., & Leonard, P. (2000). Responding to uncertainty: Critical social work education in the post-modern habitat. *Journal of Progressive Human Services, 11*(1), 23–48. https://doi.org/10.1300/j059v11n01_03

Held, V. (1995). *Justice and care: Essential readings in feminist ethics.* Westview Press.

Hillock, S. (2011). *Conceptualizing oppression: Resistance narratives for social work* [Unpublished doctoral dissertation]. Memorial University of Newfoundland.

Hillock, S., & Mulé, N. J. (Eds.). (2016). *Queering social work education.* UBC Press.

hooks, b. (1989). *Talking back: Thinking feminist, thinking black.* South End Press.

hooks, b. (1994). *Teaching to transgress: Education as a practice of freedom.* Routledge.

hooks, b. (2000). *Feminist theory: From margin to centre* (2nd ed.). south End Press.

Ife, J. (1997). *Rethinking social work: Towards critical practice.* Longman.

Jane, J., Oltmanns, T., South, S., & Turkheimer, E. (2007). Gender bias in diagnostic criteria for personality disorders: An item response theory analysis. *Abnormal Psychology, 116*(1), 166–75. https://doi.org/10.1037/0021-843x.116.1.166

Jeffery, D. (2007). Radical problems and liberal selves. *Canadian Social Work Review, 24*(2), 125–39.

Kirby, S., Greaves, L., & Reid, C. (2006). *Experience research social change: Methods beyond the mainstream.* Broadview Press.

Kirby, S., & McKenna, K. (1989). *Methods from the margins.* Garamond Press.

Kohlberg, L., & Hersh, R. H. (1977). Moral development: A review of theory. *Theory Into Practice, 16*(2), 53–9. https://doi.org/10.1080/00405847709542675

Lemieux, C. (2001). Learning contracts in the classroom: Tools for empowerment and accountability. *Social Work Education, 20*(2), 263–76. https://doi.org/10.1080/02615470120044347

Leonard P. (1996). Knowledge/power and postmodernism: Implications for the practice of a critical social work education. *Canadian Social Work Review, 11*(1), 11–26.

Levine, H. (1982). The personal is political: Feminism and the helping professions. In G. Finn & A. Miles (Eds.), *Feminism in Canada: From pressure to politics* (pp. 175–209). Black Rose Books.

Lorber, J. (2005). *Gender inequality: Feminist theories and politics* (3rd ed.). Roxbury Publishing Company.

Marsiglia, F., & Kulis, S. (2009). *Culturally grounded social work: Diversity oppression and change.* Lyceum.

Mathieson, G. (2002). Reconceptualizing our classroom practice: Notes from an anti-racist educator. In N. Nathani Wane, K. Deliovsky, & E. Lawson (Eds.), *Back to the drawing board: African Canadian feminisms* (pp. 158–74). Sumach Press.

Mellor, M. (1997). *Feminism and ecology.* New York University Press.

Mullaly, B. (2010). *Challenging oppression and confronting privilege.* Oxford University Press.

Mullings, D. (2016). Social work education: Exploring pitfalls and promises with Black queer older adults. In S. Hillock & N. Mulé (Eds.), *Queering social work education* (pp. 205–26). UBC Press.

Nash, M. (1989). Women and social work: Five principles for feminist practice. *Social Work Review, 1*(3 & 4), 9–13.

Nes, J. A., & Iadicola, P. (1989). Toward a definition of feminist social work: A comparison of liberal, radical, and socialist models. *National Association of Social Workers, 34*(1), 12–21. https://doi.org/10.1093/sw/34.1.12

Osmond, J., & O'Connor, I. (2004). Formalizing the un-formalized: Practitioners' communication of knowledge in practice. *British Journal of Social Work, 34*(5), 677–92. https://doi.org/10.1093/bjsw/bch084

Overall, C. (1998). *A feminist 1: Reflections from academia.* Broadview Press.

Pentney, B. (2006). "Oh my femagogy!": A theoretical and self-reflexive examination of feminist pedagogy in practice. *Not drowning but waving: A conference on women, feminism, and the liberal arts.* University of Alberta.

Potts, K., & Brown, L. (2005). Becoming an anti-oppressive researcher. In L. Brown & S. Strega (Eds.), *Research is resistance: Critical, Indigenous and anti-oppressive approaches* (pp. 255–86). Canadian Scholars Press.

Preston-Shoot, M. (1995). Assessing anti-oppressive practice. *Social Work Education, 14*(2), 11–29. https://doi.org/10.1080/02615479511220101

Razack, N. (1999). Anti-discriminatory practice: Pedagogical struggles and challenges. *British Journal of Social Work, 29*(2), 231–50. https://doi.org/10.1093/oxfordjournals.bjsw.a011444

Razack, N. (2002). Transforming the field: Critical antiracist and anti-oppressive perspectives for the human services practicum. Fernwood Publishing.

Razack, N. (2009). Decolonizing the pedagogy and practice of international social work. *International Social Work, 52*(1), 9–21. https://doi.org/10.1177/0020872808097748

Rebick, J. (2009). *Transforming power from the personal to the political.* Penguin.

Rossiter, A. B. (1993). Teaching from a critical perspective: Towards empowerment in social work education. *Canadian Social Work Review, 10*(1), 76–90.

Schick, C. (2005). Keeping the ivory tower white: Discourses of racial discrimination. In V. Zawilski & C. Levine-Rasky (Eds.), *Inequality in Canada* (pp. 208–20). Oxford University Press.

Schiller, L. (1997). Rethinking stages of development in women's groups: Implications for practice. *Social Work with Groups, 20*(3), 3–19. https://doi.org/10.1300/j009v20n03_02

Sinclair, R., Hart, M. A., & Bruyere, G. (2009). *Wícihitowin: Aboriginal social work in Canada.* Fernwood Books.

Sisneros, J., Stakeman, C., Joyner, M., & Schmitz, C. (2008). *Critical multicultural social work.* Lyceum Books.

Starhawk. (1987). *Truth or dare: Encounters with power, authority, and mystery.* Harper and Row.

Starhawk. (1988). *Dreaming the dark.* Beacon Press.

Starhawk. (2002). *Webs of power.* New Society Publishers.
Strega, S., & Brown, L. (Eds.). (2015). *Research as resistance: Revisiting critical, Indigenous, and anti-oppressive approaches* (2nd ed.). Canadian Scholars' Press.
The Chilly Collective. (1995). *Breaking anonymity: The chilly climate for women.* Wilfrid Laurier University Press.
Van Den Bergh, N. (Ed.). (1995). *Feminist practice in the 21st century.* NASW Press.
Weaver, A. (2009). *Choosing to be brave: A journey of mindfulness from an anti-oppressive perspective* [Unpublished Master's thesis]. University of Manitoba.
Weedon, C. (1997). *Feminist practice and poststructuralist theory* (2nd ed.). Blackwell.
Weiler, K. (1991). Freire and a feminist pedagogy of difference. *Harvard Educational Review, 61*(4), 449–75. https://doi.org/10.17763/haer.61.4.a102265jl68rju84
Westervelt, A. (2015, April 30). The medical research gap: How excluding women from clinical trials is hurting our health. *The Guardian.* https://www.theguardian.com/lifeandstyle/2015/apr/30/fda-clinical-trials-gender-gap-epa-nih-institute-of-medicine-cardiovascular-disease
Wilkin, L., & Hillock, S. (2016). Enhancing MSW students' efficacy in working with trauma, violence, and oppression: An integrated feminist-trauma framework for social work education. *Feminist Teacher, 24*(30), 189–206.
Yee, J. Y. (2005). Critical anti-racism practice: The concept of whiteness implicated. In S. Hick, J. Fook, & R. Pozzuto (Eds.), *Social work: A critical turn* (pp. 87–104). Thompson Educational Publishing.

4 Tackling Whiteness in the Classroom and Challenging/Shattering the Skills-Based Curriculum through Anti-oppression Teaching in Social Work

JUNE YING YEE AND ANNE E. WAGNER

The impact of neo-liberalism in academia is broadly acknowledged, with many authors detailing the effects of neo-liberal ideologies on learning in social work and beyond (Morley & Dunstan, 2013; Seymour, 2014; Zepke, 2015). In the contemporary audit culture of higher education, even critical scholars are unable to inure themselves to the emphasis on training for job readiness that neo-liberal thinking prioritizes. Competency-based initiatives increasingly undermine theoretically informed approaches in the field of social work. These initiatives adopt hierarchical relationships that position social workers as experts and devalue the wisdom of service users; they promote technical and procedural solutions in response to complex problems (Morley & Dunstan, 2013). Not only do these shifts put the profession at risk of losing its transformative agenda, but they also contribute to a widening divide between academia and the field of social work.

This tension between scholars and practitioners is of critical significance given the mounting challenges to the profession from historically marginalized groups who point to the ongoing inattention to systemic sources of oppression. Glaring issues include the over-representation of Black and Indigenous children coming into care (Esquao & Strega, 2015), Black children being psychiatrized and medicated at higher rates than other children (Abdillahi et al., 2017), and the expectation that LGBTQ2 populations should assimilate into mainstream agencies that are formed by neo-liberal and non-queer structures (Mulé, 2015). If social work practice is to be inclusive, anti-oppression teaching and learning must be integrated into all areas of social work curricula. In this process of integration, anti-oppression teaching and learning inevitably brings emotionally charged conversations and tensions to the classroom. Since most students come to the classroom inoculated with values and beliefs from dominant discourses, for them to engage in discussions that challenge what they have come to know as uncontested knowledge arouses discomfort and resistance. Upon learning that they are themselves implicated and a part of the problem, they will naturally rush to a place of "innocence" with claims that they "just want to help"; but as Rossiter (2001) points out, "there is no such thing as knowledge that doesn't exclude at the same time that it includes" (para. 8).

So, how might social work educators challenge neo-liberal pressures to deliver a predominantly skills-based curriculum? Critical pedagogical approaches offer a site for resisting these forces and establishing a space in which knowledge is troubled, enabling an exploration of the tensions and complexities of issues. By moving beyond dominant pedagogical practices that predominantly focus on developing skill-based competencies and striving to raise individual self-awareness regarding systems of privilege and oppression, critical approaches adopt a broader, deeper analysis of social relations. If we acknowledge that social work is a profession that is necessarily implicated in reproducing unequal power relations, classrooms may function as spaces in which to demonstrate how to productively engage in discussions and actions related to dynamics of marginalization and oppression. By engaging in critical dialogue about contentious social issues, educators may model for students how to deconstruct dominant understandings through exploring the complexities and tensions of knowledge while eschewing simple, straightforward solutions. The goal, as Zembylas (2013) suggests, is to establish a pedagogic space for "understanding troubled knowledge in more nuanced terms" (p. 186). What we propose is greater attention to the *process* of learning and how we, as educators, can consciously model critical engagement and how we mutually constitute one another within this *process* of learning in the classroom. How we talk about issues and engage across differences can create a powerful opportunity for learning.

In this chapter, we explore the ways in which this contested field of teaching and learning raises practice dilemmas in a space of diverse understandings or interpretations of social issues and the requisite actions needed to work towards social justice (Seymour, 2014). To do this challenging work, one must also ask, are educators themselves capable of navigating these difficult terrains and what is their own capacity for critical questioning? For instance, consider teaching and learning about anti-racism theory and practice. Do social work educators have the requisite in-depth knowledge and understanding of the history, theory, and phenomenology/experience behind the related core concepts of white privilege, whiteness, and white supremacy? To teach this material during the *process* of learning, educators must carefully avoid reinstating the role of the white, Western subject, that is, a removed, detached, white liberal subject of social work who is devoid of history and self, but rather must locate their own personal subjectivity and self-implication into the knowledge-making of what we come to know as the "doing" of social work practice (Jeffery, 2005).

How Being a "Good" Social Worker Promotes "Whiteness" in Social Work: A Dilemma

Schools of social work in Canada are known to be deeply embedded in reproducing whiteness through a "set of social practices, systems and values" aimed at producing "good" social workers who help others (Jeffery, 2005, p. 419). The notion of helping in social work has been constructed in a particular way, and one does not need to look far to trace its genealogical history rooted in a desire and discourse of "helping" that has been problematic for oppressed groups. In the United Kingdom, Australia, and North America, the roots of the social work profession began with two different approaches to helping: the Charity Organization Society (COS) and the Settlement House movement. COS promoted a type of social work practice that placed great emphasis on the casework method, whose purpose was to rehabilitate the poor by equipping them with the values and motivation to become productive and contributing members of society. In contrast, the Settlement House movement did try to challenge the social work profession, at the structural level, by advocating for the state to provide concrete, practical resources to help the poor.

These histories reveal a dichotomous difference on how to help; the former emphasizes individual empowerment and reform of the individual, while the latter recognizes the need to provide pragmatic resources plus advocacy for structural change. Yet both approaches, while purporting to pursue social justice, have produced and reproduced the social and cultural processes of whiteness in their practice of social work.

Whiteness operates to create and reinforce privilege and power through various social and cultural processes, including the ability to (1) shape the norms and values of society, (2) frame the representation and embodiment of white culture as the source of referential social norms and determine that of non-whites as "other"; and (3) assume that white people's own historical and sociopolitical vantage point is the dominant worldview (Gabriel, 1998, p. 13).[1] Speaking specifically to social work, some authors (Esquao & Strega, 2015; Jeffery, 2005) have noted that a less obvious role and purpose of the profession is to maintain the status

---

1 For a definition and further description of whiteness, see Yee (2015).

quo, and to do so by applying professionally designated competencies to manage difference. Those who are marginalized are seen as different and not fitting into the "social norm" of society, which is whiteness. Hence, the role of social work is constructed as the need to work with the marginalized to enable them to conform to, or at least better approximate, the norms and standards of dominant society. This focus on helping the marginalized to better fit into society positions the practice of social work as a profession that maintains whiteness; it is accomplished by narrowly defining social work practices within professional competencies that reframe social problems as technical issues to be fixed. Jeffery (2005) outlines this problem as inherent in most teaching and practice:

> Pedagogy about race and racism within social work education is structured to fit within the parameters of how practice is defined. Yet the day-to-day practices on which the profession rests, and which sustain the profession, reproduce whiteness. Thus, "doing race" following this same formula functions to reproduce whiteness and race as one more skill at which to be competent. (p. 411)

It is in this context that Jeffery (2005) cogently notes that "social work practice both produces knowledge and constitutes subjects" (p. 419). She argues further that the problematic processes involved are not easy to unearth because

> whiteness serve[s] as a deeply embedded organizing principle in social and cultural relations. It is fundamentally a process of subject formation and a construction of desire. All of these qualities shape the processes of concealment which are so integral to discourses of professional helping and mastery. (Jeffery, 2005, p. 413)

Scholars may actively work to challenge neo-liberal thinking, but its influence nonetheless penetrates the classroom. This arises in how students are most interested in learning techniques and tools to equip them in their future practice. Across Canada, there is support for this type of learning about practice, with its emphasis on social work competencies that are defined and codified as the true measure of good practice, and the basis for evaluation and assessment of the knowledge base of social work (Newfoundland & Labrador Association of Social Workers, 2016). Simultaneously, in the contemporary labour market, demonstrated acquisition of social work competencies and skills in diversity work are highly valued. Hence, students sometimes perceive critical social work teaching as another form of competency as opposed to questioning the reliance on technical competencies in itself. When this occurs, learning about critical social work becomes a useful commodity to possess upon graduation. More specifically, diversity skills come to act as a form of symbolic and cultural capital that can be used to demonstrate a commitment, albeit often superficial, to a socially just approach (Bhuyan et al., 2017). The danger in taking this approach in curriculum teaching is that students graduate with the knowledge of the language of social justice but without the requisite depth of understanding related to structural or social change (Jeffery, 2007).

Student Reactions to Critical Pedagogy That Goes Beyond Acquiring Social Work Competencies

To navigate these dynamics, students need opportunities to engage critically in discussions on the shifting terrain of knowledge and competing claims of social issues, and thus to develop the critical thinking skills required to begin deconstructing the often taken for granted dominant discourses and ideologies rooted in neo-liberal thought and white supremacy. The lack of a truly critical understanding of social justice issues leads to replicating what Schick (2014, p. 100) calls "white space":

> Reasserting white space is a performative act that accomplishes white supremacy and white identity; it also demonstrates and confirms the white racial knowledge on how to do this. As a result, "[w]hite racial knowledge limits and defines what whites are prepared to hear about a subordinate group and still "allow a self-concept of innocence to continue." (Nelson, 2002, p. 224)

In the broader historic and social context, white supremacy is what allows the social and cultural process of whiteness to be maintained in the way we do social work practice, and social work competencies can be viewed as a part of its perpetuation. Too often in the classroom, students would prefer to learn the skills based in social work competencies that emphasize the "doing" of social work practice. But this doing of social work can result in "focus[ing] on techniques" (Smith & Jeffery, 2013, p. 374) without the required deeper work of examining the troubling ways we are implicated in producing and reproducing whiteness in the practice of social work. Even when teaching from an anti-oppression approach, an umbrella term that provides theoretical analysis in areas such as anti-racism, anti-Black racism, and feminism, in relation to social work practice, many students misconstrue anti-oppression as just a "code for professional correctness" (Smith & Jeffery, 2013, p. 374). This results in the concept of anti-oppression being only superficially understood. In other words, teaching about anti-oppression is frequently not seen as part of social work practice skills and techniques in the way that designated social work competencies are. Instead, anti-oppression is viewed as more about correcting people on language and ideologically telling others what to think. Students, and at times faculty members, too, are surprised, if not threatened, by the extent to which anti-oppression social work pedagogy requires that they engage in critical self-reflexivity and in analyses of their own positioning within broader systems and structures. Students often find it especially unsettling that critical pedagogy seeks to challenge taken for granted truths and stresses the importance of discarding a binary perspective of the world to instead explore its complexities and nuances.

These tensions play out in the classroom in many ways, but a common experience is dealing with the micro-aggressions that occur between students and between students and teachers (Solorzano et al., 2000). Sue et al. (2007) define micro-aggressions as

> the brief and commonplace daily verbal, behavioral and environmental indignities, whether intentional or unintentional, that communicate hostile, derogatory or negative racial slights and insults that potentially have harmful or unpleasant psychological impact on the target person or group. (p. 271)

Micro-aggressions can refer not only to race but also to gender, sexuality, and ability. For example, in class discussions, a student may disparage certain mothering practices and express an assessment such as, "She is a bad mother," while failing to see the systemic sources of oppression that the mother experiences as a parent. In such an instance, a student in the classroom may be, or know, a mother with similar life experiences and would experience this as a denigrating micro-aggression.

Souza (2018, para. 2) notes that unaddressed micro-aggressions in the classroom have an "adverse effect on student learning and comfort." A teacher may "feel frozen, if the observer, or defensive, if the target or perpetrator" (Souza, 2018, para. 2). In these moments, it is important that social work educators maintain a supportive classroom climate (Souza, 2018) by using the opportunity to introduce a teachable moment that requires dialogue, but not debate. Debate creates competition where there are winners and losers and, worse, promotes the idea that there is only one (superior) way of viewing things and, thus, has a tendency to shut down conversations. Dialogue requires all in the room to listen to one another, to find ways to communicate with one another, and to hold one another accountable for words and actions. By not addressing micro-aggressions, teachers are complicit in perpetuating the social and cultural process of reinforcing whiteness in the classroom. In this example, the opportunity arises to explore how the use of such language and judgment is problematic and serves to further marginalize certain groups. Unless social work educators open a space to discuss the invisibility and effects of privilege, the privileged are likely to remain unaware that they have committed a micro-aggression. Such is the reality of privilege; it obscures from awareness the ways in which the actions and language of the privileged often support and are complicit in producing and reproducing whiteness. From an anti-oppressive perspective, one could argue that students may be invested in maintaining a view of the world that reproduces their own privileged worldview positions, that is, white, able-bodied, heteronormative locations.

These situations are indicative of the way in which the classroom is a microcosm of the social dynamics in society. Hence, social work educators must be prepared to intervene in these dynamics in constructive ways that may subsequently be translated into social work practice. It is not enough to call out the micro-aggression; in fact, this is not constructive and does not foster an inclusive learning environment. It may shame the student, and it is likely to shut down discussion. Some social work educators will engage the classroom in a discussion regarding language choices while still naming and addressing the micro-aggression. In this way, everyone is encouraged to critically engage in an analysis of the significance of using judgmental terms and its effects. Although students will often deflect, minimize, or speak to the "harmlessness" of using such language, it is useful to redirect the discussion to the academic literature on whiteness that unequivocally asserts that power is embedded in such instances and, even if unintentional, causes harm to those who are marginalized. Personal intent is irrelevant; it is more important to consider the impact of our actions and language. This scenario is but one example of the complexities inherent in every classroom. As Zembylas (2013) explains, the reality is that "classrooms are not homogenous environments with a common understanding of oppression, but deeply divided places where contested narratives are steeped in the politics of emotions to create complex emotional and intellectual challenges for teachers" (p. 181).

Self-Awareness and Skills Required for Teaching Dilemmas

Grounding our teaching practice in approaches that question the certainty of knowledge claims is often an anxiety-provoking experience for students (Jeffery, 2007; Seymour, 2014; Wagner & Yee, 2011). It is also a fraught endeavour for social work educators, as Seymour (2014) notes:

> In destabilising "truth" and knowledge, one's academic identity and credibility is also rendered precarious, and this, it must be said, is a somewhat uncomfortable position to inhabit given the highly corporatized and highly competitive nature of academia. (p. 8)

For these reasons, critical teaching increases the vulnerability of students and faculty members, who must be skilled at facilitating conflict and strong emotions (Zembylas, 2013) because it is likely that students' worldviews will be challenged. Beyond presenting the ideas of critical analysis and an anti-oppression approach, teachers are required to role model how to critically analyse information, engage in respectful communication and discussion, and propose alternative perspectives. Navigating these discussions in the classroom is often especially complicated for faculty members who do not approximate the norms of whiteness. They often, in effect, use their bodies as a teaching tool and must devise strategies to withstand the micro-aggressions and strong negative emotions projected at them by students who may not welcome the unsettling of their worldviews (Lawson, 2011; Macías, 2013). Student reactions may also be rooted in their perceptions of particular teachers; as considerable literature attests, those who do not approximate the white, male, heterosexual, cisgendered norm are likely to have their authority questioned and be perceived as imposing their own political agenda in the classroom (Massaquoi, 2017; Pittman, 2010; Vakalahi & Starks, 2010). Consequently, some teachers are required to navigate the dynamics and heightened emotions within the classroom as an "embodied being" since their identity may serve as a site of contestation (Zingsheim & Goltz, 2011) based on the perception that they do not "fit" or have a "right" to challenge the normativity of whiteness in the classroom.

It is important to contextualize this analysis within the current neoliberal political climate in which students are largely socialized to perceive the world in individualistic terms that maintain a we/they binary, even among oppressed groups. A fundamental challenge for social work educators is navigating the fraught terrain of competing values, beliefs, and ideologies, as well as challenging dominant assumptions. Coupled with these realities is the necessity that to immerse students in anti-oppressive approaches, social work educators must move beyond simply "managing" differences and tensions in the classroom, and undertake the emotional labour of excavating the underlying emotional landscape in which these ideological commitments are rooted. In other words, they must interrogate how these deeply held beliefs, values, and understandings are rooted in systems, structures, and social relations. Thus, when students react viscerally to ideas that challenge their worldviews, educators must establish connections between individual-level experiences and reactions and the broader context. For instance, it may be helpful to consider what is being threatened. How might this perception be challenged from another standpoint? In this way, a discussion may ensue about the fact that fear or discomfort is not solely the domain of the oppressed and is also inextricably linked to apprehensions about the privileges and security of the dominant group being challenged. In this way, the social work educator can move students away from personalizing issues and begin developing the skills to base analyses in a more comprehensive, contextual frame of reference that is grounded in anti-oppression.

Conclusion

In the contemporary academic context that is steeped in neo-liberal ideology, social work educators must be conversant with whiteness and how it operates, and be adept at translating this knowledge to prepare students for practice. Educators must resist the mounting pressures to focus on developing generic and instrumental competencies for the workplace (Morley & Dunstan, 2013). We can confront these forces by reaffirming the importance of adopting a critical stance and by preparing students to enter a contested field where experiences of oppression and marginalization will be at the forefront of practice. Critical teaching will also contribute to the project of destabilizing the white, privileged, Western moral subject in the form of the "good" social worker, "who is presumed to be the subject at the center of the management of difference discourse" (Jeffery, 2005, p. 419). By challenging students' enculturation in neo-liberal thinking that leads them to unquestioningly accept their need for a simple tool kit of practice skills, we will cultivate critical thinkers, capable of engaging in dialogue and working alongside multiple perspectives to contribute to a transformative social work agenda.

When failing to address micro-aggressions and the tensions associated with discussing social issues linked to race, gender, sexuality, and ability, social work educators deprive students of learning the fundamental skills associated with social work pedagogy: the ability to link lived experience with broader structural factors. In such instances, "innocent" discourses of helping are perpetuated and the ideology of white supremacy remains unchallenged in the classroom. Fundamentally, social work educators require the ability, skills, and willingness to engage within a pedagogy of discomfort and must be adept at handling the emotional responses often resulting from a critical pedagogy that is likely to unsettle students. This requires highly developed facilitation and conflict resolution skills to avoid shutting down or silencing students; it requires enacting the practice and the theory of social work and of transformative education.

REFERENCES

Abdillahi, I., Meerai, S., & Poole, J. (2017). When the suffering is compounded: Toward anti-black sanism. In S. Wehbi & H. Parada (Eds.), *Reimagining anti-oppression social work practice* (pp. 107–22). Canadian Scholars' Press.

Bhuyan, R., Bejan, R., & Jeyapal, D. (2017). Social workers' perspectives on social justice in social work education: When mainstreaming social justice masks structural inequalities. *Social Work Education, 36*(4), 373–90. https://doi.org/10.1080/02615479.2017.1298741

Esquao, S. A. [Jeannine Carriere], & Strega, S. (2015). Introduction: Anti-racist and anti-oppressive child welfare practice. In S. A. Esquao [Jeannine Carriere] & S. Strega (Eds.), *Walking this path together: Anti-racist and anti-oppressive child welfare practice* (2nd ed., pp. 1–24). Fernwood Publishing.

Gabriel, J. (1998). *Whitewash: Racialized politics and the media.* Routledge.

Jeffery, D. (2005). "What good is anti-racist social work if you can't master it?": Exploring a paradox in anti-racist social work education. *Race Ethnicity and Education, 8*(4), 409–25. https://doi.org/10.1080/13613320500324011

Jeffery, D. (2007). Radical problems and liberal selves: Professional subjectivity in the anti-oppressive social work classroom. *Canadian Social Work Review / Revue canadienne de service social, 24*(2), 125–39.

Lawson, T. (2011). Feminist pedagogies: The textuality of the racialized body in the feminist classroom. *Journal of Further and Higher Education, 35*(2), 317–37.

Macías, T. (2013). Bursting bubbles: The challenges of teaching critical social work. *Affilia: Journal of Women and Social Work, 28*(3), 322–4. https://doi.org/10.1177/0886109913495730

Massaquoi, N. (2017). Crossing boundaries: Radicalizing social work practice and education. In D. Baines (Ed.), *Doing anti-oppressive practice: Social justice social work* (3rd ed., pp. 289–303). Fernwood.

Morley, C., & Dunstan, J. (2013). Critical reflection: A response to neoliberal challenges to field Education. *Social Work Education, 32*(2), 141–56. https://doi.org/10.1080/02615479.2012.730141

Mulé, N. (2015). Chapter one: The politicized queer, the informed social worker: Dis/re-ordering the social order. In B. O'Neill, T. Swan, & N. Mulé (Eds.), *LGBTQ people and social work: Intersectional perspectives* (pp. 17–35). Canadian Scholars' Press.

Nelson, J. (2002). The space of Africville: Creating, regulating and remembering the urban "slum." In S. Razack (Ed.), *Race, space, and the law: Unmapping a white settler society* (pp. 211–32). Between the Lines.

Newfoundland & Labrador Association of Social Workers. (2016, May 5). *Standards for cultural competency in social work practice.* http://www.nlasw.ca/sites/default/files/inline-files/Cultural_Competency_Standards.pdf

Pittman, C. (2010). Race and gender oppression in the classroom: The experience of women faculty of color with white male students. *Teaching Sociology, 38*(3), 183–6. https://doi.org/10.1177/0092055x10370120

Rossiter, A. (2001). Innocence lost and suspicion found: Do we educate for or against social work? *Critical Social Work, 2*(1). https://ojs.uwindsor.ca/index.php/csw/article/view/5628/4598

Seymour, K. (2014). Politics and positionality: Engaging with maps of meaning. *Social Work Education, 34*(3), 275–85. https://doi.org/10.1080/02615479.2014.962504

Schick, C. (2014). White resentment in settler society. *Race, Ethnicity and Education, 17*(1), 88–102. https://doi.org/10.1080/13613324.2012.733688

Smith, K. M., & Jeffery, D. I. (2013). Critical pedagogies in the neoliberal university: What happens when they go digital? *The Canadian Geographer / Le Géographe Canadien, 57*(3), 372–80. https://doi.org/10.1111/cag.12023

Solorzano, D., Ceja, M., & Yosso, T. (2000). Critical race theory, racial microaggressions, and campus racial climate: The experiences of African American college students. *Journal of Negro Education, 69*(1), 60–73.

Souza, T. (2018, April 30). Responding to microaggressions in the classroom: Taking action. *Faculty Focus: Higher Education Teaching Strategies from Magna Publications.* https://www.facultyfocus.com/articles/effective-classroom-management/responding-to-microaggressions-in-the-classroom/

Sue, D. W., Bucceri, J., Lin, A. I., Nadal, K. L., & Torino, G. C. (2007). Racial microaggressions in everyday life: Implications for counseling. *American Psychologist, 62*(4), 271–86. https://doi.org/10.1037/0003-066x.62.4.271

Vakalahi, H. F. O., & Starks, S. H. (2010). The complexities of becoming visible: Reflecting on the stories of women of color as social work educators. *Affilia: Journal of Women and Social Work, 25*(2), 110–22. https://doi.org/10.1177/0886109910364343

Wagner, A., & Yee, J. Y. (2011). Anti-oppression in higher education: Implicating neo-liberalism. *Canadian Social Work Review, 28*(1), 89–105.

Yee, J. Y. (2015). Whiteness and white supremacy in social work. In J. Wright (Ed.), *International encyclopedia of social and behavioral sciences,* Social Work (2nd ed., pp. 569–74). Elsevier.

Zembylas, M. (2013). Critical pedagogy and emotion: Working through "troubled knowledge" in posttraumatic contexts. *Critical Studies in Education, 54*(2), 176–89. https://doi.org/10.1080/17508487.2012.743468

Zepke, N. (2015). What future for student engagement in neo-liberal times? *Higher Education, 69*(4), 693–704. https://doi.org/10.1007/s10734-014-9797-y

Zingsheim, J., & Goltz, D. B. (2011). The intersectional workings of whiteness: A representative anecdote. *Review of Education, Pedagogy, and Cultural Studies, 33*(3), 215–41. https://doi.org/10.1080/10714413.2011.585286

5 Classrooms as Circles: The Pedagogy of Sharing Indigenous Worldviews

CYNDY BASKIN AND CASSANDRA CORNACCHIA

Challenging dominant worldviews begins with the belief that decolonization *must* happen and that we all have something to teach each other, which is supported by the growing literature on this crucial topic. From an Indigenous perspective, the decolonization of settler colonialism is meant to implicate and unsettle everyone. It is meant to change everything and thus is in line with Fanon's (2007) understanding of decolonization as a process of complete disorder that aims to transform the complete order of the world. In the settler colonial context, decolonization must involve the repatriation and the recognition of Indigenous sovereignty, while recognizing that relations to the land have always been understood much differently by Indigenous Peoples than by colonizers/settlers (Tuck & Yang, 2012). Both learners and educators from diverse cultures, spiritualties, genders, sexual orientations, beliefs, and life experiences have much to offer one another. When we begin to think in circles, rather than hierarchies, we have opportunities to gain from the knowledge sharing from the best of the world's knowledges.

We have chosen to use the term *Indigenous* throughout this chapter, which is inclusive of status and non-status First Nations, Inuit, and Métis peoples in Canada and those who identify globally as Indigenous. A universal definition of Indigenous has not been adopted on a global level; however, as documented by the United Nations, the one most commonly used was created by Jose R. Martinez-Cobo (1986):

> Indigenous Peoples, Nations, and Communities have a historical continuity with the land, long before the invasion of colonial societies that developed on their territories. Indigenous Peoples consider themselves as distinct from the dominant sectors of society that are prevailing over their territories or parts of them. They form sectors of society that are committed to preserve, develop, and transmit to future generations their ancestral territories and ethnic identities, in alignment with their own cultural patterns,

social institutions, and legal systems, as a way to ensure continued existence as people. (p. 379)

The Context

Most Canadians have never had the opportunity to learn through education, or in day-to-day life, about Indigenous perspectives and knowledges because of the hidden history of colonization in this country. Non-Indigenous learners cannot be expected to know the truth of colonization when it has been purposely hidden from their education curriculum. Often, these typically young adult Canadians are learning about these topics for the first time when they enter postsecondary educational institutions. After they are exposed to the history of colonization, including the rape of land, residential schools, and the degradation of Indigenous women, they are typically aghast. They demand to know why their education and their government has lied to them their entire lives. Meanwhile, Indigenous learners often do not see themselves, their worldviews, or their lived experiences represented in education curriculum, sometimes making their learning not only irrelevant but painful.

Exploring education for Indigenous and non-Indigenous learners is timely with the Truth and Reconciliation Commission's (TRC, 2015) focus on education in Canada. The TRC, established in 2009, was commissioned to undertake a truth telling and reconciliation process to form a report on the residential school system and its repercussions while creating recommendations and Calls to Action. For education specifically, there are seven Calls to Action (TRC, 2015), which include eliminating educational and employment gaps between Indigenous and non-Indigenous Peoples, removing the discrepancy in federal education funding for children being educated in First Nation communities, and drafting of new Indigenous education legislation with the fully informed consent of Indigenous Peoples. As has been stated in the past by scholars such as Regan (2010), the TRC's Calls to Action also emphasize the need for the education of all Canadians from an Indigenous perspective, including pre-contact, colonization, and present realities of Indigenous Peoples.

Classrooms as Circles: Application

Importance of Values

Learning about Indigenous values within an educational context arises repeatedly among Indigenous learners because mainstream education continues to be infused with dominant, Eurocentric worldviews, which often contradict values within Indigenous perspectives. Therefore, educators and learners alike need insight into their assumptions, values, and biases and where these originate, especially those that place Western knowledge as superior to Indigenous ways of knowing.

Once these values are explored, many non-Indigenous educators and learners realize that they do not adhere to all Western values. This finding was revealed through in-class activity, carried out in Indigenous-specific social work courses, at both the graduate and the undergraduate levels. Learners were presented with two lists, created by the instructor, based on the oral teachings that she received from Elders and Knowledge Keepers over many years. Referred to as *Indigenous Values* and *Dominant Society Values*, the activity asked learners to consider to which values they adhere. These values (as listed below) are generalizations, representing the societies we live in, and not necessarily our personal values.

Indigenous Values	Dominant Society's Values
Extended family	Nuclear family
Interdependence	Independence
Cooperation	Competition
Non-interference	Interference
Group/clan	Individual
Harmony with nature	Conquest over nature

Typically, during this activity, learners discover that they live by a combination of these two sets of values. Most learners believe in some of the Indigenous values, even though they live by those of the dominant society, or they state that the world would be a better place if more people adhered to Indigenous values. As co-author Cassandra found:

> Taking part in this activity provided great insights into my identity and the values that I hold. I often feel that many of my values, as well as those of other students that I have taken Indigenous courses with, are not present in dominant, Western society. Seeing the list of Indigenous values felt like a breath of fresh air and offered insight into other ways of being in this world. This activity revealed that my upbringing through an extended familial structure is respected, honoured and held as sacred within Indigenous values, whereas much of elementary and high school education consisted of a strong emphasis on nuclear family dynamics. Interdependence is another value that has been incredibly transformative in my life. Learning to understand that every being is in relation to one another has led me to an earth-based spirituality that has enriched my life in several ways. Cyndy's classrooms allowed space to

> reflect, feel, and respect multiple ways of knowing, through our emotional, mental, physical, and spiritual selves. The classes offered a refreshing focus on cooperation, sharing, and reciprocal learning.

The classroom was a space where students were finally able to question and reflect upon the values shaping their existence, their identities, and what was guiding their current and future actions.

The Circle

It could be stated that every Indigenous Nation sees the circle as a sacred symbol, with many cultural and spiritual teachings. The symbolism of the circle is that everything in the universe is circular: the planets, moon, and sun; seasons; the cycles of animals and human beings of birth, death, and rebirth; and structures on Mother Earth shaped into circles, such as Stonehenge in the United Kingdom and Medicine Wheels in western Canada. In fact, the circle is represented in various ways by Indigenous Peoples across the planet. For example, African American scholar Mambo Ama Mazama (2002) refers to the circle as "the African symbol par excellence" (p. 221).

Sitting in circles replicates this symbolism. There is no seat in the circle that represents a place of power. In Indigenous classrooms, there are often no desks between the learners and educators, which creates, as much as possible, an egalitarian energy. Everyone sits in a circle so that they can see the faces of everyone else. Such a classroom sends out a number of messages that are remarkably different from one where the teacher stands at the front of the room or behind a lectern and learners sit in rows, looking at the backs of those in front of them.

Being in a circle helps learners to connect with themselves, classmates, and the world around them. The circle offers support to learners through connectedness and belonging. A bonding occurs among learners over a course because they are not only listening to words but also being receptive to body language, facial expressions, tone of voice, and presence. In circles, learners develop a responsibility to support each other's learning and build one another's trust. Trust, in turn, means that learners can learn through their hearts, as well as their minds. Learning with one's heart includes the expression of feelings. Feelings, such as anger and sadness, as well as their expression through tears, are welcome in circle classrooms.

Although I have not experienced it, some colleagues report student resistance to sitting in circles. Perhaps some students, particularly those new to working in groups and those who are not Indigenous, find it awkward to form or join into a circle for learning purposes, as it challenges the traditional didactic ways they have previously been taught.[1]

Hearing Indigenous Voices

The stories shared by Indigenous learners about their social work education, in both an undergraduate and a graduate program in downtown Toronto, over ten years shape this chapter and provide real-life examples that support the writing of Indigenous scholars in diverse disciplines. For instance, Indigenous learners want to have their unique circumstances accounted for in their education. Importantly, they want other learners to understand that they have a relationship with the government that no other group in Canada has; their ancestors signed treaties with colonial governments, thereby acknowledging their ongoing sovereignty, living under legislation called the *Indian Act*, which has an impact on all aspects of their lives. This legislation defined who was and is an "Indian" according to governmental law, the regulation of band membership, government, taxation, management, and land (Joseph, 2018). There have been long-standing objections to the *Indian Act* because of its inherent paternalism and failure to meet the needs and aspirations of Indigenous Peoples. However, opinions regarding how to move forward with or without the *Indian Act* are multifaceted because although it serves as an instrument of external regulatory authority and assimilation, the Act also provides some protection of Indigenous Peoples' inherent rights (Hurley & Simeone, 2010).

Furthermore, Indigenous learners want an education that is driven by Indigenous needs, values, and visions, education that highlights their many strengths and acts of resistance while privileging their ways of seeing the world. Most educators have a limited understanding of Indigenous Peoples and perspectives, which has led to Indigenous community members and their allies advocating for the infusion of Indigenous content into mainstream teacher education and doctoral programs (Blimkie et al., 2014). Eurocentric culture has dominated educational perspectives and approaches for far too long; it is time for a new educational process rooted in Indigeneity, which will welcome Indigenous Peoples to participate more fully in their education (Harms et al., 2011).

Learners stress that it is important for their worldviews to be represented in their education because they need to feel a sense of belonging in educational institutions, know that their ways of learning are

1 See chapter 2 for a greater exploration of this theme.

respected and valued, and see that their knowledges are recognized as making important contributions in all disciplines. This is in keeping with research that shows that there is a vital relationship between learners' cultures and the way in which they acquire knowledge, engage with information, and synthesize ideas (Barnhardt, 1999; Bell et al., 2004; Kanu, 2005, as cited in Deer, 2013). This argument implies that educational institutions should be environments where educators engage learners in ways that affirm and explore aspects of their identities, which in turn facilitates academic success (Deer, 2013). A substantive caution, however, is that when Indigenous Peoples are the students of non-Indigenous educators, they do not want to be the ones to educate their professors or other learners in the classroom. Rather, they emphasize that professors need to be responsible for their own learning, which includes participating in their own critical self-reflexivity, without shying away from discomforting points of discussion in the classroom.

Another significant point that Indigenous learners routinely stress is that members of their communities, such as Elders, Knowledge Keepers, professionals, and natural Helpers, must have input into curriculum development, as well as professional development for faculty and other instructors. Such a stance is supported by research, which states that to integrate Indigenous knowledges into postsecondary education, it is crucial that scholars develop relationships with members of local First Nations communities and learn about their perspectives and ways of understanding the world (Moore, 2012). This is emphasized by social work scholar Kathy Absolon (2016) who writes:

> There is wisdom in Indigenous knowledge, traditions, ceremonies and teachings ... [It is important to] show respect for Indigenous knowledge and wisdom through authentic inclusion. What I mean by authentic inclusion is inclusion that Indigenous people feel and experience as real, genuine and meaningful. (p. 51)

Going beyond the incorporation of Indigenous knowledges and further examining the appropriate delivery method of narratives related to ongoing colonial violence, Cote-Meek (2014) directs educators and learners' attention towards the importance of adopting a holistic pedagogy:

> Professors who are teaching difficult material must engage in holistic pedagogical approaches that give attention to the emotive aspects of a student's being. I acknowledge the fine line between the political and therapeutic

> in this regard. However, in this context it is impossible to separate as the degree of trauma demands a pedagogical response that is holistic. The mind, body and spirit are typically disconnected in most postsecondary classrooms. To further expect that students only focus on one aspect of their being, the mind, in the classroom is to perpetuate that the body and spirit are of no matter. (p. 317)

Student Voices

The following statements and quotes are from Indigenous and non-Indigenous students, at both the undergraduate and the graduate levels, who participated in Indigenous-specific courses within the School of Social Work at Ryerson University in Toronto during the 2016–2017 academic year. At the end of each course, learners were invited to provide feedback on the content and pedagogy of the courses. The sharing of information from the learners was done informally while sitting in circle with permission granted by some of the learners to use their actual names.

LISTENING TO INDIGENOUS LEARNERS

Indigenous learners echo the scholarship of Indigenous educators regarding the impacts of a (w)holistic pedagogy with insightful first-hand perspectives. In looking at all the suggestions raised by Indigenous learners over the years, everything fits together in a (w)holistic, seamless way: Indigenous faculty means there will be Indigenous curriculum, which, in turn, means the presence of Indigenous learners. One undergraduate learner emphasized that in addition to the above needs, high-quality content within courses is equally important:

> We have to have our own writers writing books and curriculum. Since non-Indigenous people come to teaching with a totally different perspective, they cannot write in ways that will be representative of Indigenous values.

Many learners with Indigenous heritage share how being in a safe educational circle of learning helps them to acknowledge that learning can come from other places of the self, besides the intellect. An example of this came from Alex Cahuas, with ancestry from Ayacucho, Peru, who while completing a master of social work course on Indigenous knowledges at Ryerson University said, "The biggest impact the course had on me was that it reminded me that learning takes some vulnerability and sharing … Our learning happened from what we felt when discussing the material: the anger, sadness, frustration, love and passion." This same learner also took up how learning in the circle made space for him to explore his identity, which he had not had the opportunity to do in other courses:

> When speaking about colonialism, the course became a place for me where I could grieve the loss of my culture through the intergenerational trauma my family went through and allow myself to feel pain and sadness. [This] was my learning as I could finally stop hiding it away from myself, look at it and grow from it.

Another master of social work student who took a course on Indigenous knowledges, Marguerite Marges, echoed how the course impacted her search for her identity:

> This course, unlike any before it, provided me with the privilege to gain invaluable insight into both my Indigenous and settler ancestry, while fuelling my lifelong journey of decolonization. The way the entire course was structured provided an atmosphere that felt familiar, despite my overwhelmingly colonial, Eurocentric upbringing.

Sense of self and Indigeneity is another common theme among Indigenous learners in courses on Indigenous worldviews and knowledges. As recounted by Emily Blackmoon, another master of social work student:

> As a person of mixed Algonquin, French, and British descent, I always struggled with my identity and my relationship to indigeneity. I knew I was a part of the legacy of colonization [and] genocide, [as well as the] resilience and resistance of Indigenous Peoples, but I didn't know which part that was. Being in Cyndy's classes helped me to recognize that I am both settler and Indigenous, and that I carry the duality of the oppressor and the oppressed within my very existence.

LISTENING TO NON-INDIGENOUS VOICES

When non-Indigenous learners discuss how learning in circles impacts them, they often speak of education itself in terms of what it can be. One of the undergraduate learners in an Indigenous-specific social work course at Ryerson University, which took place in the winter of 2017, especially appreciated how many knowledges were invited to be a part of the circle setting, saying, "This class embraced the knowledge of all the students and encouraged our expression. Within [Cyndy's] class, I experienced the most progressive and liberating teaching that I have ever had." Another learner highlighted, "Being a part of [Cyndy's] class allowed me to see a clear vision of what education will look like in the future, when more freedom fighters like yourself gain positions of power in this system." This last quote also speaks to the need for Indigenous faculty hires within postsecondary education.

Another common theme that arises about courses on Indigenous content from non-Indigenous learners is that of being an ally. As one undergraduate noted:

> Thank you for teaching me a whole new way to think about being an ally and about being honest with myself. Thank you for laying your stake in educating those of us who are not familiar with Aboriginal worldviews and history, so we can make a difference.

Allies are those who recognize the unearned privileges they receive from society's patterns of injustice and take personal responsibility for resisting and changing these patterns (Bishop, 2015). Within Indigenous courses, something that often arises within settler learners, when they come to understand how deeply they are implicated within the ongoing oppression of Indigenous Peoples and lands, is guilt and feelings of helplessness. However, it is crucial that learners move past guilt because it is a position that does not inspire action; on the contrary, it causes inaction. Tongue in cheek, I often say to learners, "Now is your time to feel guilty. You have five minutes." I am only half joking. One of the ways to combat feelings of individual guilt in the classroom is through critical engagement with the structural and historical nature of oppression. In this way, learners gain a realistic understanding of their place within the broader societal environment. They are then able to learn practical, genuine ways of taking part in truth telling, justice, resistance, and, eventually, action and reconciliation, while stepping into a critical understanding of allyship and contributing to real differences (Bishop, 2015).

Many non-Indigenous graduate learners also spoke of diverse ways of knowing, as well as the value of learning in a circle. The following quotation, from a master of social work student emphasizes the practical aspects of learning to implement Indigenous worldviews while expressing emotions about what one learns:

> [This course was] a collaborative, respectful space to learn and practise the many ways that Indigenous knowledges can inform those in the helping

> professions take steps to decolonize our practice. With all classes taking place in the circle format, we were able to create a culture of support and dedicated learning that enhanced both our practical knowledge and our emotional strength.

Another graduate learner, Siobhan Cassidy, explained the impact this particular learning approach has had on students' ability to engage with education: "In Cyndy's class, we learned how to be in relation with each other and to process the course content together. I was learning through my body, spirit, emotions, and my mind, rather than just my mind."

What about Non-Indigenous Educators?

In recent years, the question of who teaches about Indigenous knowledges, and how they are taught, has been a contested discussion. With the 2015 TRC's Calls to Action, certainly these questions are now being asked in many educational institutions. These questions are often about whether non-Indigenous educators can teach Indigenous content; if so, should they be teaching these in circle formats? Non-Indigenous educators are sometimes leery of raising Indigenous content out of ignorance and lack of comfort with the topics and materials. Others appropriate various cultural practices, thinking this is inclusion. Neither of these approaches is helpful. Instead, those who belong to the settler population need to begin with acknowledging and appreciating whose lands they are on and role model this recognition to learners and their colleagues (Aboriginal Education Council, 2016; University of Alberta, 2016; University of Manitoba, 2016).

Both Indigenous learners and educators agree that non-Indigenous educators who hold their own identities, know who they are, have their own cultural understandings, and are not threatened by the idea of not knowing everything are needed. These scholars role model, for both Indigenous and non-Indigenous learners alike, how to be allies and develop relationships. At the same time, non-Indigenous educators need to closely look at the meaning of "truth" in connection to the TRC's report (2015). Within a relationship with Indigenous Peoples, there are responsibilities to learn about the true history of Canada, a country that was founded on colonization. With these responsibilities comes the acknowledgement of the ongoing devastating impacts of colonization upon Indigenous Peoples and the benefits non-Indigenous people receive because of this. Upon learning this truth, responsibilities can morph into teaching from the perspective of an ally.

Just as important, however, is that non-Indigenous scholars see Indigenous Peoples as strong contributors to the world, rather than as merely victims. They need to teach about the strengths that Indigenous Peoples have and the incredible achievements that are happening in their communities, which have been outlined as crucial factors in delivering purposeful Indigenous education where learners can thrive (Kitchen & Hodson, 2013). In this way, educators will be contributing to decolonization within educational institutions by disclaiming stereotypes and identifying the ongoing successes of Indigenous Peoples in the face of extreme adversity.

To move forward, educators have to be prepared to take risks in the following ways:

- Do not be afraid to make mistakes.
- Be honest with yourself about contributing to relationships of dominance.
- Learn about the historical context and current events that are impacting Indigenous People's livelihoods and rights globally.
- Do not ignore difference as Indigenous Peoples are not all the same.
- Be mindful of language.
- Invite many ways of knowing and seeing the world from all learners in the classrooms.
- Invite input from Indigenous communities but ensure reciprocity when doing so.
- Support colleagues who are also attempting to teach Indigenous content.
- Work with others inside the educational institution who have the power to make systemic changes.

The Closing Circle

The spoken word below was inspired by Cassandra's experiences as a learner in Cyndy's classes. Spoken word and poetry is an opportunity to passionately express the raw, heartfelt emotions, insights, and experiences that have had a very significant effect on a person's life. This spoken word is titled "The Closing Circle":

I step into Cyndy's classroom for the last time
I feel a sense of sadness for the end
A sense of love for new beginnings
We sit in a closing circle today
Closure from the heart wrenching, eye-opening, mind-expanding experiences we have all had together

This is a space where we could be who we are
A space for the emotions that inform our ways of being in this world, to flow out of us
Without judgment
In this classroom our hearts mattered
Our bodies, our spirits, our mental health
Our whole beings
They mattered
This class fostered connection and community through circle
Circles to share tears of pain and sorrow
Circles to share laughter and light hearts
Circles to learn from one another, as mentors, teachers, and friends
Circles where it is okay to be vulnerable
Circles where we move past guilt and learn that the true beginning of reconciling is truth, justice, and action
Circles to heal
Circles to embody our ability to become powerful warriors of peace

Conclusion

Teaching and learning in circles is not simply a classroom setting. Sitting in circles and teaching from an Indigenous lens creates inclusion, a measure of safety, and opportunities for (w)holistic learning. It opens the door for learners to gain knowledge through their hearts, spirits, and bodies, rather than only their minds, and to consider their values, as well as those of Indigenous Peoples, as they navigate their learning in postsecondary education. At the beginning of this journey of truth, decolonization, and reconciliation within Canada, as well as other countries, such (w)holistic learning is greatly needed.

REFERENCES

Aboriginal Education Council. (2016). *Ryerson land acknowledgement.* Ryerson University. https://www.ryerson.ca/aec/land-acknowledgement/

Absolon, K. E. (2016). Wholistic and ethical: Social inclusion with indigenous peoples. *Social Inclusion, 4*(1), 44–56. https://doi.org/10.17645/si.v4i1.444

Barnhardt, C. (1999). Kuinerrarmiut Elitnaurviat: The school of the people of Quinhagak. In J. W. Kushman & R. Barnhardt (Eds.), *Study of Alaska rural systemic reform: Final report.* Alaska Native knowledge Network. http://www.ankn.uaf.edu/curriculum/Books/JamesKushman/index.html

Bell, D., Anderson, K., Fortin, T., Ottmann, J., Rose, S., Simard, L., Spencer, K., & Raham, H. (2004). *Sharing our success: Ten case studies in Aboriginal schooling.* Society for the Advancement of Excellence in Education. Research Gate.

https://www.researchgate.net/publication/48878867_Sharing_Our_Success_Ten_Case_Studies_in_Aboriginal_Schooling

Bishop, A. (2015). *Becoming an ally: Breaking the cycle of oppression in people* (3rd ed.). Fernwood Publishing.

Blimkie, M., Vetter, D., & Haig-Brown, C. (2014). Shifting perspectives and practices: Teacher candidates' experiences of an Aboriginal infusion in mainstream teacher education. *Brock Education, 23*(2), 47–66. https://doi.org/10.26522/brocked.v23i2.384

Cote-Meek, S. (2014). *Colonized classrooms: Racism, trauma and resistance in post-secondary education.* Fernwood Publishing.

Deer, F. (2013). Integrating Aboriginal perspectives in education: Perceptions of pre-service teachers. *Canadian Journal of Education, 36*(2), 175–211.

Fanon, F. (2007). *The wretched of the earth.* Grove/Atlantic.

Harms, L., Middleton, J., Whyte, J., Anderson, I., Clarke, A., Sloan, J., & Smith, M. (2011). Social work with Aboriginal clients: Perspectives on educational preparation and practice. *Australian Social Work, 64*(2), 156–68. https://doi.org/10.1080/0312407x.2011.577184

Hurley, M. C., & Simeone, T. (2010). Bill C-3: Gender equity in Indian Registration Act: Legislative summary. Parliamentary Information and Research Service. https://lop.parl.ca/staticfiles/PublicWebsite/Home/ResearchPublications/LegislativeSummaries/PDF/40-3/40-3-c3-e.pdf

Joseph, B. (2018). *21 things you may not know about the Indian Act: Helping Canadians make reconciliation with Indigenous Peoples a reality.* CBC Books.

Kanu, Y. (2005). Teachers' perceptions of the integration of Aboriginal culture into the high school curriculum. *The Alberta Journal of Education Research, 51*(1), 50–68.

Kitchen, J., & Hodson, J. (2013). Enhancing conditions for Aboriginal learners in higher education: The experiences of Nishnawbe Aski teacher candidates in a teacher education program. *Brock Education: A Journal of Educational Research and Practice, 23*(1), 97–115.

Martinez-Cobo, J. R. (1986). *Study on the problem of discrimination against Indigenous populations.* United Nations Sub-Commission on Prevention of Discrimination and Protection of Minorities. https://www.un.org/development/desa/indigenouspeoples/publications/2014/09/martinez-cobo-study/

Mazama, M. A. (2002). Afrocentricity and African spirituality. *Journal of Black Studies, 33*(2), 218–34.

Moore, S. (2012). A trickster tale about integrating Indigenous knowledge in university-based programs. *Journal of Environmental Studies and Sciences, 2*(4), 324–30. https://doi.org/10.1007/s13412-012-0089-5

Regan, P. (2010). *Unsettling the settler within: Indian Residential Schools, truth telling, and reconciliation in Canada.* UBC Press.

Truth and Reconciliation Commission of Canada. (2015). *Calls to action, education.* http://trc.ca/assets/pdf/Calls_to_Action_English2.pdf

Tuck, E., & Yang, K. W. (2012). Decolonization is not a metaphor. *Decolonization: Indigeneity, Education & Society, 1*(1), 1–40.

University of Alberta. (2016). *Acknowledgement of traditional territory.* University of Alberta. https://www.ualberta.ca/toolkit/communications/acknowledgment-of-traditional-territory

University of Manitoba. (2016). *Acknowledgement.* http://umanitoba.ca/admin/president/acknowledgement.html

6 The Crying White Woman and the Politics of Emotion in Anti-oppressive Social Work Education

DAPHNE JEYAPAL AND LIZ GRIGG

Indigenous, postcolonial, feminist, queer, and disability theorists have long supported the embodiment of being and learning (Peters, 2016; Price & Shildrick, 1999; Ritenburg et al., 2014; Thomas, 2016). Rationalist, positivist, masculinist, and Eurocentric approaches have been criticized for privileging the mind over the body while ignoring emotion (Barlow & Hall, 2007). Acknowledging emotion in teaching and learning allows for inclusion of a fuller range of people's humanity. Anti-oppressive pedagogical and andragogic approaches recognize and incorporate these important critiques (Barlow & Hall, 2007; Rajan-Rankin, 2014). Emotion is a key component for deconstructing and challenging the social and racial relations inherent in our profession and in broader society. Indeed, we encounter emotion as we learn, unsettle, and disrupt our positions of power and marginalization.

Drawing both from the literature that positions emotions as more than just psychological states and as cultural and social practices (Ahmed, 2004, 2017; Lutz & Abu-Lughood, 1990; White, 1993) and from our own student and teaching experiences, we, the co-authors, have often considered and debated the ways emotion emerges in social work classrooms. Our classrooms exist within institutions that were created by white settlers on unceded Indigenous territories. Our experiences of the classroom, and the emotions that emerge, represent the complexities that Ahmed (2004) speaks to in her conceptualization of "orientation." Orientation refers to how subjectivities are constructed as normal and others deviant, and how space and place are organized to demarcate who belongs and who is out of place. In this configuration, we, the co-authors of this chapter, occupy the two locations of "insider" and "outsider." While we both entered into social work as an academic discipline, our paths were in some ways carved along racialized trajectories. I (Daphne), a first-generation Canadian, born in the Middle East to parents who are

Sinhalese and Tamil, embody the conditions and contradictions of racialization, citizenship, coloniality, and belonging in the "age of terrorism." Today, I live and work on the Tk'emlups te Secwepemc territory, the unceded traditional lands of the Secwepemc Nation. I (Liz) was born on traditional beaver trapping lands of the Attawandaran, Algonquin, and Haudenosaunee peoples, to the descendants of British settlers and Dutch farmers. My identity has been informed as "insider" with the ability to navigate spaces within Canada through whiteness and, as such, embody a degree of race-privilege taken through colonization. Embodying our own social identities, as a racialized woman and a white woman, who have both worked to dismantle the politics of race through our work, we ask: *what* do "we" construct as "good"/"bad" emotion; *who* is socially sanctioned to be "emotional"; and *when* and *how* can the expression of emotion challenge and contradict anti-imperial complicities and anti-racist pedagogies?

The Inevitability of Whiteness in Anti-oppressive Social Work Classrooms

Social work is deeply embedded within a context of whiteness: "The centrality of whiteness as an unmarked social, cultural, and epistemological orientation continues to organize social work education and practice" (Jeyapal & Bhuyan, 2016, p. 130). It is also a feminized, one could even argue a mainstream feminist, discipline dominantly constructed through the work, visions, and intentions of white women. The legacy of white female social workers is complex and contradictory. While engaged in myriad of progressive social justice projects, their tradition is also implicitly and ideologically entrenched within a discriminatory past and present. Social work as a profession has been complicit, if not directly active, in numerous racist state projects: from the Daughters of the Imperial Order across the British Empire to its role in Japanese internment, oppressive forms of immigrant "settlement," and Indigenous Peoples' marginalization and murder (Blackstock, 2011; Johnstone, 2015; Park, 2008).

In present day social work, this history is not that far behind us: the last federally operated residential school in Canada closed in 1997; there continues to be an over-representation of Indigenous and racialized young people in care of the government, at a rate surpassing that of the Sixties Scoop (Blackstock, 2011; Blackstock & Trocmé, 2005); and challenges to the theoretical orientations of social work as rooted in whiteness remain a topic of debate in schools of social work across the country. Featherstone (2001) and Turner and Maschi (2015) have unpacked the ways that feminist theory in social work has evolved and advanced the profession through strategies of empowerment, equality, and critiques of domination and subordination, in particular, patriarchy. As social work's engagement with social justice has evolved, intersectionality (Collins, 1999) has informed our understanding of equity both in the profession and in service provision. However, there remains a struggle to completely shed the influence of whiteness as social work's main building block. As Jonsson (2015) has suggested, the problematic function of whiteness is that it works to remain the centre of the story of feminism. This reality underpins our critique of white feminists, those that focus on issues affecting white women, at the erasure or expense of racialized women. At worst, white feminists are intentionally white supremacist. At best, white feminists position themselves as colour-blind. Yet even this flawed attempt at anti-racism simultaneously functions to subsume the unique narratives of women of colour as a part of the larger schema for gender-based justice, neutralizing their distinct experiences.

Intersectionality, anti-racist theories, and classroom pedagogies (Nylund, 2006) have interrupted this impetus to centre whiteness, making it visible, while opening space to move racialized voices from the margins. According to Reason et al. (2005), allyship is difficult to navigate as "allies have action-oriented identities, they have their feet in the worlds of both the dominant and the oppressed, they need to continually and accurately judge when it is most appropriate, to listen, to speak up, or to absent the discussion" (p. 1). There are significant contradictions inherent within ally work, including the space that one takes up, how and who benefits, and how someone's own privilege is, and needs to be, challenged and interrogated (Patton & Bondi, 2015). Ally work can become performative. In their discussion of white allyship, Patton and Bondi (2015) identify that "performing" occurs when social justice work is considered "helping" or remains at the individual, not systemic, level. Performing white allyship is cemented by a lack of desire to decentre whiteness in institutions. In this context, ally work is used to advance one's own position or as refusal to engage with issues that may involve personal risk. It may also occur in situations where people may not be aware of their racial biases, reconciled through a logic of colour-blind neutrality.

The Inevitability of Emotion in Anti-oppressive Social Work Classrooms

Attending to emotion is inevitable when we challenge our own racial and imperial complicities. As Friedman (1995) points out, discussions of race even among feminists "often collapse in frustration, anger, hurt, yelling, silence, withdrawal and a profound belief that different sides are unable to listen and learn from the other" (p. 5). Yet Canada's new chapter in its settler colonial relations, marked by the Truth and Reconciliation Commission of Canada (TRC, 2015), requires us to mobilize essential, at times emotional, considerations for our country and our profession. The TRC's Calls to Action challenge social workers to disrupt their colonial role in child welfare from the Sixties Scoop to the present (TRC, 2015). It urges us to confront the racist, paternalistic, and dehumanizing values and behaviours guiding our relations with Indigenous Peoples. The Canadian Association for Social Work Education – l'Association canadienne pour la formation en travail social (CASWE-ACFTS, 2017) recently vowed to disrupt its complicity in colonial processes by urging social work educators to acknowledge and address the colonizing narratives, policies, and practices implicated through education, research, and social work practice. Despite this declaration, educating to challenge complicity in racism towards Indigenous and racialized peoples often elicits strong emotion and can lead to backlash.

This new chapter of settler colonial relations requires educators not only to contextualize and temporalize social work's role in constructions of race but also to create a space that promotes confronting one's own position. Social work education's engagement with theories of privilege and power dates back over three decades (Phillips, 2010). Yet the mobilization of education that successfully incorporates critical race discourses that rupture whiteness is often met with challenges. Social work classrooms are a microcosm of broader social relations of power, especially as it relates to whiteness. As such, the identities, histories, and structures of domination that operate outside the classroom must also be negotiated within the classroom. In social work as a professional discipline in the West, space is often given to and taken up by white women as their identity and experience is constructed as most relevant, true, and valid. The "unmarked" nature of whiteness allows its construction as a "universal" experience of humanness (Daniels, 2015).

Here, we explore the construction of white women as social work students. Our emphasis on this social category adopts a critical race feminist lens to examine white women's complicity in other(ed) women's lives and disrupts the often-recognized counter-representation of the "angry black woman scholar" (Williams, 2001, p. 88). To accomplish this, we centre on one recurring archetype: the crying white woman. We do not aim to exclude white men or those who identify as transgender but to highlight the particular social and cultural embodiment of white women, and emotional tears, drawing attention to how social work commonly confronts hetero-patriarchy. We evoke this binaried colonial gender identity, exemplified by the idealized "white woman," who represents much of the characteristics of patriarchal desire and is cisgendered, heterosexual, and able-bodied, to reify rather than concretize its construction. As such, examining this archetype requires confronting white women's tears, the role of femininity, and the logic of white feminism as areas of sociological study, not realms of personalized, individual identity. Rather than an indictment that women who are white cannot or should not cry, this critical analysis challenges us to problematize when, why, and what happens socially and culturally when we, as social work educators, encounter the crying white woman. Since "we" are not a unified group but embody different social locations, we encourage readers to consider the following critique through a lens of their own privileges and oppressions.

The Archetype of the Crying White Woman

> We come to know and perform ourselves in ways that reproduce social hierarchies. Tracing our complicity in these systems requires that we shed notions of mastering differences, abandoning the idea that differences are pre-given, knowable and existing in a social and historical vacuum.
>
> (Razack, 1998, p. 10)

The archetype of the crying white woman is often evoked in anti-racist social work classrooms. She emerges when difficult realities about race and racism are taught. She emerges when personally challenged to confront her role in perpetrating racist acts, words, or behaviours. She emerges when her privilege is destabilized through conversations on racial injustice. Sometimes, she cries in silence. Sometimes, she cries while defending her position. Other times, she cries to express her own victimization triggered through her learning. In sum, she is a, "familiar representation of the 'tearful white woman' who cannot deal with anti-racism: she is described as 'balling [*sic*] her eyes out,' 'freaking-out,' 'weeping,' and 'blubbering' when racism is raised" (Srivastava, 2006, p. 83). Are her tears an expression of fear, guilt, learning, or defensiveness? Are her tears for the displacement of her own oppressions and victimhood? Are they evidence of her "race to innocence" (Fellows & Razack, 1998, p. 335)? When evoked in response to the charge of racism, where do her tears place non-white students and social work educators?

The Politics of the Crying White Woman

White women are oppressed. Historically and presently, Canadian society is shaped, informed, and negotiated through gender oppression. While women now have the right to education, property, and political representation, their lives are still socially, politically, and economically constructed through sexist and patriarchal discourses. As a group, women face disproportionate rates of violence, are over-represented in low-paying occupations, experience more precarious employment, earn less, are less represented in politics, and occupy fewer political leadership positions when compared to men (Johnstone & Jeyapal, 2019). However, being oppressed does not automatically make one understand all forms of oppression, nor does it make any woman unconditionally relate to the oppression all women face. White women are at the top of the racial hierarchy of all women. While they face elevated risks of violence, they are still significantly less vulnerable than Indigenous women, who are three times as likely to be murdered by a stranger than non-Indigenous women (Native Women's Association of Canada, 2015). In the hierarchy of oppression, white women are the most advantaged; affirmation action policies have primarily benefited white women over racialized others (Ruparelia, 2014).

White women are also oppressors. Critical race scholars have long critiqued white women's roles in maintaining, sustaining, and valorizing white supremacy. They suggest that white women experience constructed superiority through their interactions with their racialized counterparts. In *Home and Harem*, a study of the interaction of ideas between English and Indian cultures, Grewal (1996) demonstrates how the construction of the othered Indian woman as victim allowed all classes of nineteenth-century English women to elevate their own status through racialized, gendered constructions of self and other, home and abroad. We continue to see evidence of this binary between "civilized" Western women and non-civilized oppressed "Third World Women" in dominant discourse. As Razack states, "a message of Southern cultural inferiority and dysfunction is so widely disseminated that when we in the North see a veiled woman, we can only retrieve from our store of information that she is a victim of her patriarchal culture or religion" (1998, p. 7). Razack (1998) and Salazar (2012) assert that we are all implicated in systems of oppression that inform our understanding of ourselves and others. While racialized women are made inferior through constructed forms of cultural oppression, white women are made superior through their Western (read: comparatively less-oppressed) status. Studies of gender power uncover how

> the rationed privileges of race all too often put white women in positions of decided, if borrowed, power, not only over colonized women but also over colonized men. As such, white women were not the hapless onlookers of empire but were ambiguously complicit both as colonizers and colonized, privileged and restricted, acted upon and acting. (McClintock, 1995, p. 6)

Despite white women's complicities in imperialism and white supremacy, mainstream (white) feminism forefronts gender as a dominant form of oppression.

White women's tears foster and further their privilege. In addition to maintaining racial equilibrium, by paradoxically assuming equal speaking positions and powers, crying nurtures social capital on the backs of racialized others. This privilege is typically awarded through white women's proximity to white men and the benefits accrued through patriarchy. Importantly,

> white men also get to authorize what constitutes pain and whose pain is legitimate. When white men come to the rescue of white women in cross-racial settings, patriarchy is reinforced as they play saviour to our damsel in distress. By legitimating white women as the targets of harm, both white men and women accrue social capital. (Diangelo, 2015, para. 14)

Through crying, white women deflect their whiteness and are reinscribed through patriarchy; they simultaneously deflect their complicity in patriarchy and are reinscribed through their defence of white supremacy.

Privileging an essentialized narrative of gender over race is not a new phenomenon (Watters, 2017). In Canada, as in many Western nations, the first two waves of liberal feminism excluded Indigenous and racialized women. For example, white women earned the right to vote in 1916; decades later, in 1947, racialized women earned this right. It was not until 1960 that Status Indigenous women did. The unique struggles of othered women, in contrast to dominant white women, highlight the tension between and among race-based categories of women (Lugones, 2016).

In the United States, white women's role in electing President Trump surfaces this ongoing, insidious reality. According to exit polls, 53 per cent of white women in America voted for him (Schaffner et al., 2018). This fact incited contentious conversations about the pattern of white women allying with white men and white men's priorities over racialized others to uncover the history of racism ingrained in white feminism and its scholarship, which theoretically assumes womanhood as a universal category (Watters, 2017). It demonstrates that "race animates voting patterns even more than gender" (Filipovic, 2016, para. 11). Trump's win was interpreted to mean that "to white men, Trump promises the restoration of diminishing supremacy over both women and people of color. To white women, he promises a return to a simpler time, when their race alone made them exceptional and worthy of special protection" (Filipovic, para. 16). Dominant public debates framed this outcome as white women's historical abandonment of racialized women by adopting white supremacist rhetoric when it advances their own privilege and social status (Jacobsen, 2016). It has challenged the limitations of white feminism and called assumptions of gender solidarity across racial lines into question (Watters, 2017). Are white women genuine allies to racialized and Indigenous women, or are they foremost allies to white men and each other in their own conquest for equality through the eradication of gender oppression and white supremacy?

What Happens When White Women Cry?

In cross-racial classrooms, the act of crying over racial injustices has specific political motivations and requires an analysis as it relates to the complexities of these spaces. White privilege transcends individual intentions and reflects structural powers and benefits rewarded to many for simply being white. Confronting white privilege requires placing oneself within the larger sociopolitical context. Similarly, our emotions must be placed within a larger context of racial inequities. Tears are more than an outcome of emotional expression. They also signal an "emotional attachment to innocence" when confronting race and racism (Fellows & Razack 1998, p. 343). This emotional attachment is informed by the construction of white women's identities: as feminine and feminized. Insidiously, "the problem for White women is that their privilege is based on accepting the image of goodness, which is powerlessness" (Palmer, 1994, p. 170). They continue to earn this privilege by being viewed as "respectable," ultimately subscribing to the colonial project's bourgeois notion that to be feminine requires white women be constructed in contrast to the racialized other, specifically, docile and not aggressive, emotionally expressive in a civilized fashion, not unruly (Salazar, 2012). Embodying this binary advances white women through the presence of their tears, thereby operationalizing forms of racial innocence.

Diangelo (2015) reminds us that white tears are evidence of white fragility and the inability of white people to respond constructively when white privilege and superiority are challenged. She argues that people cry, defend, withdraw, minimize, or ignore because they so rarely have to face the true depth of their white privilege, and they use these strategies to retain racial equilibrium. These tactics deflect and realign challenging moments that may otherwise unsettle the racial status quo. Being moved to cry insinuates that one is experiencing something troubling but also something novel. While potentially heartfelt, attending to racial oppression should not be new. Racialized people encounter it daily and in profound ways. When and why are white people moved to tears by this reality, and when and why are they not? How brutal and shocking must racism be to elicit an emotional response? By highlighting this distinction, white tears reinscribe the invisibilized lived experience of systemic racism.

The act of crying shifts the terms of the conversation. A white woman's tears transform her into a victim. When she cries, her individualized distress and suffering become central: she takes up space and energy by performing her innocence while racialized others are put in the position to be consolatory, blamed, or ignored. It shifts difficult but necessary conversations about systemic racism and accountability into "let's talk" approaches, conversations that assume and further universalize "the role of emotional disclosure in political life and analysis ... [neglecting] to understand how this practice may be shaped by inequitable relations of race" (Srivastava, 2006, p. 83). Furthermore, "white woman's reality is visible, acknowledged, and legitimized because of her tears, while a woman of color's reality, like her struggle, is invisible, overlooked, and pathologized based on the operating 'standard of humanity'" (Accapadi, 2007, p. 210). While the white woman becomes a feminized casualty, her racialized counterpart is read simply as angry (Williams, 2001). While white feminists may be read as angry when resisting injustice, a range of identities is provided to them. Whereas white women can be described as *passionate, progressive,* and an *ally*, racialized women's identities are informed by tropes of aggression in most public domains, including the grocery store, academia, and the criminal justice system (Jones & Norwood, 2017). This construction is exacerbated in typically white spaces such as academia, which requires performing the fragility of whiteness for inclusion, and activates its binary opposition, the "angry black woman" (Baxley, 2012; Pitts, 2017). Within academia and feminist spaces, Ahmed (2017) refers to feminists of colour as "killjoys." The killjoy, who often represents what goes unnoticed when happiness is the benchmark of experience, disrupts not only the status quo and the opportunity for (white) happiness but the ideology itself (Ahmed, 2010, 2017) by critiquing the notion that challenging patriarchy and the design of happiness tailored to women is the key to *all* women's freedom. Ahmed (2010) cautions women in the pursuit of white-bred happiness, in that unhappiness does not need to be a decidedly political act and, perhaps, requires an analysis of the privileging of whiteness.

In this sense, white tears as part of the disruption of white happiness are self-indulgent and destructive. When racism is learned or debated, who gets to cry, when, and where, becomes a political act. As racialized students bear witness to the realities of their racialization, white women "steal their pain" (Razack, 2007, p. 376) to commodify it as their own. This theft operates in a sociopolitical context where the power of white women's victimization has been a useful strategy to enact and justify racial injustices from racial segregation to lynching. It fosters a false performance of innocence and sanitizes the political project of white supremacy through a personal project of emotional expression. Responding to white tears increases the disproportionate emotional labour racialized people already experience within academia. Validating white women's feelings can also be experienced as coercive, where racialized others, whether they are students or academics themselves, feel constrained to "have to" hear the confessions of their white peers (Bannerji, 1992, p. 10).

A Critical Race Critique of Emotion for Social Work

> Learn why people of color hate it when you cry. When you cry, you are shifting the focus off the policies, events, and people who target, harm, and murder people of colour – and putting the focus on you and your emotional reaction. It is at best self-centered, and at worst complicit in racism.
>
> (Malsbary, 2016, para. 19)

As social work educators, we face the challenge of validating emotion as integral to learning while pushing our students beyond enacting their own emotion. We acknowledge and respect acts of emotion as learning edges and learning opportunities: emotive expression may mark the very encounters where learning becomes possible and necessary. That said, we must foster classroom and workplace cultures where we can problematize emotion's meanings. Connecting our own personal and professional accountability and privileges is one starting point; our own histories, identities, and the bodies we inhabit inform how students learn from and respond to us. A white social work educator arguably experiences different resistances and to lesser degrees than racialized educators, who are "presumed incompetent" (Gutiérrez y Muhs et al., 2012, p. 3). Acknowledging these differences allows us to be supportive of educational processes while challenging our colleagues and peers.

To truly engage in critical social work pedagogy, we must move beyond the personal, whether that is an individualized and apoliticized intellectual analysis or an individualized and apoliticized act of emotion. A structural analysis of the space of the classroom and the social and cultural politics of emotion challenge us to do this. We must consider the demographics of the social work classrooms we teach, the profession as a whole, and those we serve: who are we teaching and for whom? In the classroom, we have to include othered students and decentre social work education as the teaching of, for, and by white people only. As the recruitment and retention of Indigenous, racialized, and other equity-seeking students becomes increasingly important, we must ask ourselves how our classroom practices authentically include different bodies, knowledges, and ways of being. In so doing, not only must we unsettle our classrooms away from masculinist, positivist, and modernist approaches to learning that erase emotion from intellectual projects, but we also must navigate the politics of emotion more constructively in an effort to genuinely problematize the Eurocentric biases within our profession, our classrooms, and ourselves.

White social work students and educators must both be held accountable for their learning and their complicities. They must be challenged to face, and be made responsible for, their complex interplay of identities as oppressed and oppressor, in the classroom and in their social work practice. The oppressiveness of racial privilege should be placed within a broader understanding of structural and systemic racism's power and pervasiveness, students' best intentions notwithstanding. White social work students must be taught to regulate their emotions constructively, whether this involves pausing to think before sharing, leaving the room when overwhelmed, finding alternative ways to communicate, or accessing resources or support outside the classroom. They must be taught to understand and embody anti-racist politics, not only in their words but also through their actions and their emotions.

It is challenging to support and confront white tears in ways that do not marginalize the experience of racialized others. In our personal journeys, through social work education and transitions to educators, the work of challenging race requires different emotional and intellectual labour, based on social positioning. For white women, this requires a reorientation of both advocacy and allyship, understanding that providing a "voice" for racialized women, inclusion, or elevating their concerns can fall short. As Su'ad Abdul Khabeer tweeted in 2017, "You do not need to be a voice for the voiceless. Just pass the mic." White intersectional feminists must realize that there are times where we must remain silent, as our voice and our presence detracts and can threaten the labour and solidarity of racialized women. In the pursuit of racial justice, our work must be focused on supporting racialized women in ways determined by them. We must accept that there may be consequences to our personal and professional identities, as we must challenge our white colleagues, friends, and families for covert and overt acts of racism. To genuinely be an ally as a white woman, we must work to educate other white people and avoid the traps of white solidarity or performative racial allyship for social status. We must work from a standpoint of equity for all, independent of caveats of deserving, such as conditions of who works hard or who should have their rights respected. We must understand that when we respond with the defence of "not all white people," we centre our own experience and imply that we, as allies, deserve special treatment or recognition. Being an ally should not include expectations of being acknowledged or accepted, especially when demanding the emotional labour of racialized women to be appreciative and "nice" (not "angry"). It is our role to confront the crying white women, in ourselves and in others.

The classroom provides the context for invaluable learning students can acquire and transfer to their future work as social work professionals and as allies for social and racial justice. Without centring a critical understanding of racial difference within social work's feminist inclination, racialization, and racism within our classrooms, pedagogies, and practice will thrive. White supremacy continues to be maintained and reinscribed through these problematic classroom encounters. Therefore, social work pedagogy must meld its feminist politics with an anti-racist agenda to confront these ongoing challenges. The infamous title of Terri Lee Flavia Dzodan's (2011) article can serve as inspiration: "My feminism will be intersectional or it will be bullshit."

REFERENCES

Accapadi, M. M. (2007). When white women cry: How white women's tears oppress women of color. *College Student Affairs Journal, 26* (2), 208–15.

Ahmed, S. (2004). *The cultural politics of emotion.* Edinburgh University Press

Ahmed, S. (2010). Feminist killjoys. *The promise of happiness* (pp. 50–87). Duke University Press.

Ahmed, S. (2017). *Living a feminist life.* Duke University Press.

Bannerji, H. (1992). Re: Turning the gaze: Racism, sexism, knowledge and the academy. *Resources for Feminist Research, 20*(3/4), 5–11.

Barlow, C., & Hall, B. L. (2007). "What about feelings?" A study of emotion and tension in social work field education. *Social Work Education: The International Journal, 25*(4), 399–412. https://doi.org/10.1080/02615470601081712

Baxley, T. P. (2012). Navigating as an African American female scholar: Catalysts and barriers in predominantly white academia. *The International Journal of Critical Pedagogy, 4*(1), 47–64.

Blackstock, C. (2011). The Canadian Human Rights Tribunal on First Nations Child Welfare: Why if Canada wins, equality and justice lose. *Children and Youth Services Review, 33*(1), 187–94. https://doi.org/10.1016/j.childyouth.2010.09.002

Blackstock, C., & Trocmé, N. (2005). Community-based child welfare for Aboriginal children: Supporting resilience through structural change.

Social Policy Journal of New Zealand, 24(12), 12–33. https://doi.org/10.4135/9781412976312.n7

Canadian Association for Social Work Education – l'Association canadienne pour la formation en travail social. (2017, June 26). Board of directors endorses a statement of complicity and commits to change [Press release]. https://caswe-acfts.ca/media-release-board-of-directors-endorses-a-statement-of-complicity-and-commits-to-change/

Collins, P. H. (1999). Moving beyond gender: Intersectionality and scientific knowledge. In M. Ferree (Ed.), *Revisioning gender* (pp. 261–84). Sage

Daniels, J. (2015). The trouble with white feminism: Whiteness, digital feminism and the intersectional Internet. SSRN. https://doi.org/10.2139/ssrn.2569369

Diangelo, R. (2015, September 19). *White women's tears and the men who love them.* The Good Men Project. https://goodmenproject.com/featured-content/white-womens-tears-and-the-men-who-love-them-twlm/

Dzodan, T. L. F. (2011, October 10). My feminism will be intersectional or it will be bullshit. *Tiger Beatdown.* http://tigerbeatdown.com/2011/10/10/my-feminism-will-be-intersectional-or-it-will-be-bullshit/

Featherstone, B. (2001). Where to for feminist social work. *Critical Social Work, 2*(1). https://ojs.uwindsor.ca/index.php/csw/article/view/5619/4592

Fellows M., & S. Razack. (1998). The race to innocence: Confronting hierarchical relations among women. *Journal of Gender, Race and Justice, 1*(2), 335–52.

Filipovic, J. (2016, November 9). *Trump's win boils down to white women.* CCN. http://www.cnn.com/2016/11/09/opinions/trumps-win-women-filipovic/index.html

Friedman, S. (1995). Beyond white and other: Relationality and narratives of race in feminist discourse. *Signs, 21*(1), 1–49. https://doi.org/10.1086/495041

Grewal, I. (1996). *Home and harem: Nation, gender, empire, and the cultures of travel.* Duke University Press.

Gutiérrez y Muhs, G., & Niemann, Y. F., Gonzalez, C. G., & Harris, A. P. (Eds.). (2012). *Presumed incompetent: The intersections of race and class for women in academia.* Utah State University Press.

Jacobsen, M. (2016, November 4). *White women, you need to talk about racism.* Bitch Media. https://www.bitchmedia.org/article/white-women-you-need-talk-about-racism

Jeyapal, D., & Bhuyan, R. (2016). Theorizing the racial orientation of the social work classroom: The making and unmaking of whiteness in social work. *As/Us: A Space for Writers of the World, 6*, 130–46.

Jones, T., & Norwood, K. J. (2017). Aggressive encounters & white fragility: Deconstructing the trope of the angry black woman. *Iowa Law Review, 102*(5), 2017–69.

Johnstone, M. (2015). The pervasive presence of the discourse of white civility in early Canadian social work in immigration services (1900–30). *British Journal of Social Work, 46*(6), 1724–40. https://doi.org/10.1093/bjsw/bcv104

Johnstone, M., & Jeyapal, D. (2019). Women, intersecting oppressions, and social policy in Canada. In R. Harding & D. Jeyapal (Eds.), *Canadian social policy for social workers* (pp. 141–60). Oxford University Press.

Jonsson, T. (2015). *White feminist stories: Locating race in the narratives of British feminism* [Doctoral dissertation, London Metropolitan University]. London Met Repository. http://repository.londonmet.ac.uk/959/

Khabeer, S. A. [@DrSuad]. (2017, February 12). *You don't need to be a voice for the voiceless. Just pass the mic* [Tweet]. Twitter. https://twitter.com/drsuad/status/830838928403988480

Lugones, M. (2016). The coloniality of gender. In W. Harcourt (Ed.), *The Palgrave handbook of gender and development* (pp. 13–33). Palgrave Macmillan.

Lutz, C. A., & Abu-Lughood, L. (1990). *Language and the politics of emotion.* Cambridge University Press.

Malsbary, C. (2016, November 11). Dear white people: Things you can do instead of cry or try to hug us. Sincerely, people of color. *Passionate People.* https://cultureraceimmigration.com/2016/11/11/dear-white-people-things-you-can-do-instead-of-cry-and-try-to-hug-us-sincerely-people-of-color/comment-page-1/

McClintock, A. (1995). *Imperial leather: Race, gender, and sexuality in the colonial contest.* Routledge.

Native Women's Association of Canada. (2015). *Missing and murdered Aboriginal women and girls* [Fact sheet]. https://www.nwac.ca/wp-content/uploads/2015/05/Fact_Sheet_Missing_and_Murdered_Aboriginal_Women_and_Girls.pdf

Nylund, D. (2006). Critical multiculturalism, whiteness, and social work: Towards a more radical view of cultural competence. *Journal of Progressive Human Services,* 17(2), 27–42. https://doi.org/10.1300/j059v17n02_03

Palmer, P. M. (1994). White women/black women: The dualism of female identity and experience. In R. Takaki (Ed.), *From different shores: Perspectives on race and ethnicity* (2nd ed., pp. 167–74). Oxford University Press.

Park, Y. (2008). Facilitating injustice: Tracing the role of social workers in the World War II internment of Japanese Americans. *Social Service Review, 82*(3), 447–83. https://doi.org/10.1086/592361

Patton, L. D., & Bondi, S. (2015). Nice white men or social justice allies? Using critical race theory to examine how white male faculty and administrators engage in ally work. *Race Ethnicity and Education, 18*(4), 488–514. https://doi.org/10.1080/13613324.2014.1000289

Peters, S. (2016). The politics of disability identity. In L. Barton (Ed.), *Disability and society: Emerging issues and insights* (pp. 215–36). Routledge.

Phillips, C. (2010). White, like who? Temporality, contextuality and anti-racist social work education and practice. *Critical Social Work, 11*(2). https://doi.org/10.22329/csw.v11i2.5825

Pitts, M. (2017). Uses of my anger: Negotiating mothering, feminism, and graduate school. In M. A. Massé & N. Bauer-Maglin (Eds.), *Staging women's lives in academia: Gendered life stages in language and literature workplaces* (pp. 41–52). State University of New York Press.

Price, J., & Shildrick, M. (Eds.). (1999). *Feminist theory and the body: A reader.* Edinburgh University Press.

Rajan-Rankin, S. (2014). Self-identity, embodiment and the development of emotional resilience. *British Journal of Social Work, 44*(8), 2426–42. https://doi.org/10.1093/bjsw/bct083

Razack, S. (1998). *Looking white people in the eye: Gender, race, and culture in courtrooms and classrooms.* University of Toronto Press.

Razack, S. (2007). Stealing the pain of others: Reflections on Canadian humanitarian responses. *Review of Education, Pedagogy, and Cultural Studies, 29*(4), 375–94. https://doi.org/10.1080/10714410701454198

Reason, R. D., Broido, E. M., Davis, T. L., & Evans, N. J. (Eds.). (2005). *Developing social justice allies. New directions for student services* (no. 110). Jossey-Bass.

Ritenburg, H., Leong, A. E. L., Linds, W., Nadeau, D. M., Goulet, L. M., Kovach, M., & Marshall, M. (2014). Embodying decolonization: Methodologies and indigenization. *AlterNative, 10*(1), 67–80. https://doi.org/10.1177/117718011401000107

Ruparelia, R. (2014). Legal feminism and the post-racism fantasy. *Canadian Journal of Women and the Law, 26*(1), 81–115. https://doi.org/10.3138/cjwl.26.1.81

Salazar, E. M. (2012). *Global coloniality of power in Guatemala: Racism, genocide, citizenship.* Lexington Books.

Schaffner, B. F., MacWilliams, M., & Nteta, T. (2018). Understanding white polarization in the 2016 vote for president: The sobering role of racism and sexism. *Political Science Quarterly, 133*(1), 9–34. https://doi.org/10.1002/polq.12737

Srivastava, S. (2006). Tears, fears and careers: Anti-racism and emotion in social movement organizations. *Canadian Journal of Sociology, 31*(1), 55–90. https://doi.org/10.1353/cjs.2006.0028

Thomas, C. (2016). On being post-normal: Heterosexuality after queer theory. In N. Giffney & M. O'Rourke (Eds.), *The Ashgate research companion to queer theory* (pp. 35–50). Routledge.

Truth and Reconciliation Commission of Canada. (2015). *Honouring the truth, reconciling for the future: Summary of the final report of the Truth and Reconciliation Commission of Canada.* http://www.trc.ca/assets/pdf/Honouring_the_Truth_Reconciling_for_the_Future_July_23_2015.pdf

Turner, S. G., & Maschi, T. M. (2015). Feminist and empowerment theory and social work practice. *Journal of Social Work Practice, 29*(2), 151–62. https://doi.org/10.1080/02650533.2014.941282

Watters, J. (2017). Pink hats and black fists: The role of women in the Black Lives Matter Movement. *William and Mary Journal of Women and the Law, 24*(1), 199–207.

White, G. M. (1993). Emotions inside out: The anthropology of affect. In M. Lewis & J. M. Haviland (Eds.), *Handbook of emotions* (pp. 41–51). Guilford.

Williams, C. (2001). The angry black woman scholar. *National Women's Studies Association Journal, 13*(2), 87–97. https://doi.org/10.1080/00335630.2011.585169

7 The Practice of Critically Reflective Analysis

CAROLYN CAMPBELL AND GAIL BAIKIE

A reflective stance has long been recognized as an essential component of social work (Kondrat, 1999; Oterholm, 2009). Developing skills of critically reflective analysis is especially important for practitioners who want to advance social work's contribution to social transformation (Fook, 2004; Fook & Gardner, 2007; Heron, 2005; Keenan, 2004; Macfarlane & Bay, 2011). However, developing a critically reflective stance, and the skills congruent with such a stance, is often difficult for students. Similarly, social work educators frequently struggle to develop meaningful methods for teaching skills of self-reflection and critical analysis. These challenges are particularly evident among educators and students whose primary experiences of teaching and learning are rooted in didactical methods. What is needed, then, is a process that provides pedagogical guidance for teachers and specific skill development tools for learners. We, the authors, have been working together for over 15 years to develop and refine such a process, a process that we call critically reflective analysis (CRA). CRA serves as both our core pedagogical praxis and a central learning outcome for students. Our theorizing and analysis of CRA are also informed by our dissatisfaction with and critique of our own experiences with what is commonly referred to as *diversity training*.

We have previously discussed the teaching and learning of CRA in an online context (Baikie et al. 2012; Campbell et al., 2011) and introduced students to the fundamentals of a critical stance (Campbell & Baikie, 2012). We also explored the theoretical foundations and practice implications of our pedagogical praxis in the context of a first-year BSW course called Advancing Social Justice (Campbell & Baikie, 2013). We invite you to consider this chapter as a demonstration of how we have built upon our earlier work to further refine our teaching of CRA.

Preparing Educators for the CRA Process

Adopting our CRA process requires educators to work within a specific theoretical perspective and pedagogical framework.

Theoretical Perspective

For us, Fook and Gardner's (2007) theory and method of critical reflection form the basis of CRA. However, we have expanded this perspective and practice, with our own groundings in feminist, experiential, transformative, transcultural, and Indigenous perspectives and pedagogies (Baikie & Campbell, 2005; Baikie et al., 2012; Campbell & Baikie, 2012). A primary difference in our respective approaches is that while Fook and Gardner rely on individualized critical incidents as the material for reflection, we more broadly use generic experiences as the basis for reflection and analysis.

Underpinning CRA is the understanding that knowledge is socially constructed and, as such, is open to scrutiny and rethinking. Knowledge is also related to one's positionality: this means that one's social location influences what is known, how it is understood, and the meaning given to experiences. Therefore, within the CRA process, the emphasis is on asking context-specific questions with the intent to elicit provisional and partial knowledge over definitive truths. The unearthing of power relations is a primary objective. Mattson (2014) explains that

> critical reflection ... focuses on the social worker and her unconscious assumptions and actions as part of reinforcing and maintaining oppression. By critical reflection, the social worker is getting knowledge and insights of how social structures work in everyday life, and therefore becomes capable of working against oppression and injustice. (p. 9)

Thus, the overall goal of CRA is to enable mindful and empowered practice in the social world.

What makes CRA transformative is that its aim is to explicitly and intentionally unearth, scrutinize, and, if necessary, change problematic fundamental values, assumptions, and beliefs (VABs) that inform personal, cultural, and professional perspectives, as well as behaviours. This contrasts with conventional diversity training that typically focuses on differences in the behaviours and practices of the "other." In such training, change efforts are targeted at behaviours and to a lesser degree, attitudes; however, the roots of injustice, namely, the unexamined differences in VABs, especially those within the dominant Eurocentric worldview, remain unscrutinized.

The goal of the CRA process then is to connect one's individualized assumptions, values, and beliefs with broader societal dominant and marginalized worldviews, to dig beneath the surface to unearth the broader social discourses that influence each person's understandings of social phenomenon. In this manner, connections are made between one's personal meanings and broader social, cultural, and political influences. The process of making connections between the personal and the political is a long-standing characteristic of many social justice liberation movements such as feminism (Firestone & Koedt, 1970; Steinem, 2010), the educational work of Paulo Freire (Giroux, 2010), and some critical research methodologies, specifically, memory work (Haug & Others, 1987) and collective biography (Davies & Gannon, 2006).

Pedagogical Framework

CRA is grounded in what we call *transformative experiential education*, a hybrid teaching-learning theory. The basis of the theory is Kolb's (1984) experiential learning cycle. In teaching diversity, we begin the cycle by analysing experiences designed to explicitly disrupt and facilitate the transformation of the students' current "habits of mind" (Mezirow, 1997). We either work with spontaneously occurring incidents within the classroom or introduce specifically designed exercises.

Such a process is not without risks to learners and needs to be thoughtfully managed by educators (Fook & Askeland, 2007). For instance, Fook and Askeland (2007) assert that in Western society, we tend to be guided by cultural norms related to "silence, individualism and secrecy" (p. 523) that mitigate against us exposing our vulnerabilities and that view direct questioning as intrusive. Such a culture works against forming an educational environment that is collaborative, supportive, egalitarian, and open to a diversity of knowledges and understandings. Fook and Askeland (2007) also question whether critical reflection is appropriate for all types of learners and recommend a number of strategies to mitigate the risks and maximize the learning potential. They suggest that some groups may need more preparation then others. Indeed, our approach is to scaffold the learning over the course.

While there may be therapeutic implications, as educators, we must also be clear that the purpose of the process is professional development, not personal therapy. Any level of self-disclosure should be based on informed consent. Along with ensuring students are provided with enough information and understanding to make informed choices, educators must strive to create a learning climate that is conducive to critical reflection and the overall principles of adult learning; that welcomes challenges but also is non-judgmental; and that creates the ideal conditions for interaction and discussion (Mezirow, 1997). As educators, in this environment, we act as "*facilitator* and *provocateur* rather than as an authority on subject matter" (Mezirow, 1997, p. 11).

Preparing Learners for the CRA Process

Understanding Assumptions

Assumptions are our taken-for-granted beliefs about the world and our place within it; they seem so obvious to us as not to need to be stated explicitly. Assumptions give meaning and purpose to who we are and what we do. In many ways, we are our assumptions.

(Brookfield, 2005, p. 49)

Should I Sleep with My Boyfriend? To prepare students for the CRA process, we introduce the concept of *assumptions.* We begin by asking them to imagine they are working in a teen health clinic offering education and counselling regarding teen sexual health. A youth comes to the clinic seeking information and advice. The youth says, "My boyfriend wants me to have sex: he says we have a good relationship and that we are mature enough to be more intimate than we have been. My friends say 'go for it' but I know my parents would be distressed and worried. I really care about him. What do you think I should do?"

We ask students, individually or in groups, depending upon time, to consider what they might want to say to, or ask of, this youth and, after a few minutes of individual reflection, solicit their responses. While there are considerable variations, a common response is something like, "I would encourage her to focus on what she wants to do, not on what others want her to do."

Default Assumptions. We then draw upon the work of Tina Lopes and Barb Thomas (2006) to introduce the idea of *default assumptions.* Using computers as an illustration, we point out that when you begin to type in a program, Times New Roman is the usual or default font. The power of the program is behind this default choice. You either use this font or take intentional action to change it. Even if you change it, the next time you start the program, it often returns to Times New Roman. As humans, our values, beliefs, and experiences are the power behind our default choices.

We point out that heterosexuality and individualism are two default assumptions frequently surfaced by the "Should I sleep with my boyfriend?" exercise. Students are often surprised by their default assumptions. We encourage them to accept the reality that such hidden assumptions will impact their social work practice by influencing how they define problems, informing the actions or interventions they choose, and shaping the very words they speak. We reinforce the idea that active intention is needed to recognize and change default assumptions.

Creation Stories. We then use the metaphor of a tree to engage students in a more theoretical analysis of assumptions with particular attention to the roots of the tree, specifically, the axiological, ontological, epistemological, cosmological, spiritual, and temporal assumptions that are usually not evident to students. One way to illuminate the fundamental assumptions of a given worldview is to look at creation stories.

Usually beginning with the Christian creation story, we engage the whole class in a pantomime wherein the instructor is a narrator and calls upon students to act out the elements of the story. We then surface the assumptions embedded in the story, assumptions about gender, humans' place in the world, time, and knowledge. Students are then divided into groups and asked to present a pantomime illustrating different creation stories. A similar reflection follows each presentation. This has proven to be both a valuable and a fun means of giving life to the theoretical material.

Practising CRA

After students have been prepared for the CRA process, they must become adept at using it. The challenge, as we have previously articulated (Campbell & Baikie, 2013), is to develop instructional aids that give students explicit guidance while not oversimplifying the complexity or epistemological foundation of CRA. In the chapter appendix we share an instructional aid called "Critically Reflective Analysis: A Practice Handout."[1] We distribute this to all students as it offers specific prompts to

1 This is our sixth iteration of this instructional tool. An earlier version can be found in Campbell and Baikie (2013).

assist them in practising the CRA process. The handout also suggests helpful metaphors to use in the teaching of social work. For instance, the wondering why wand, lightning bolt, mirror, linked chain, tissue box, compass, puzzle pieces, and megaphone serve as further prompts for reflection and analysis.

Assessment

In an earlier writing (Campbell & Baikie, 2013), we demonstrated how another metaphor – the tree – serves as the base for a comprehensive group project. We have created another assignment to help students develop a critically reflective stance, and the skills congruent with such a stance, called Before and After.

Before and After. At the beginning of the course, we give students a handout with the following instructions: "Below are several mini-practice scenarios that put you in various social work roles. Describe your thoughts and feelings in response to each scenario. Then describe what you would do or say: be specific – write *exactly* what you would do and say." We have developed six practice scenarios, two of which are presented here:

SCENARIO 1

You are doing a presentation on "domestic violence" to an interagency group. One of the participants states that they are having a difficult time understanding the issues involved and they ask, "Why don't the women just leave the situation and make a better life?"

What might be your internal reaction (thoughts, feelings, behaviour) to this question and what answer would you give the participant? Be specific – write *exactly* what you would do and say.

SCENARIO 2

As a student doing a placement in a rehabilitation centre, you are observing your social work placement supervisor conducting an initial assessment interview with a person who uses a wheelchair. The social worker asks the service user the following question: "What is it about your disability that makes it difficult for you to manage your daily routine?"

What might be your internal reaction (thoughts, feelings, behaviour) as you listen to this question? Would you ask the question in the same way: why or why not? If not, how might you re-phrase the question? Be specific – write *exactly* what you would do and say.

We collect their responses and return them as part of a final assignment, by which time the students have typically forgotten what they had initially written. The final assignment asks them to use the practice handout to complete a CRA of their practice as demonstrated by their initial responses. We are frequently encouraged by the depth and insightfulness of their reflections. The prompts in the handout also serve as a convenient shorthand in providing evaluative feedback. For example, we might comment, "There is considerable evidence of the lightning bolt being used to aid your reflection. It could be enriched if you used the mirror to a similar extent."

Conclusion

CRA, an essential skill for progressive social workers, can be challenging for educators to teach and students to learn. In this chapter, we have described a CRA process to assist educators and students to improve their critical reflection and analysis skills. We recognize that critical reflection is not a uniformly defined concept and not well researched in terms of the factors and characteristics of educators and learners that promote it. While reviews of the empirical studies in the literature are generally silent regarding the impact of factors such as age, social identity, cultural and ideological discourses, as well as educational context, in advancing critical reflection and transformative learning (Baikie et al., 2012; Fook et al., 2016; Taylor, 2000, 2007), our experience and observations lead us to believe that relatively young postsecondary education students are able to acquire foundational skills in critical reflection. Furthermore, many students experiencing marginalized positionalities seem to arrive in the classroom already with a degree of skills in reflexivity and critical analysis. As a helpful tool, our CRA method enables social work students to dig beneath the surface of their experiences to unearth underlying assumptions and associated values and beliefs. As demonstrated in the chapter appendix, the metaphor of a shovel helps to guide students in this process. In addition, insight into CRA and skill development is achieved through structured classroom exercises, several of which have been described in this chapter. Most importantly, while students may initially struggle with the challenge to their traditional modes of thinking, many provide feedback that the learning has been profound, even life altering.

REFERENCES

Baikie, G., & Campbell, C. (2005, May 31). *Critical reflection in decolonizing and creating Aboriginal centered social work theory and practice* [Conference presentation]. Congress/CASSW Conference, London, ON, Canada.

Baikie, G., Campbell, C., Thornhill, J., & Butler, J. (2012). An online critical reflection dialogue group. In J. Fook & F. Gardner (Eds.), *Critical reflection in context: Specific applications in health and social care* (pp. 219–30). Routledge.

Brookfield, S. (2005). Overcoming impostership, cultural suicide, and lost innocence: Implications for teaching critical thinking in the community college. *New Directions for Community Colleges,* (130), 49–57. https://doi.org/10.1002/cc.195

Campbell, C., & Baikie, C. (2013). Teaching critical reflection in the context of a social justice course. *Reflective Practice, 14*(4), 452–64. https://doi.org/10.1080/14623943.2013.806299

Campbell, C., & Baikie, G. (2012). Beginning at the beginning: An introduction to critical social work. *Critical Social Work, 13*(1). https://ojs.uwindsor.ca/index.php/csw/article/view/5849

Campbell, C., Baikie, G., Thornhill, J., & Butler, J. (2011, April 26–8). *Critical reflection dialogue groups: Promoting critical reflection within as online environment* [Conference presentation]. Partnerships in Learning Conference, Halifax, NS, Canada.

Davies, B., & Gannon, S. (2006). *Doing collective biography: Investigating the production of subjectivity.* McGraw-Hill Education.

Firestone, S., & Koedt, A. (1970). *Notes from the second year: Women's liberation: Major writings of the radical feminists.* Radical Feminism.

Fook, J. (2004). Critical reflection and transformative possibilities. In L. Davies & P. Leonard (Eds.), *Social work in a corporate era: Practices of power and resistance* (pp. 16–30). Routledge.

Fook, J., & Askeland, G. A. (2007). Challenges of critical reflection: "Nothing ventured, nothing gained." *Social Work Education, 26*(5), 520–33. https://doi.org/10.1080/02615470601118662

Fook, J., & Gardner, F. (2007). *Practising critical reflection: A resource handbook.* Open University Press.

Fook, J., Psoinos, M., & Sartori, D. (2016). Evaluation studies of critical reflection. In J. Fook, F. Collington, Ross, G. Ruch, & L. West (Eds.), *Researching critical reflection: Multidisciplinary perspectives* (pp. 90–105). Routledge.

Giroux, H. (2010). Rethinking education as the practice of freedom: Paulo Freire and the promise of critical pedagogy. *Policy Futures in Education, 8*(6). https://doi.org/10.2304/pfie.2010.8.6.715

Haug, F., & Others. (1987). *Female sexualization: A collective work of memory* (E. Carter, Trans.). Verso.

Heron, B. (2005). Self-reflection in critical social work practice: Subjectivity and the possibilities of resistance. *Reflective Practice, 6*(3), 341–51. https://doi.org/10.1080/14623940500220095

Keenan, E. (2004). From sociocultural categories to socially located relations: Using critical theory in social work practice. *Families in society: The Journal of Contemporary Social Services, 85*(4), 539–48. https://doi.org/10.1177/104438940408500412

Kolb, D. (1984). *Experiential learning: Experience as the source of learning and development.* Prentice Hall.

Kondrat, M.-E. (1999). Who is the "self" in self-aware: Professional self-awareness from a critical theory perspective. *The Social Service Review, 73*(4), 451–77. https://doi.org/10.1086/514441

Lopes, T., & Thomas, B. (2006). *Dancing on live embers: Challenging racism in organizations.* Between the Lines.

Macfarlane, S., & Bay, U. (2011). Teaching critical reflection: A tool for transformative learning in social work? *Social Work Education: The International Journal, 30*(7), 745–58. https://doi.org/10.1080/02615479.2010.516429

Mattson, T. (2014). Intersectionality as a useful tool: Anti-oppressive social work and critical reflection. *Afflilia: Journal of Women and Social Work, 29*(1), 8–17. https://doi.org/10.1177/0886109913510659

Mezirow, J. (1997). Transformative learning: Theory to practice. *New Directions for Adult and Continuing Education, 74,* 5–12. https://doi.org/10.1002/ace.7401

Oterholm, I. (2009). Online critical reflection in social work education. *European Journal of Social Work, 12*(3), 363–75. https://doi.org/10.1080/13691450902930738

Preskill, S., & Brookfield, S. (2009). *Learning as a way of leading: Lessons from the struggle for social justice.* Jossey-Bass.

Steinem, G. (2010). *Revolution from within: A book of self-esteem.* Phoenix Books.

Taylor, E. (2000). Fostering Mezirow's transformative learning theory in the adult education classroom: A critical review. *The Canadian Journal for the Study of Adult Education, 14*(2), 1–28.

Taylor, E. (2007). An update of transformational learning theory: A critical review of the empirical research (1999–2005). *International Journal of Lifelong Education, 26*(2), 173–91. https://doi.org/10.1080/02601370701219475

APPENDIX: CRITICALLY REFLECTIVE ANALYSIS: A PRACTICE HANDOUT

So far, in this course, we have claimed that social injustice is maintained through the privileging of hidden and unexamined Eurocentric values and assumptions. We have reviewed multiple types of assumptions. We have engaged you in exercises to illustrate the concept of *default assumptions.* We have introduced the tree metaphor as a way of illustrating the importance of "digging up" the default assumptions that inform our society, the social work profession, and social work praxis. Finally, we have offered you a metaphorical shovel to help you with this digging up process. With this handout, we introduce you to critically reflective analysis (CRA): a process to help you use your shovel to dig up hidden assumptions.

Learning from Experience

> Myles Horton famously observed that we don't automatically learn from experience; we learn only from those experiences we learn from. By this he meant that experiences don't teach us anything until we probe deeply into their meaning. To analyze experience is to break it down and examine it in depth so that it is placed in some larger personal and social context. Analyzing experience improves our understanding, helps us make connections, and sometimes leads to alternative means for addressing problems.
>
> (Preskill & Brookfield, 2009, p. 105)

CRA is a professional development process that helps us probe deeply into the meaning of experience. CRA promotes active and intentional engagement with experience and draws upon cognitive, affective, and spiritual ways of "meaning-making." CRA is a non-linear, complex, challenging, and dynamic process with no specific end point.

The ability to reflectively and critically analyse professional practice experiences is an essential component of good social work. Engaging in critical reflective analysis (CRA) ensures that we learn from our practice experiences, helps us improve our practice, opens new avenues for action, and contributes to the development of "practice wisdom," which is the essence of social work praxis. Such processes are particularly useful for practitioners who are committed to social work's contribution to social transformation.

Practising the CRA Process

CRA is not a straightforward process. We will practise and practise this process throughout the rest of the course. Begin by thinking of a **specific** practice experience that is meaningful to you. It should be an experience in which you were actively involved and that you can describe clearly and in detail. The event may be either negative or positive and may or may not involve your direct work with service users and perhaps even colleagues and other agencies. The event may be large or small. (If you are not able to recall a practice experience think about the "Should I sleep with my boyfriend?" exercise we did in class.)

Grab your shovel and, as you are digging up your assumptions, use the following prompts to help your reflection and analysis.

Prompt 1: The Wondering Why Wand

Posing questions and wondering *why*? are fundamental to the CRA process. But we are not asking *why* in the usual sense that calls upon us to defend ourselves and our ideas. Rather, it is the *why* of the two-year-old child who is trying to understand their world. The Wondering Why Wand prompts us to consider

- what was said and why it might have been said
- what might have been the various perspectives of those involved in the event
- what might have influenced the thoughts and ideas of those involved in the experience
- what might be the implications of those thoughts and ideas

Prompt 2: The Lightning Bolt

Promoting social transformation requires a sophisticated understanding of the complexities of power. Power is best understood as a shifting attribute of relationships, not as a static, quantifiable commodity. The Lightning Bolt prompts us to

- consider how power is exercised and shifted within the experience
- ponder the role of language
- note what voices/perspectives are absent or marginalized
- determine who has structured the argument or experience – who has set the terms and who's interests are served

Prompt 3: The Mirror

Turning the gaze inward and considering *the self* as opposed to *the other* is an essential component of CRA. The Mirror prompts you to consider

- how you describe the truth of the experience
- what values, assumptions, and beliefs you bring to the experience
- what there is about your positionality that might contribute to your understanding of the experience
- how you are positioned (both historically and currently) in relation to privileged and marginalized assumptions, concepts, and practices
- how your fundamental values, assumptions, and practices might be impacted by privileged and marginalized assumptions, concepts, and practices

Prompt 4: The Linked Chain

CRA asks us to consider personal experiences in their political context. This "personal is political" analysis asks us to consider how societal assumptions and structures might be influencing the thoughts, feelings, and actions of individuals involved. Use the Linked Chain as a prompt to consider

- the history behind the experience
- popular assumptions that might be evident
- how personal reactions might be linked to these popular assumptions
- how these popular assumptions uphold social systems and structures

Prompt 5: The Tissue Box

Affective learning processes are those that involve our emotions/feelings. CRA asks us to deconstruct (un-learn) and reconstruct (re-learn) fundamental values and beliefs, and such learning engages our hearts and minds. Exploring our emotional and intuitive reactions to any experience offers valuable learnings. Use the Tissue Box to help you learn from your emotions/intuitions by considering

- how you felt about the experience and what assumptions, values, and beliefs are linked to these feelings
- if there is anything about your positionality that might have contributed to your feelings/senses

- what you learned from the experience and from your feelings/senses
- how the emotional/intuitive responses of those involved in the experience might be influenced by respective positionalities and relationships to various social structures

Prompt 6: The Compass

The assumptions, institutions, and practices of any society are the result of individual and collective choices made by human beings. By digging deep and using the various prompts, you begin to understand these choices and to analyse them for internal congruency. The Compass prompts you to

- return to the metaphor of the tree to determine if there is congruency among the roots, the branches, and the leaves in any experience
- make intentional choices about the direction of your personal and professional life
- consider if the language you use, the way you define problems, and the actions you take are congruent with your values and beliefs

Prompt 7: Puzzle Pieces

Using the thoughts, words, and writing of others to advance our own thinking and understanding is another central CRA skill. The point of drawing on the wisdom of others is not to "prove" you are right or wrong. While it is fine to use the work of others to extend and support your ideas, integrating the wisdom of others with your own ideas and feelings is often more powerful learning. Use the Puzzle prompt to consider

- what you learned from others that sparked a new idea for you
- your emotional reactions to the work of others
- the values, assumptions, and beliefs of other worldviews that might offer you alternative understandings of your experience
- how the ideas or feelings of others connect with each other and with your ideas and feelings

Prompt 8: The Megaphone

Social work is rooted in effective communication with others; communication can take multiple forms, but effectively expressing your thoughts and ideas to others is an essential skill. The image of the Megaphone reminds you to

- express yourself succinctly but clearly
- change your communication style depending upon the context
- use language that is appropriate to your audience

Critically reflective analysis is a complex process that invites you to situate yourself in the context of rigorous theoretical analysis; embrace cognitive, affective, and spiritual learning; search for questions, not answers; become comfortable with discomfort; link the personal and the political; and engage in dialogue, not debate. It is an exciting journey, and we look forward to sharing it with you.

8 Teaching and Learning Critical Reflection of Practice: Why Was It So Engaging?

LAURA BÉRES

In this chapter, I describe why and how I developed and taught a required course in critical reflection of practice (CRoP) for an advanced standing master of social work (MSW) program. In offering the course for the first time, we, Jan Fook – the originator of this model of critical reflection – and I, decided to incorporate a research study. This study involved pre and post surveys, as well as weekly questionnaires, to examine if and how students' understanding of critical reflection had changed. As part of the study, I also wrote critical incident reflections, which will be described, each time I experienced anything in my role as facilitator that I believed was worthy of more in-depth analysis. In this chapter, I comment upon my own reflections, post-course surveys, and weekly questionnaires. Through this examination of the process of teaching and learning CRoP, I consider how this course might have contributed to the "re-enchantment" of the academy for students.

Re-enchantment

I was recently asked to write a review of *Re-enchanting the Academy* (Béres, 2018) and was inspired by the authors' reflections on how we might lead "future generations of students out of the cave of policy-led consumerism into the creative freedom of their own souls" (Voss & Wilson, 2017, p. 13). The authors suggest that "enchantment" involves imagination and creativity, allowing for a true connection to self, others, and the world. Although they admit disenchantment may have always been an element of academia, they worry it has recently been more prevalent and pervasive. Looking to the European Enlightenment for the effective severing of the rational from the mysterious, they acknowledge how much we must go against the grain in our contemporary context, where scientific rationality and even secular humanism rule, if we want to bring spirituality, wisdom, and imagination back into the classroom. Voss and Wilson (2017) argue for locating the process of re-enchanting the academy in the field of transformative learning, which they describe as being concerned with "individual 'soul-work'" (p. 18). They suggest this requires "advocating a variety of methods for engaging both the critical mind and the intuitive/emotional heart" (p. 18). This offers a way beyond the dualism of rationality and creativity, and argues for the ongoing need for a true liberal arts education.

Why Critical Reflection of Practice?

As a result of a thorough review of our MSW program at King's University College, we shifted from a generalized focus to one of direct practice in the 2016–2017 academic year. This meant developing new program expectations and courses to ensure students would learn not only advanced direct practice skills but also necessary evaluation skills. We decided to include one required research course to provide skills in traditional methodologies like case studies and pre and post measurements. In addition, we agreed to offer a required course on an alternative form of practice evaluation, which we called Critical Reflection and Appraisal of Social Work Practice. In this course, I teach Fook's (2002, 2012) model of CRoP, which provides students with a structured approach to identifying what Fook and Gardner (2007, p. 27) call "gaps" in their theory and practice, as well as to developing new skills and theories based on their own experiences. It is a model that assists students in articulating their implicit and explicit understandings and values, as well as identifying challenges they have had applying theory to practice. It provides a method for building upon what they learn from reflecting on their reactions to these insights as an aid to developing practice-based theory. In this way, it complements traditional research courses, requiring students to engage in holistic learning rather than relying solely on scientific-rational skills.

Moreover, Fook has written extensively on the value of CRoP as a form of accountability and practice-based research, which responds to a need for professional development at a time when economic stress and heavy workloads often result in lack of supervision in many social work agencies (Fook, 2002, 2012; Fook et al., 2016; Hick et al., 2005; White et al., 2006). Although much of Fook's teaching of CRoP occurs for post-qualified social workers, literature (Brookfield, 2009) suggests it is beneficial to teach CRoP within academic professional programs before post-graduation employment so that new graduates are familiar with the model and can use it for ongoing practice development.

Fook's Model of Critical Reflection

Fook's CRoP model is a two-stage approach. Stage 1 involves the discovering and unsettling of assumptions that are underpinning a reaction to a critical incident. Stage 2 involves focusing on changed thinking arising from reflecting on the critical incident and considering the potential resulting implications for practice (Fook & Gardner, 2007, p. 52). In other words, stage 1 involves deconstruction of thinking and assumptions while stage 2 involves the chance for reconstruction of theory and practice. This process offers the opportunity for being surprised and enriched by new possibilities (Béres, 2017).

In Fook's model, a critical incident can be any event that practitioners have experienced that has remained in their minds and on which they continue to dwell periodically. It may be an event that did not go well and still concerns the individual, or it might be an event that causes pride, resulting in the individual revisiting it for reassurance. Although the critical incident can be either positive or negative in content, Jan and I have found, in our experience of teaching this model, that participants are generally more inclined to choose *negative* critical incidents on which to reflect for this process. However, students in my course commented that they also took into consideration not wanting to appear "too incompetent" to their future colleagues so were carefully selective about the incident to be shared. CRoP then provides a formalized approach for clearly articulating the details of this critical incident and identifying any gaps in the movement from theory to practice. *Gaps* are practice moments when an espoused theory that is being used appears to have let the practitioner down, resulting in the need to draw upon creativity and intuition to fill what would have been a missing step in the theory to practice process. Fook's (2002) model then proposes viewing critical incidents through the lenses of four theoretical traditions (Fook & Gardner, 2007, p. 23):

1 The reflective approach to theory and practice (reflection)
2 Reflexivity
3 Postmodernism and deconstruction
4 Critical social theory

Interestingly, Fook (2016) has recently been integrating a fifth lens, that of spirituality.

Describing the four theoretical lenses, Fook and Gardner (2007) begin by distinguishing between reflective and reflexive practice. In terms of reflective practice, they draw upon Schön's (1983) work in the field of education, where he proposes that teachers need to both "reflect-in" (during) and "reflect-on" (after) their practice. This initially responded to a divide that teachers felt between theories they were taught in academic settings and the practice in which they actually engaged in classrooms. Therefore, practitioners are encouraged not only to rationally attempt to apply theories that have been taught but also to use artistry, emotion, and intuition in their practice to recognize the limitations of those taught theories. Catching the manner in which gaps in taught theory have been filled in this way can assist in articulating new practice-based theory. Reflexivity, on the other hand, is influenced by social science research, particularly in the field of anthropology (Fook & Gardner, 2007). It involves recognizing that researchers and social workers cannot be completely objective and so need to examine their own subjectivity, which influences how and what they observe in people.

The third theoretical framework, postmodernism and deconstruction, encourages an examination of the language and discourses used within the description of the critical incident to highlight the relationships between knowledge, power, and the social construction of any particular "one truth" (Fook & Gardner, 2007). This process also assists students in recognizing dualisms they have set up in their thinking and promotes a movement beyond either-or thinking.

Finally, CRoP is *critical* because of the role of the fourth theoretical framework, critical social theory, as influenced by Marx, Marcuse, and Habermas. Critical social theory articulates "that power, or domination, is both personally experienced and structurally created" (Fook & Gardner, 2007, p. 35). As a consequence, introspective unearthing of assumptions in the process should not occur on its own but rather within theories of structures of power and injustice within society.

Structure of the Critical Reflection of Practice Research Project and Course

Research Design

Because this Critical Reflection and Appraisal of Practice course was being offered in the MSW program for the first time, and because very little has been written about teaching CRoP in a university setting, we designed a research study to examine if, and in what way, students' understanding of critical reflection changed over the program time and what facilitated their learning. Before the course, during orientation week, students completed a questionnaire regarding what they understood critical reflection to be. Three months following completion of the course, when the students were involved in field placement settings, they were invited to complete questionnaires about what they believed they had learned about CRoP and whether they were integrating it into their ongoing practice. We received 45 completed pre-course questionnaires and 10 post-course questionnaires. As often occurs with an online request for follow-up surveys, the response rate was only 22 per cent, which limits the interpretation of the findings.

In addition to the pre and post questionnaires, all students completed Brookfield's (2009) Critical Incident Questionnaire at the end of each week's class. Questions asked students to consider moments in class when they had been most and least engaged and what actions any other people had taken that had supported their engagement and learning. The questionnaires allowed students to retain one copy for themselves and anonymously submit the other to me. I then reviewed all 45 questionnaires each week, analysing them for themes that I then reported back to each class the following week. This provided us with weekly feedback about what was helpful for their learning and what we could adjust. Early on, although a handful of students appreciated PowerPoint slides and more formal lectures, most found they were least engaged during these. This was simple to adjust. Since the CRoP framework requires small-group work, as students slowly became more comfortable with the theory and framework of the approach, I was able to provide additional small-group time, and I circulated among the groups and assisted students as they attempted to put into practice what they were learning.

Structure of the Course

Before beginning stage 1 of CRoP, it is crucial to set the tone and assist with the development of a "trusting and collegial climate" (Fook & Gardner, 2007, p. 49), since students will be asked to share descriptions of their critical incidents within small-group settings and in the classroom. Fook and Gardner (2007) suggest that the group culture requires a climate of "critical acceptance" (p. 78) and provide a description of the requirements for this: a commitment to confidentiality and lack of judgmental comments, presentation of an incident rather than a case, no advice-giving, willingness to ask and respond to why questions that promote deconstruction of the incident, and the right to draw limits (p. 84).

Stage 1 involves individuals writing, in a few pages, a detailed account of their critical incident and presenting it to their small group of six to eight other students. The group then assists in developing and asking questions based upon the four theoretical frameworks described above. Before working on their own, I provided time in the class for students to immerse themselves in the four theoretical frameworks and to learn how to ask questions informed by those frameworks. I also provided a critical incident of my own from a practice experience, and we practised creating questions together. Learning to develop well-crafted questions can cause students to feel deskilled initially when their first reactions to hearing the details of an incident are often either to empathize or to attempt to problem solve. Since many MSW students with practical experience have developed skills in basic counselling, they tend to initially depend on questions they have used in generic interviewing situations and struggle with developing questions based on the four theoretical frameworks that underpin the CRoP process. Fook has reported (personal communication, 2016) that social workers and students often ask to be given a list of questions to use in the CRoP process. However, I agree with her that it is more important for people to develop an in-depth understanding of the theories and create their own questions specific to each critical incident. Although Fook and Gardner provide a few example questions in their 2007 book, the difficulty with providing questions is that students may use them as a checklist. This stymies thorough theoretical understanding and skill development. Checklists are apt to provide a quick and superficial account of the incident, whereas it is important to encourage students to take time to immerse themselves in the story of the critical incident, and from that immersion consider how each theory provides a lens to promote further exploration.

Stage 2 involves continuing small-group work, summarizing insights that have resulted from exploring the critical incident, and, most importantly, articulating the resulting implications for practice. This can involve a greater awareness of important personal implicit values, increased sensitivity regarding the complex relationship between structures of power and knowledge, and descriptions of new specific practice-based wisdom and skills.

Fook and Gardner (2007) present the CRoP model as facilitated in three full-day sessions, with time provided between the first and second stages. In contrast, I was required to adjust the model to fit within the usual 13-week academic term, with one three-hour class each week. I committed the first two weeks to considering the classroom culture required for the type of work in which the small groups were expected to engage, to review definitions and descriptions of critical incidents, and to review the four theoretical frameworks.

Weeks three through five focused on supporting students in beginning to consider their critical incidents and then, in their small groups, developing and asking questions based on the four theories. In week six, I gave an in-class test in which students were asked to complete a written description of their critical incident, describe each of the four theories, and develop a series of questions for each. This test was important for their learning since it motivated them to practise more carefully; several students suggested it was only through the process of writing the test that they suddenly understood the process more clearly. In weeks seven through twelve, we reviewed research literature and theory that had been developed through the two-stage process of CRoP, practised stage 2, and prepared for group presentations that occurred in week thirteen. Students were then also required to complete a final essay. However, we all required more time to learn and engage thoroughly in stage 1 and did not require as much time for stage 2, so I would restructure the course in future, taking a week or two from stage 2 and giving it to stage 1.

Pre and Post Surveys and Weekly Critical Incident Questionnaires

Pre-course surveys suggested that students had all been taught in their undergraduate programs that critical reflection was an important part of professional practice, but they did not remember having been taught what it was or how to engage in it. The following provides a summary of the types of comments made in the pre-course survey regarding what they believed they already knew about CRoP:

- It is crucial.
- It relates to self/growth/improvement/change.
- It is linked to clinical practice improvement.
- There is a psychodynamic influence, so it requires understanding our own background, triggers, as well as transference and countertransference issues.
- I do not know much or anything about it.

In general, students thought CRoP entailed reviewing emotions in relation to interactions with service users and so it was to be done in supervision or in personal journaling.

In responding to a general question about what they thought they had learned from the course in the post-course survey, they offered the following range of comments:

- CRoP was new to me. It was useful. I can apply it in a practice setting and it is useful as a form of resistance.
- All perspectives from an incident can be reflected upon.
- My ideas changed greatly. I had a narrow idea that it was connected to theory and practice, but had not considered deconstruction, nor critical social theory.

- I gained good understanding of the two stages, what CRoP means, and how useful it is in practice.
- My ideas changed totally. I did not understand it before. I thought it was about just thinking on a deeper level.
- My ideas changed totally, and I have new clarity. I look at everything through these lenses now and they add a level of empathy and compassion.
- I realize now that idle reflection only goes so far when it comes to improving practice. CRoP allows me to change practice in a vibrant way.
- The framework allows better use of time, and better ability to identify gaps in practice. It provides a better understanding of the many influences of power.
- It provides a systematic model to engage with an incident. Taking the time to do this can help resolve feelings of responsibility and self-blame, with a new stance helping me resolve challenges.
- I learned how CRoP can be applied to professional experiences. It has prompted me to explore different experiences and has allowed me to go further and expand my practice.

Similarly, Jan Fook (personal communication, 2017; and in her role as co-researcher in this study) indicated that the pre-course surveys were consistent with her experiences of teaching CRoP over many years. Practitioners almost always indicate that they are already reflecting on their practice but usually have not been relying on a particular model to move the reflection beyond either a personal examination of emotions on the one hand, or an overly rational attempt to problem solve on the other. We have both found it rewarding to read how students came to appreciate learning the structured CRoP model, as well as how it provided them with different perspectives for filling gaps in theory and practice, the resolution of issues of self-blame, the opportunity for personal and professional change, and greater empathy and compassion.

For the weekly critical incident questionnaires (CIQs), students indicated that the demonstration of other students' interest, shown through questions and comments, was appreciated in terms of their growing confidence and engagement with the topic. They also indicated that they found it helpful when I spent time with them in small groups providing immediate feedback and suggestions as they attempted to develop the kinds of questions required for each theoretical framework. In addition, they indicated valuing being able to watch me facilitate an interview of a volunteer student regarding a critical incident, in front of the class, providing examples of how to generate appropriate questions from each of the theories.

The CIQs also provided students the opportunity to share worries and frustrations about the learning process and group dynamics. In one CIQ, a student indicated she was extremely upset with the other students in her small group. She explained her frustration in detail on the back page of her CIQ (usually students only completed the front of the sheet) and when she handed me her CIQ, she pointed out the amount she had written, thereby purposefully not maintaining her anonymity that week. She explained that although she was attempting to engage fully in the process, the other members in her group were not as fully engaged, and she felt this was having a detrimental impact on her learning. I contacted her and offered to provide individual assistance to her to support her learning, and I suggested that I spend longer with her group the following week assisting with developing and asking questions. She declined to meet individually, but she and other members of her group provided feedback that the extra time I spent with them was very helpful in consolidating the process for them and assisting them in becoming more engaged with their learning. This example demonstrates that using CIQs weekly does require the instructor's time and commitment to promptly review and respond to feedback.

Unfortunately, another group also experienced difficulties and conflicts in their group process, but none of the group members raised their problems until two of them included a description of the process in their final papers. These two incidents, and other less dramatic group dynamics, reinforce the contention that a culture of critical acceptance, as described above, is required within the group for it to support the CRoP process. I will know to stress this even more in future years when I teach this course again and will explore with students what they may want to do if they experience difficulties.

There was also a class-wide incident that caused tension in one section of the course, which was brought up in the CIQs. Although I had been aware of the interaction that had caused some difficulty and had spoken in a small group with the student who was most annoyed, verbal feedback suggested those students most impacted did not want me to engage more fully with the incident at that time, whereas the CIQs showed that many students were unsettled by it. This was one of two incidents that occurred within the larger classroom context that I also experienced as critical incidents, since they stayed with me and continued to unsettle me. Using these as an opportunity to more fully engage in the CRoP process myself, I wrote descriptions of both critical incidents for my own personal learning. Since I was not involved in a group as a participant, I was required to use the four theories as lenses upon the incidents by myself, asking and answering questions from the four approaches, in a written format. This process was very helpful and provided a much fuller examination of incidents and a wider understanding of the possible elements contributing to them. It allowed me to see more clearly how I could have dealt with the incidents differently at the time and how I might move forward with greater sensitivity. This gave me the opportunity to learn how to both engage in CRoP within a different format and improve my teaching of CRoP through modelling the process. Although I did not share my writing about the incident with the students, I did describe my process and the learning with the students in class. This added a certain feeling of vulnerability to my experience, but nonetheless, feedback has suggested that students appreciated my commitment and my willingness to be vulnerable with them in this whole teaching and learning process.

Concluding Thoughts

I have been asked why this process of teaching and learning CRoP was so engaging, despite the ups and downs we experienced. There are a few possible answers to this question. First, students were given time to examine and learn from an incident that many of them had been worrying about for a year or longer and of which they had previously experienced professional shame, anxiety, or frustration. For many students, the incident was related to a field placement experience in their undergraduate degree. The opportunity to examine the fullness of the context of their incidents and develop greater confidence in their professional identities appeared to give many of them more hope regarding their upcoming graduate-level placements. Second, students were able to engage in the classroom setting not only with their intellects but also with their intuition, their creativity, and their personal and professional values. Engaging with all these skills provided an opportunity for transformative learning as described by Voss and Wilson (2017). Third, the need to develop a stance of curiosity in uncovering implicit and explicit values in their accounts of their critical incidents was initially difficult for some students but eventually seemed to intrigue them. They seemed to enjoy the process of coming to think about and know themselves in a different way. Fourth, students also learned that their insights are worthy of publication. Five students were contracted to rework their final papers as chapters for a book that Jan Fook and I edited, titled *Learning Critical Reflection: Experiences of the Transformative Learning Process*, published by Routledge (Béres & Fook, 2020).

Finally, one of my greatest surprises from teaching the CRoP course for the first time was how overwhelmingly positive the feedback was from students. Students indicated that they found it to be one of the few courses in their advanced standing MSW program that provided what they had hoped for from graduate education, saying that the course stimulated new ways of thinking and engaging with the world. I now think part of the reason the course was so successful was because students found it "re-enchanting." It seems, then, that social work education would benefit from providing more opportunities for students to engage their souls and creativity along with their rational intellects.

REFERENCES

Béres, L. (2017). Maintaining the ability to be unsettled and learn afresh: What philosophy contributes to our understanding of "reflection" and "experience." *Reflective Practice: Multidisciplinary and International Perspectives, 18*(2), 280–90. https://doi.org/10.1080/14623943.2016.1269003

Béres, L. (2018). Re-enchanting the academy, *Journal for the Study of Spirituality, 8*(1), 101–3. https://doi.org/10.1080/20440243.2018.1431367

Béres, L., & Fook, J. (Eds.). (2020). *Learning critical reflection: Experiences of the transformative process.* Routledge.

Brookfield, S. (2009). The concept of critical reflection: Promises and contradictions, European *Journal of Social Work, 12*(3), 293–304. https://doi.org/10.1080/13691450902945215

Fook, J. (2002). *Social work: Critical theory and practice.* Sage.

Fook, J. (2012). *Social work: A critical approach to practice* (2nd ed.). Sage.

Fook, J. (2016). Finding fundamental meaning through critical reflection. In L. Béres (Ed.), *Practising spirituality: Reflections on meaning-making in personal and professional contexts* (pp. 17–29). Palgrave Macmillan.

Fook, J., Collington, V., Ross, F., Ruch, G., & West, L. (Eds.). (2016). *Researching critical reflection: Multidisciplinary perspectives.* Routledge.

Fook, J., & Gardner, F. (2007). *Practising critical reflection: A resource handbook.* Open University Press.

Hick, S., Fook, J., & Pozzuto, R. (Eds.). (2005). *Social work: A critical turn.* Thompson.

Schön, D. (1983). *The reflective practitioner.* Basic Books.

Voss, A., & Wilson, S. (Eds.). (2017). *Re-enchanting the academy.* Rubedo Press.

White, S., Fook, J., & Gardner, F. (Eds.). (2006). *Critical reflection in health and social care.* Open University Press.

PART TWO

Practice

The practice of social work has greatly evolved since it was first taught in postsecondary institutions at both the undergraduate and the graduate levels. Beginning with casework, with its roots intertwined with the medical model, to generalist social work practice that took on more systems and ecological orientations, to a contemporary focus with an increasing emphasis upon evidence-informed anti-oppressive practice, social work has become a more rigorous and progressive academic domain. Part II explores a broad range of contemporary social work practice issues, beginning with the intersection of the academic setting with field practice. It also explores issues of diversity and mindfulness while touching on all three levels of social work practice: micro, mezzo, and macro. Though we may debate whether fieldwork is our signature pedagogy, there is no argument about its fundamental function in social work and that students need to begin their preparation for the field in the classroom. The opening chapter, "Preparing for Social Work Practice: Effective Educational Approaches to Bridge Class and Field," by Marion Bogo, offers ways to make that connection and links the previous section on pedagogy to this one, which concentrates on practice and examines demonstrated approaches to unite the classroom and the field.

Bogo, appointed as an Officer to the Order of Canada as a result of her practice and teaching in social work, writes that students enter social work programs with the specific intention of becoming professional practitioners. While many Canadian schools focus on developing critical thinking and a social critique, students and alumni often report that this approach does not prepare them adequately for their future roles as organization-based social work practitioners. Bogo's long-standing program of research on social work education has resulted in educational innovations and a range of valuable methods to develop students' practice competence. Her chapter presents a model of holistic competence in social work that guides the use of systematic, well-designed simulations in classes; intensive preparation for field learning that integrates theory and practice; an objective structured clinical examination for assessment of holistic competence; and methods that integrate learning in the class and field.

Bogo is followed by Claude Olivier and Akin Taiwo of King's University College, who discuss "Preparing Social Workers for Practice with Diverse Populations." Their chapter outlines teaching approaches designed to equip social work students with the values, knowledge, and skills to work purposefully with individuals, families, groups, and communities that reflect the diversity of Canadian society. They apply a critical theoretical perspective in examining conceptual frameworks related to diversity, including multiculturalism, anti-oppressive practice, cultural competency, and cultural humility. Their intent is for students to grasp both the strengths and the limitations of these various frameworks in understanding and responding to issues of diversity. Olivier and Taiwo emphasize how, for them, theory informs practice. Thus, they present approaches used to foster the integration of theory in practice at micro, mezzo, and macro levels of intervention. Inevitably, students' own social locations enter the mix as new practitioners grapple with issues of privilege and vulnerability to oppression. The authors have found that their own use of self-disclosure related to social location, intersectionality, and positionality facilitates this important, yet difficult, examination of self. Overarching the teaching approaches outlined in this chapter is a positive and affirming perspective on diversity, accompanied by a discussion of social work practices, aimed at disrupting oppression and advancing social inclusion and justice.

Another critical practice theme for social work educators is examined by Diana Coholic, in her contribution, "Teaching Mindfulness." Coholic writes that there are many rationales for teaching mindfulness-based practices and concepts to social work students. For example, practising mindfulness has been found to improve therapeutic presence, self-awareness, emotion regulation, and abilities to cope with stress and anxiety. Thus, learning mindfulness can have both personal and professional benefits. Coholic's chapter discusses how to teach the philosophy and practice of mindfulness and some of its important concepts, such as self-compassion, non-judgment, acceptance, gratitude, curiosity, loving-kindness, beginner's mind, and trust. The focus of Coholic's writing is on a social work approach to mindfulness that is holistic, strengths-based, and anti-oppressive, using creative arts-based and experiential methods to engage students.

Next, in "Teaching Change: Navigating the Tensions in Social Change Pedagogy," Kathy Hogarth discusses the fundamental social work practice principle of teaching social change. The relationship between social change and social work is a well-established and long-existing one. Despite this, significant challenges remain in teaching social change and having students envision themselves as agents of it. Hogarth worked with 90 students for a year, exploring a number of elements involved in the pedagogy of change. The findings of her work suggest that teaching social change meets with degrees of resistance, reimagining, anxiety, and satisfaction – not only for students but also for instructors and the institutions that employ social work educators.

Jan Yorke, Scott Grant, and Rick Csiernik use two intriguing metaphors to examine social work practice in their contribution "Horses and Baseball: Social Work's Cultivation of the Third Eye." The authors write that active self-reflection is a sophisticated and subtle multilayered process that requires learning how to constantly self-monitor. This fundamental interactive skill, which is at the core of being a competent social worker, is important in any social work context. However, the authors argue that in current social work education curricula, the use of self is not consistently prioritized, practised, or well understood.

Bharati Sethi and Tracy Smith Carrier then explore "Bridging the Micro-Macro Divide: Making Policy Relevant to Social Work Students." Despite the recognition of the importance of macro-level practice, students and instructors in schools of social work continue to be wary of a perceived, if not actual, micro-macro divide. Historically, and as the profession has migrated to various specializations, a schism between micro and macro levels of practice has emerged, and forms of macro-level practice, such as policy analysis and advocacy, have often been cast aside or undervalued. This chapter is also framed by a social justice approach to teaching. Sethi and Smith Carrier argue that bridging the micro-macro divide and strengthening the integration of policy in direct practice education are essential to equip social work graduates with the skills and tools necessary for work with oppressed populations. Having heard their students state that social policy courses are considered "dry" or "abstract," they discuss how direct practice at the macro level can be reimagined, and revitalized, not as ancillary knowledge for social workers but as a quintessential expression of the profession.

Rachel Birnbaum's contribution to this section on practice in social work teaching is entitled "Navigating Real-World Research Steps: Behind the Scenes." Birnbaum, a member of the Royal Society of Canada, writes that many studies fail to explore the context of research activities or discuss issues raised by participants as a result of their involvement in a study. Birnbaum challenges the traditional assumption that research activities/contexts can be separated from process. Her chapter employs a case example that highlights how the context of the research can be a contributory and/or challenging factor in carrying out the research process. Issues such as the research question, theoretical framework, sampling, methodology, results, and practice, research, and policy implications are examined as each stage has real-world implications to consider in teaching research to social work students. This is of particular importance because research remains among the most daunting teaching and practice areas in which to engage social work students.

The closing chapter, by Nancy Freymond, Gissele Damiani-Taraba, Sherri-Lynn Manto, Sarah Robertson, Leigh Savage, Marilee Sherry, and Andrew Koster, explores a fundamental social work practice area: child welfare. This collaboration between academics and field instructors links us back to Bogo's opening chapter. Their chapter, "Charting a New Course for Community-University Partnership for Teaching Child Welfare Social Work," explores an approach to undergraduate social work education in which lived experience is the core practice approach that drives teaching. They see teaching and learning as being situated not only inside university classrooms but also across community child welfare sites. These authors, writing in a collectivist style, present their experiences as part of a circle of educators that includes service users, university instructors, service providers, and students, all of whom share a vision and hope for transformed practice. They view the classroom environment as a learning context that should be designed to critically examine beliefs, values, and knowledge about, in their case, child welfare service users and workers, and the role of the academy in preparing students for child welfare practice. They conclude their chapter by reflecting on how journeying together has inspired their own transformation of practice.

9 Preparing for Social Work Practice: Effective Educational Approaches to Bridge Class and Field

MARION BOGO

The Purpose of Education for Professional Social Work

What is the purpose of university-based education for any profession? Lee Shulman (2005), education scholar and former president of the Carnegie Foundation for the Advancement of Teaching, identified unique aspects of professional education. In contrast to traditional education in disciplines, education for the professions is preparation for "accomplished and responsible practice in the service of others … They [students] must come to understand in order to act, and they must act in order to serve" (Shulman, 2005, p. 53). Consequently, professional educational programs are responsible for instilling in their students the profession's fundamental ways of thinking, performing, and acting with integrity. This vision suggests the need for close links between university-based educators and professional practitioners and leaders. Such links address the ever-evolving nature of the specific profession's mission, roles, relevant issues faced, and capacities needed to function effectively in contemporary and future environments. The quality of Canada's health and social programs is highly dependent on the effectiveness of the social workers who deliver these services. Hence, social work educators are eager to find useful methods to prepare students for contemporary and future practice.

Theorizing Competence: A Model of Holistic Competence in Social Work

Committed to educating students for effective social work practice, scholars at the University of Toronto have conducted a multi-project program of research aimed at identifying dimensions of competence.

In-depth interviews were held with experienced social work field educators from a range of specializations and practising at micro (Bogo et al., 2006), mezzo, and macro levels (Regehr et al., 2012). The aim was to illuminate the internal constructs field educators used when describing and evaluating students' practice. Qualitative data analysis led to the development of a model of holistic competence. In subsequent studies, the model guided the conceptualization, teaching, and assessment of students' and practitioners' generic practice competence (Bogo et al., 2014). Recently, the model has been successfully applied to analysing and teaching competent practice in a range of specializations and with diverse populations and practice situations. This includes discussing the application in acute care hospital settings (Craig et al., 2017); using it with service users who are "coming out" (Logie et al., 2015); applying it to potential child neglect situations (Tufford et al., 2015); and using the model to teach practice with ethnically diverse service users (Asakura et al., 2018) and in social work education in mental health, addictions, and suicide risk assessment (Kourgiantakis et al., 2019). The view of holistic competence has proven robust and applicable to these multiple contexts.

Unlike traditional competence models, which usually define competencies as consisting of knowledge, skills, and attitudes or values, the holistic model recognizes a more complex view of practice: that there are multidimensional and interrelated components. What social workers actually do is illustrated in the centre of Figure 9.1. These are the complex practices, such as engaging in and maintaining mutual relationships with service users, arriving at shared understanding of issues to be addressed, developing agreed upon goals and ways of achieving those goals, and implementing those plans. These practices are enacted through the use of verbal and non-verbal communication and attending behaviours and are identified in the upper left quadrant. Additionally, the use of these behaviours, sometimes referred to simply as skills, are informed by the humanistic values of the profession: acceptance, non-judgmental stance, respect, and positive regard for the service user. As well, social workers draw on rich and multifaceted sources of knowledge to guide their use of skills, as depicted in the lower left quadrant of Figure 9.1. Sources of knowledge include generic concepts; specialist knowledge related to populations; substantive issues, such as interpersonal violence, substance use, types of mental illness, and family functioning, where they exist; empirically supported intervention models; and practice principles derived from practice wisdom.

Figure 9.1. A Model of Holistic Competence in Social Work

Source: Reprinted with permission of the Council on Social Work Education from Bogo, Rawlings, Katz, & Logie (2014). *Using simulation in assessment and teaching: OSCE adapted for social work.* Alexandria, VA: Council on Social Work Education.

Holistic competence, however, is more than the application of knowledge and skills through procedures. As described by Bogo and colleagues (2013):

> One dimension, *meta-competence*, refers to higher order, overarching qualities and abilities of a conceptual, interpersonal, and personal/professional nature. This includes students' cognitive, critical, and self-reflective capacities. The second dimension, *procedural competence*, refers to performance and the ability to use procedures in various stages of the helping process and includes the ability, for example, in direct practice, to form a collaborative relationship, to carry out an assessment, and to implement interventions with clients and systems. (p. 261)

Meta-competencies are captured on the right side of Figure 9.1, the section that identifies the role of thinking and feeling in practice. Similar to contributions from cognitive neuroscience, regarding the role of emotions in behaviour, studies showed that participants' feelings and thoughts were intricately interwoven with their actions in practice (Bogo, Regehr, et al., 2017). Specifically, participants' emotional state, ability to manage and regulate strong reactions, and degree of self-awareness influenced their ability to use social work knowledge frameworks and concepts. They reported that their emotions affected their ability to reflect on complex problems, engage in critical thinking, exercise judgment, and make decisions in a thoughtful manner. It became apparent that practitioners' and students' cognitive and affective processes affect the way social workers engage in their actual practice, whether they are intentional and thoughtful or reactive and not purposeful in a professional manner (Bogo, 2018). This view of meta-competence has also been expressed by scholars in related human services and health professions and in studies of over 20 professions (Cheetham & Chivers, 2005). Finally, consistent with the person-in-environment social work framework (Kondrat, 2013), the holistic competence model depicted is nested within the multiple systems that affect social work practice such as professional values and ethics, organizational policies and processes, community context and norms, and societal structures.

A holistic perspective requires recognition of these interrelated dimensions of competence. To reiterate, practising in an organizational context and using social work professional values, competence involves social workers carrying out complex practices informed by knowledge, filtered through their own cognitive and affective processes, and delivered through the use of skills. So, are social work educators confident that their current forms of teaching facilitate such integration? Typically, content areas deemed important are taught and assessed in stand-alone courses in a curriculum (Crisp & Lister, 2002). Aspects of competence are also divided between class and field; primarily, content and cognitive processes are addressed in courses and practice is considered in the field. Attention to affective processes related to the self is frequently discussed in both domains through an emphasis on reflective practice. Reflection is defined in many ways but generally refers to the way in which social workers use their unique characteristics, assumptions, and beliefs, or "self," in their professional roles (Ferguson, 2018). For example, many courses address reflective practice in relation to the specific content in each course and, in field, in relation to the population served and the particular service user's response to the student. There is a vast literature on reflection generated from a variety of paradigms. In general, reflection refers to encouraging students to engage in critical self-awareness, to surface assumptions of which they may be unaware, and to acknowledge power differences between workers and service users (Ferguson, 2018).

A holistic conceptualization of competence requires approaches that bring together the various dimensions of competence rather than teaching and assessing them separately. Ultimately, what matters is how the student brings these dimensions together in effective practice. It is therefore not sufficient for students to learn *about* concepts that inform practice without learning *how* to apply them in practice. As importantly, it is not sufficient for students to learn skills without learning about the conceptual and empirical rationale for intentionally choosing particular interventions. What is needed are educational approaches that systematically provide learning opportunities that articulate knowledge in a way that students see how to apply concepts and simultaneously examine actual practice to deconstruct the concepts guiding interventions. Also needed are reflective practices to deconstruct and surface how individuals' thoughts, assumptions, biases, and emotions are influencing their reactions to practice situations. Studies conducted by our team used reflection immediately after simulated interviews to illuminate students' and experienced practitioners' perspectives on influences on their practice (Bogo et al., 2013; Bogo, Lee, et al., 2017). A dominant theme emerged from this work. Students and practitioners reported that when practice situations led to experiences of high anxiety and emotional dysregulation, their ability to use the knowledge frameworks they possessed was compromised. In such situations, they described their practice as unfocused and arbitrary and had difficulty conceptualizing the practice situation and interacting in an intentional manner. Thus, by creating an increased awareness, students are in a better position to learn how to practise purposefully and intentionally rather than reacting to situations as they arise.

A Promising Teaching Approach to Develop Holistic Competence: The Use of Simulation

Social work educators have embraced experiential learning and the use of simulation as an effective method in classrooms to assist students in learning practice skills (Logie et al., 2013). Simulation can be defined as a method "to replace or amplify real experiences with guided experiences, often immersive in nature, that evoke or replicate substantial aspects of the real world in a fully safe, instructive and interactive fashion" (Gaba, 2007, p. 136). A critical review of studies using simulation and role-plays found 18 studies showing students' and faculty members' high satisfaction with the approach (Logie et al., 2013). Instructors develop scenarios depicting typical social work situations, and students take turns enacting roles of social worker and service users. In this approach, peers and the instructor both provide feedback on skill performance. Simulation using human actors builds on this tradition; however, as adapted for social work, Bogo et al. (2014) recommend a specific systematic design and execution format.

A series of iterative phases are used to create simulation-based teaching for developing holistic competence (Bogo et al., 2014):

1 Articulating competencies as outcomes
2 Designing authentic scenarios
3 Creating teaching and learning tools and methods
4 Evaluating and refining the content and method

In the first phase, the holistic competence model guides the instructor to consider and articulate competencies related to all dimensions as they apply to the practice issue. Since the view of competence provided in this chapter rests on intentional use of concepts, students must have the opportunity in courses or modules to learn the foundational knowledge for skillful complex practice. Instructors also need to develop observable indicators of students' behaviour consisting of specific descriptions of those practices. For example, the broad competence of developing and using a collaborative relationship can be broken down into component parts, such as students' ability to respond to content and process, as well as issues in the specific situation. These indicators are used to create teaching and learning tools. Such tools include these broad competencies, as well as more specific behavioural indicators. By specifying practice behaviours, teaching becomes transparent and students have enhanced clarity regarding expectations. Indeed, our recent studies found students reporting that such descriptions of competencies and related behaviours helped them recognize how concepts were actually used in practice (Kourgiantakis et al., 2018).

The second phase includes designing authentic scenarios. Scenarios must provide the factual content or data with which students can engage to learn and to demonstrate the identified competencies. Instructors can begin this process by defining a presenting problem and the beginning details for a scenario, such as service users' factors, history, and background; intersecting diversity factors; the emotional state of the service user; verbatim statements for the actor; social worker goals; and instructions for students. Involving social workers who are experts in specific fields strengthens the likelihood of producing an authentic situation. Actors trained to portray the service users in each scenario require sufficient information to enable them to respond, based on each student's interview.

The third phase involves creating teaching and learning tools and methods that link concepts and practices. Tools consist of examples of competencies and video recordings of interviews. Instructors use these tools to explicitly articulate these links, guide students' performance, and guide students' observations as they watch classmates' interviews and provide focused feedback. An additional useful teaching tool is the creation of video-recorded interviews to demonstrate examples of effective enactment of the competencies. Our studies revealed that students regularly struggle to link theory and practice (Bogo et al., 2013; Katz et al., 2014). This finding led to teaching that intentionally and frequently drew explicit attention to instances where students could see the theory in the action and where students could examine the practice and deconstruct it using the concepts being taught. Current studies reveal the usefulness of employing learning strategies that allow students to have multiple opportunities to engage in practice that is observed and receive focused feedback on the positive enactment of a limited number of identified skills and areas for further development (Kourgiantakis et al., 2018). As well, observed practice with feedback, referred to as deliberate practice, further strengthens learning and performance (Chow et al., 2015).

Given that the model of holistic competence underpinning this teaching method involves attention to procedural competencies, those that can be observed, *and* meta-competencies, those that are internal to students' cognitions and affective reactions, post-interview reflection questions elicit these later dimensions. Instructors can use these reflections in a variety of ways: to determine students' reactions to the simulations, for debriefing in class or individual discussions, or to determine conceptual material that requires more attention in teaching.

Data for evaluation and refinement of the content and method come from observations of students' performance, information gleaned from their reflective responses, and instructors' own perceptions of areas needing strengthening in teaching. Increasingly, schools of social work are using adapted versions of the objective structured clinical examination (OSCE), originally developed in medicine (Harden & Gleeson, 1979) and now broadly used in most health professions, to assess students' competence (Bogo et al., 2014; Logie et al., 2013). Following similar design steps as described above, students conduct 15-minute interviews with actors trained to consistently and uniformly portray a service user's situation. A trained observer uses a rating scale to assess student performance (Bogo et al., 2011; Bogo et al., 2012). Raters used in these studies have been volunteers interested in the method and include faculty colleagues, field instructors, and experienced social workers. Since numerous studies in social work have noted the leniency bias of instructors who have a relationship with the student being evaluated (Finch & Taylor, 2013), the rater should not be the student's instructor. Students' performance on the OSCE also contributes to curriculum development as instructors note dimensions that have been taught effectively and areas needing additional emphasis. While resources are needed to develop scenarios and train and hire actors to offer the type of simulations and OSCE described here, programs with limited funds have also successfully integrated the use of simulation for undergraduate and graduate students. Creative approaches have witnessed programs accessing university teaching funds and awards (Rawlings, 2012), building relationships with university drama departments where drama students portray service users (Dennison, 2011), developing interprofessional simulations with health professions' educators who have established simulation resources (Wilcox et al., 2017), and obtaining grants to fund the teaching of specific approaches using simulation (Sacco et al., 2017).

Time is a critical resource in using this approach. Despite increased time requirements, students report benefits, from going beyond reading texts and writing about practice to actually learning how to put concepts into practice (Kourgiantakis et al., 2018). Instructors also need to spend time to observe students' interviews in vivo or on video recordings and provide useful feedback. This requires considering the most effective use of instructors' time and priorities; workload may need to be re-ordered when implementing this approach.

Bridging Class and Field

At the University of Toronto, first-year students in the master of social work program enter the field practicum after spending the first semester in two companion foundation practice courses. These courses use multiple simulations to teach core holistic competence, provide an optional enhancement for students to practise and receive feedback, and use an OSCE to assess students' learning at the end of the courses. The course instructor prepares a final written summary evaluation of each student's competence based on participation as interviewer and peer in numerous simulations, assignments that involve analysis of interviews and self-assessments, and performance in the OSCE. Each student shares this evaluation with the field instructor when beginning the field practicum in the winter semester. Together, student and field instructor review the information and integrate into the field learning plan recommendations for areas for transfer and learning goals. Faculty field liaisons review these plans to ensure continuity between learning in these courses and in the field.

A follow-up study found field instructors and field liaisons value the preparation students receive before engaging in the field (Bogo, Lee, et al., 2017). They noted that the focus in these courses and learning activities prepared students for practicum learning. The information on the evaluation summary is referred to as providing a baseline, a foundation, and a place to begin, noting strengths and areas for development. Thorough reviewing of the material with the field instructors enhanced students' ability to be open and think critically about their learning needs, in turn facilitating meaningful engagement in the supervisory relationship. High student satisfaction with learning through simulation is consistently found in our studies and in a critical appraisal of 14 studies on the use of simulation in social work (Logie et al., 2013). In addition, students report greater confidence in their ability and readiness to engage in field learning.

Conclusion

This model has stimulated innovations in education that promote integrative teaching necessary for this multidimensional understanding of practice. Using simulation in teaching and in assessing competence has proven effective as it provides students with realistic scenarios to practise and develop as social workers without placing service users at risk. When coupled with the provision of knowledge frameworks and attention to cognitive and affective aspects of competence, the integration of theory and practice comes alive.

REFERENCES

Asakura, K., Bogo, M., Good, B., & Power, R. (2018). Social work serial: Using video-recorded simulated client sessions to teach social work practice. *Journal of Social Work Education, 54*(2), 397–404. https://doi.org/10.1080/10437797.2017.1404525

Bogo, M. (2018). *Social work practice: Integrating concepts, processes, and skills* (2nd ed.). Columbia University Press.

Bogo, M., Katz, E., Regehr, C., Logie, C., Mylopoulos, M., & Tufford, L. (2013). Toward understanding meta-competence: An analysis of students' reflections on their simulated interviews. *Social Work Education, 32*(2), 259–73. https://doi.org/10.1080/02615479.2012.738662

Bogo, M., Lee, B., McKee, E., Ramjattan, R., & Baird, S. L. (2017). Bridging class and field: Field instructors' and liaisons' reactions to information about students' baseline performance derived from simulated interviews. *Journal of Social Work Education, 53*(4), 580–94. https://doi.org/10.1080/10437797.2017.1283269

Bogo, M., Rawlings, M., Katz, E., & Logie, C. (2014). *Using simulation in assessment and teaching: OSCE adapted for social work.* Council on Social Work Education.

Bogo, M., Regehr, C., Baird, S., Paterson, J., & LeBlanc, V. R. (2017). Cognitive and affective elements of practice confidence in social work students and practitioners. *British Journal of Social Work, 47*, 701–18. https://doi.org/10.1093/bjsw/bcw026

Bogo, M., Regehr, C., Katz, E., Logie, C., Mylopoulos, M., & Regehr, G. (2011). Developing a tool to assess student reflections. *Social Work Education, 30*(2), 186–95. https://doi.org/10.1080/02615479.2011.540392

Bogo, M., Regehr, C., Katz, E., Logie, C., Tufford, L., & Litvack, A. (2012). Evaluating the use of an objective structured clinical examination (OSCE) adapted for social work. *Research in Social Work Practice, 22*(4), 428–36. https://doi.org/10.1177/1049731512437557

Bogo, M., Regehr, C., Woodford, M., Hughes, J., Power, R., & Regehr, G. (2006). Beyond competencies: Field instructors' descriptions of student performance. *Journal of Social Work Education, 42*(3), 579–93. https://doi.org/10.5175/jswe.2006.200404145

Cheetham, G., & Chivers, G. (2005). *Professions, competence and informal learning.* Edward Elgar.

Chow, D. L., Miller, S. D., Seidel, J. A., Kane, R. T., Thornton, J. A., & Andrews, W. P. (2015). The role of deliberate practice in the development of highly effective psychotherapists. *Psychotherapy, 52*(3), 337–45. https://doi.org/10.1037/pst0000015

Craig, S. L., McInroy, L. B., Bogo, M., & Thompson, M. (2017). Enhancing competence in health social work education through simulation-based learning: Strategies from a case study of a family session. *Journal of Social Work Education, 53*(Supp. 1), S47–S58. https://doi.org/10.1080/10437797.2017.1288597

Crisp, B. R., & Lister, P. G. (2002). Assessment methods in social work education: A review of the literature. *Social Work Education, 21*(2), 259–69. https://doi.org/10.1080/02615470220126471

Dennison, S. T. (2011). Interdisciplinary role play between social work and theatre students. *Journal of Teaching in Social Work, 31*(4), 415–30. https://doi.org/10.1080/08841233.2011.597670

Ferguson, H. (2018). How social workers reflect in action and when and why they don't: The possibilities and limits to reflective practice in social work. *Social Work Education, 37*(4), 415–27. https://doi.org/10.1080/02615479.2017.1413083

Finch, J., & Taylor, I. (2013). Failure to fail? Practice educators' emotional experiences of assessing failing social work students. *Social work education, 32*(2), 244–58. https://doi.org/10.1080/02615479.2012.720250

Gaba, D. M. (2007). The future vision of simulation in healthcare. *Simulation in Healthcare, 2,* 126–35. https://doi.org/10.1097/01.sih.0000258411.38212.32

Harden, R. M., & Gleeson, F. A. (1979). Assessment of clinical competence using an observed structured clinical examination. *Medical Education, 13*(1), 41–7. https://doi.org/10.1111/j.1365-2923.1979.tb00918.x

Katz, E., Tufford, L., Bogo, M., & Regehr, C. (2014). Illuminating students' pre-practicum conceptual and emotional states: Implications for field education. *Journal of Teaching in Social Work, 34*(1), 96–108. https://doi.org/10.1080/08841233.2013.868391

Kondrat, M. (2013). Person-in-environment. In C. Franklin (Ed.), *Encyclopedia of Social Work*. National Association of Social Workers; Oxford University Press. https://doi.org/10.1093/acrefore/9780199975839.013.285

Kourgiantakis, T., Bogo, M., & Sewell, K. M. (2018). Practice Fridays: Using simulation to develop holistic competence. *Journal of Social Work Education*. https://doi.org/10.1080/10437797.2018.1548989

Kourgiantakis, T., Sewell, K. M., Lee, E., Adamson, K., McCormick, M., Kuehl, D., & Bogo, M. (2019). Enhancing social work education in mental health, addictions, and suicide risk assessment: A teaching note. *Journal of Social Work Education*. https://doi.org/10.1080/10437797.2019.1656590

Logie, C., Bogo, M., & Katz, E. (2015). "I didn't feel equipped": Social work students' reflections on a simulated client "coming out." *Journal of Social Work Education, 51*(2), 315–28. https://doi.org/10.1080/10437797.2015.1012946

Logie, C., Bogo, M., Regehr, C., & Regehr, G. (2013). A critical appraisal of the use of standardized client simulations in social work education. *Journal of Social Work Education, 49*(1), 66–80. https://doi.org/10.1080/10437797.2013.755377

Rawlings, M. (2012). Assessing BSW student direct practice skill using standardized clients and self-efficacy theory. *Journal of Social Work Education, 48*(3), 553–76. https://doi.org/10.5175/jswe.2012.201000070

Regehr, C., Bogo, M., Donovan, K., Anstice, S., & Kim, A. (2012). Identifying student competencies in macro practice: Articulating the practice wisdom of field instructors. *Journal of Social Work Education, 48*(2), 307–19. https://doi.org/10.5175/jswe.2012.201000114

Sacco, P., Ting, L., Crouch, T. B., Emery, L., Moreland, M., Bright, C., Frey, J., & DiClemente, C. (2017). SBIRT training in social work education: Evaluating change using standardized patient simulation. *Journal of Social Work Practice in the Addictions, 17*(1–2), 150–68. https://doi.org/10.1080/1533256x.2017.1302886

Shulman, L. S. (2005). Signature pedagogies in the profession. *Daedalus, 134*(3), 52–9. https://doi.org/10.1162/0011526054622015

Tufford, L., Bogo, M., & Asakura, K. (2015). How do social workers respond to potential child neglect? *Social Work Education, 34*(2), 229–43. https://doi.org/10.1080/02615479.2014.958985

Wilcox, J., Miller-Cribbs, J., Kientz, E., Carlson, J., & DeShea, L. (2017). Impact of simulation on student attitudes about interprofessional collaboration. *Clinical Simulation in Nursing, 13*(8), 390–7. https://doi.org/10.1016/j.ecns.2017.04.004

10 Preparing Social Workers for Practice with Diverse Populations

CLAUDE OLIVIER AND AKIN TAIWO

This chapter examines the conceptual and theoretical underpinnings, pedagogical approaches, and use of self as related to teaching diversity in social work. It also examines teaching approaches designed to prepare social work students for practice with diverse populations. We have both taught courses focusing on diversity and social justice, with anti-oppressive theory and practice as the foundation. We have also taught courses encompassing various levels and areas of social work, such as direct practice skills, group work, social welfare, and community organization. In our experience, these courses are enriched with content on diversity. Underlying our teaching is a positive and affirming perspective on diversity, along with social work practices aimed at disrupting oppression and advancing social justice and inclusion. We believe that issues of diversity need to be infused into all social work teaching, as an important complement to designated courses on this topic.

In our teaching, we apply a critical theoretical lens in examining conceptual frameworks related to social work practice and diversity. The intent is for students to grasp both the strengths and the limitations of each framework. We incorporate experiential activities that contribute to critical reflection of content and self, as well as the application of knowledge and insight to practice. Inevitably, students' own identities enter the mix as they grapple with issues of privilege and oppression. Our use of self-disclosure facilitates this important, but sometimes difficult, examination of self.

Conceptual and Theoretical Underpinnings

This section outlines concepts and theories fundamental to teaching diversity and social justice. Our intent is not to examine each concept or theory in depth, but rather to point out how each contributes to students' understanding of diversity, oppression, and privilege and, ultimately, informs practice. The presentation of the concepts and theories parallels their sequencing in our courses and includes oppression and privilege, anti-oppressive and structural social work practice, and culturally informed approaches.

Oppression and Privilege

Consistent with critical theory, we situate our teaching about diversity within an anti-oppressive framework. Typically, we begin a course with discussion on what is meant by diversity, thus setting the direction for responding to issues of diversity in ways that are affirming, culturally informed, and non-oppressive. Thompson's (2011) examination of diversity informs this discussion, as he links valuing diversity to promoting equality, which "involves valuing fairness, while diversity involves valuing difference – and these are entirely compatible" (p. 9).

Next, we define oppression inclusive of theoretical and applied dimensions. The concept of oppression becomes more meaningful if students grasp how oppression affects people's lives. Mullaly and West's (2018) description moves the concept from the abstract to the applied:

> Oppression is determined by whether a person is blocked from opportunities to self-development, is excluded from full participation in society, does not have certain rights that the dominant group takes for granted, or is assigned a second-class citizenship, not because of individual talent, merit, or failure, but because of their membership in a particular group or category of people. (p. 8)

Similarly, it is useful to define privilege from theoretical and applied perspectives. Students' understanding is enhanced with examples of privileges associated with various identities. To that end, Mullaly and West (2018) have listed privileges "associated with being middle or upper class, a member of the white race, male, heterosexual, non-disabled, a member of a two-parent family, and of an adult age that precedes old age" (p. 51). In addition, students are more receptive to the concept of privilege when we underscore that privilege stems from group membership and so can be independent of an individual's actions or intent.

We find some early contributions to the discourse on oppression continue to be valuable in our teaching. Young's (1990) five "faces" or forms of oppression – exploitation, marginalization, powerlessness, cultural imperialism, and violence – provide language for describing how individuals and groups experience oppression. More recently, Thompson's (2012) personal-cultural-structural (PCS) framework conceptualizes levels or locations of oppression. These three levels are useful in examining how various groups experience discrimination and oppression. They also point to locations for actions aimed at disrupting oppression at the micro, mezzo, and macro levels in line with generalist social work practice.

Of course, every person or group is affected in some ways by each identity associated with oppression or privilege. Therefore, an intersectional analysis is vital, with the recognition that people can experience multiple forms of oppression or privilege depending on where they fall on a continuum related to an identity, and that oppressions and privileges intersect and interact, affecting people's lives in numerous ways (Mullaly & West, 2018).

Anti-oppressive and Structural Social Work Practice

Teaching diversity and social justice is not simply about understanding concepts and theories; it is also about applying this knowledge to social work practice. The literature on anti-oppressive social work provides direction for practice (Baines, 2017), inclusive of personal, cultural, and structural levels (Mullaly & West, 2018). The structural social work literature also informs practice (Hick et al., 2010; Mullaly 2007; Olivier, 2010). In discussing practice approaches with students, we also point out that it is appropriate to draw from social work's extensive range of practice approaches and methods, provided they are applied in a non-oppressive and culturally informed manner.

Culturally Informed Approaches

We introduce students to culturally informed approaches to practice by examining the concepts of cultural competence and cultural humility. Sue et al. (2016) have outlined four major competencies for effective multicultural social work practice:

1 becoming aware of one's own values, biases, and assumptions about human behavior;
2 understanding the worldviews of culturally diverse service users;
3 developing appropriate intervention strategies and techniques; and
4 understanding organizational and institutional forces that enhance or diminish components of cultural competence. (p. 60)

Accordingly, cultural competence is described as "a set of attitudes, skills, behaviours and policies enabling individuals and organizations to establish effective interpersonal and working relationships that supersede cultural differences" (Cross et al., 1989, as cited in Fisher-Borne, Cain, & Martin, 2015, p. 178). Cultural competence supports obtaining cultural knowledge in advance of working with service users from a particular culture or group. We have found that such knowledge enables practitioners to conduct assessments with greater intentionality. Without prior cultural knowledge, there is potential to place full responsibility on service users to teach social workers about their group identities. However, cultural competence has been challenged for its uncritical focus on the "Other"; its use of *culture* as a proxy for racial/ethnic minority groups; its emphasis on knowledge, competence, or mastery regarding the culture of another; and its failure to challenge systemic inequalities or the lack of a transformative social justice agenda (Fisher-Borne et al., 2015). There is also the risk of the social worker overgeneralizing and coming across as the expert. Indeed, Pon (2009) characterized cultural competence as a form of new racism partly because it does not consider power relations as it promotes an obsolete and absolutist view of culture, marginalization, and colonization; therefore, Pon called for its elimination in social work discourse, though we do not necessarily share his view.

A cultural humility/safety orientation to multicultural practice, on the other hand, has been suggested by some scholars as an alternative to cultural competence (Fisher-Borne et al., 2015). Cultural humility is defined as "having an interpersonal stance that is other-oriented rather than self-focused, characterized by respect and lack of superiority toward an individual's cultural background and experience" (Hook et al., 2013, p. 353). Hence, this approach emphasizes learning about service users' experiences of cultural identity from their perspectives. Fisher-Borne et al. (2015) identified the core elements of cultural humility as having institutional and individual accountability, engaging in lifelong learning and critical reflection, and mitigating inequality and power imbalances at both individual and institutional levels. However, Danso (2018) has critiqued cultural humility as being a mere repackaging of the principles of anti-oppressive practice and education. In our experience, the cultural competency and cultural humility orientations can offset each other's limitations.

We emphasize in our teaching that to the extent that culture is complex, multidimensional, and fluid, generalization or universalization is impossible. Likewise, someone may not be able to definitively know or attain competence or mastery in the culture of another.

Moreover, the status, power, and privilege of the "knower" needs to be explored to deconstruct the dominant role of the "white saviour" (Danso, 2018) and mitigate the probability of oppression in the therapeutic relationship. We admit that we can have broad knowledge or understanding about specific cultures and peoples but recognize that we cannot know for certain as the "Other" may be unknowable (Pon, 2009). Hence, we embrace ambiguity, curiosity, and humility, and promote critical self-awareness regarding the practitioners' own culture and position. We use cultural humility as a complement to cultural competence as we integrate both in our approach to culturally informed practice.

Our Use of Self

From our experience, to prepare social workers for practice with diverse populations, teachers must be consciously aware of their own values and visions, assumptions and biases, passions and prejudices, certainties and uncertainties, fears and concerns, as well as what identities to disclose or not disclose relative to class composition and discussion topics. We have both realized that our intersecting identities have had a profound effect on our students over the years, an issue discussed by several others (Bell et al., 2007; Heydt & Sherman, 2005; Mandell, 2007).

I (Akin) make use of self-disclosure as a foreign-born, racialized man from a working-class background. Most of my students (easily over 90 per cent) are White, with most of them admitting (when asked) that I am their first Black professor. As a means of highlighting the obvious, I have started some classes by asking students to reflect on what they think on seeing me as the professor vis-à-vis their perception of the Black male in Canadian society. Interestingly, some students talk about being colour-blind, yet they identify me as a Black man. I often steer the conversation to being colour-aware to not erase or ignore the master status by which people like me are perpetually marginalized in a White-normed society (Badwall, 2014). I also freely talk about my African, specifically Nigerian, accent, emphasizing that I need them to understand every word I say, and to be free to ask questions when I seem unclear to them. To demystify my own accent, I speak slowly, clearly, and emphatically, welcoming questions about words and mannerisms that may not be as familiar to them.

I also inform students that most of my examples will come from my African, Black, and social work experiences. This is not intended to impose Blackness on them or to minimize their own subjectivities, but they should see it as an opening for them to inject their own stories, examples, and experiences as they relate to course materials. While maintaining confidentiality, I ask them to draw on their lived, practice, and practicum experiences. I encourage dialogue about and celebration of diverse viewpoints. To the extent that most of my students are White, I am very sensitive to how they might feel about stories of oppression and discrimination. I constantly assure them that they are not personally responsible for the way society has been set up to benefit some at the expense of others, but that, being complicit or implicated, we all have the responsibility to restructure the system in a way that will benefit everyone.

I (Claude) also disclose details related to my various identities to illustrate content and facilitate discussion. Initially, I anticipated that sharing my experiences as a gay man would provide the most learning opportunity. However, I have come to realize that talking about the identities that afford me privilege as a White, able-bodied male also has tremendous teaching potential. I usually preface my disclosure of being gay by stating that I would feel inauthentic discussing issues related to the LGBTQ+ community without acknowledging that I am part of this group. This frees me to use my experiences to illustrate content related to oppression, resistance, and anti-oppressive practice. For example, I share experiences related to seeking counselling and adopting children. Students regularly ask me what it was like to adopt children as a gay man. My response serves to illustrate intersectionality, as I cannot separate this one aspect of my identity from having privilege related to professional status, gender, race, non-disability, and income level. I am certain that these privileged identities have mediated my vulnerability to oppression related to my sexual orientation. In addition, I discuss how awareness of my privilege informs my attempts to disrupt unearned advantage (Mullaly & West, 2018).

Both of us encourage the expression of multiple and conflicting perspectives regarding current affairs as they relate to course materials. Promoting diversity of opinions encourages students to express themselves. It also enables us to address beliefs and biases that should be challenged. Likewise, we ask our students to challenge assumptions and content that they find inaccurate. We exhibit patience and understanding as students try to express themselves and provide guidance regarding how issues could be better addressed. We encourage students to wrestle with the complexity of social problems, recognizing that there may not be a perfect answer for any issue. Doing this, we also make ourselves vulnerable to queries, questions, and challenge from our students.

We recognize that not all students are uniformly articulate or willing to share their experiences, so we alleviate anxiety and discomfort by announcing at the beginning of the course that students are not under any obligation to disclose identities or share personal information. For me (Akin), usually a small number of racial minorities are represented in my class, and I try not to put these students under a spotlight. They should not feel the burden of educating their peers (Deepak et al., 2015). Some of my stories, however, often validate the experiences of these minority students. Though it has been noted that White students may be defensive, disinterested, or deny minority oppression (Deepak et al., 2015; Le-Doux & Montalvo, 2008), as a Black professor, I cultivate their understanding regarding the difficulties of others and encourage them to not dismiss or disrespect the experiences of others or attribute their oppression to other reasons. A few White students have challenged some of my stories of oppression as fables and I have used that to illustrate the discrimination, marginalization, slights, and injustices that most of them do not experience. I also endeavour to not have a chip on my shoulder because of my lived experience of oppression.

Pedagogical Approaches

In selecting and developing pedagogical approaches to teach about oppression, and diversity more broadly, we are cognizant of making links to social work practice. We emphasize how theory informs practice, thus fostering the integration of theory in practice. What follows are approaches we have found helpful in teaching, including experiential exercises, class discussions, guest speakers, and student assignments.

Experiential Exercises

Experiential exercises are widely used in diversity and social justice education (Cramer et al., 2012). Cramer et al. (2012) provide a categorization of experiential activities in teaching about diversity consisting of three models:

1. EXPERIENCING

Experiencing activities, such as role-play and game play, "provide students with an opportunity to actually take on a disadvantaged or discriminated role and experience life from the viewpoint of an oppressed population" (Cramer et al., 2012, p. 2).

2. SELF-DISCOVERING

Self-discovering exercises "assist students in identifying their own cultural identities and biases toward people from different cultures" (Cramer et al., 2012, p. 2). These could be based on group discussions or case studies.

3. LEARNING

The learning model "refers to exercises that deepen students' knowledge of life experiences of diverse populations" (Cramer et al., 2012, p. 2) such as field trips or guest speakers. We use several in-class experiential exercises, discussed below, to move concepts and theory from the abstract to the applied.

Bishop's (2015) Conquest of a Peaceful Culture activity is an example of an experiencing model (Cramer et al., 2012), where students take on the role of a dominant group member. In this group activity, participants assume membership in "a society with a social structure based on separation, hierarchy, and competition" (Bishop, 2015, p. 14), conquering another nation whose society is "based on connection, equal value, and cooperation" (p. 14). Participants are instructed to develop strategies that would enable them to assimilate the conquered nation, moving from armed occupation to covert and systemic means of control. The outcome, once drawn out, produces a "web of oppression" that illustrates concepts of competition, separation, and hierarchy and underscores the interaction of various sources and locations of oppression. Students frequently disclose discomfort with their assigned power and privilege while gaining insight into the dynamics of oppression and identifying historic and current examples of assimilation strategies.

Likewise, the Intersectional Analysis Self-Rating assessment tool (Box 10.1) enables students to reflect upon their social identities and indicate with a dot the degree to which an identity affects their lives on a continuum from disadvantage to privilege. By connecting the dots, students obtain a visual sense of how identities intersect and interact to affect their overall experience, pulling them towards oppression or privilege. The "other" categories provide space for students to insert an identity that they have found important in shaping their lived experience such as "body size" or "tattoos and piercings." This activity serves as an example of self-discovery (Cramer et al., 2012), as students gain greater awareness of their oppressed and privileged identities. Students have also shared that they have found this assessment tool useful in exploring identities with service users. Other exercises are available that help facilitate self-examination of identities, including The Web by Sisneros et al. (2008, p. 87) and The Flower Power exercise described by Lundy (2004, pp. 71–2).

Box 10.1 Intersectional Analysis Self-Rating Exercise

Place a dot on each line to indicate the degree to which your social identity contributes to your vulnerability to oppression or provides you with privilege.

Identity	Oppression/Disadvantage	Privilege/Advantage
Income level		
Skin colour		
Sex		
Gender identity		
Sexual orientation		
Age		
(Dis)Ability		
Culture/ethnicity		
Religion		
Other		
Other		

Social identity is "the way society or the world surrounding an individual views them" (Mullaly & West, 2018, p. 117). Now join the dots. The joined line represents the interaction of your various identities and how identities combine to shape one's experience of oppression and privilege. The "Other" categories provide space to insert an identity that you have found important in shaping your lived experience.

Class Discussions

Like Deepak et al. (2015), we have also found that basic group work skills are useful in establishing ground rules, mediating conflict, and selecting activities that support participation. Thus, we regularly have students discuss in small groups concepts that are relevant to diversity and use questions to help them identify implications for social work practice. We argue that an important first concept to explore through discussion is *social justice*. Students are generally aware of the importance of this concept in social work but are less familiar with practice activities and policy directions that bring practice, the social work profession, and society closer to exemplifying key components of social justice. The results of these small-group discussions are then used to inform a full class discussion. Another topic covered in this manner is how culture and diversity shape preferences related to such lived experiences as disciplining children, structuring spousal and partner relationships, and problem solving. This topic assists students in understanding how they have come to acquire their own approaches to day-to-day living and that others may have differing preferences. This greater awareness can reduce bias and judgment towards people who hold other perspectives. As a final example, discussion on multiculturalism serves to illustrate the interplay between cultural and structural locations of oppression and privilege. It is also an entry point to exploring policy directions at the macro level of practice.

Guest Speakers

We make extensive use of guest speakers to bring the community into the classroom. This can exemplify the learning model of experiential learning (Cramer et al., 2012). Typically, the invited speakers are members of social groups vulnerable to oppression and/or workers who provide services to such groups. The presentations and accompanying discussion have great impact on the students, who hear first-hand of the struggles, challenges, histories, programs/services, or lack thereof, and strengths associated with the various population groups. Guest speakers also offer suggestions and guidelines for providing culturally informed services, as well as orienting students towards the need for advocacy and social change. As one example, I (Claude) invite a group of women who use theatre to tell their stories related to poverty, homelessness, addictions, trauma, and mental health. The performances enhance the students' understanding and empathy related to the women's experiences. In addition, the women use forum theatre techniques (Boal, 1985), which give the students an opportunity to temporarily interrupt the performance and take the place of one of the actors. This enables the student, now actor, to take the skit in a different direction, opening possibilities for more positive interaction such as replacing an actor playing an unsympathetic social worker.

We also use guest speakers to link students to the world of practice and volunteer activities. I (Akin) have invited social workers from diverse ethno-racial groups and fields of practice to present to students. These practitioners not only bridge university and community but also facilitate meaningful community-based opportunities for students. I have observed many students make lasting connections through this avenue. As one measure of the impact of guest speakers, students frequently mention in their course evaluations that guest speakers are one of the highlights of the course.

Student Assignments

Student assignments also provide an important means of furthering the integration of theory in practice. As one example, in an undergraduate course on diversity and oppression, I (Claude) give students two connected assignments that incorporate case studies. In the first assignment, an individual paper, students reflect on their own intersectionality of identities and social location, as well as on how these dynamics, along with positionality, may impact upon their relationship and interaction with the service users in their case study. Typically, students gain greater insight into their identities that afford privilege, along with those that contribute to their vulnerability to oppression. In their discussion of the service users in the case study, students examine how their various identities, which can lead to bias, may affect their interaction with service users, who bring in their own identities, social location, and perceptions of others.

In the second assignment, students who were assigned the same case study in assignment one deliver a class group presentation. The case studies cover service-user identities related to class and poverty, (dis)ability, sexual orientation, gender and gender identity, and age, although the interaction of multiple service-user identities is ever present. The presentations cover identification of the service user's identities and social location; background information about the group(s) of which the service user is a member, inclusive of the types of oppression and strengths associated with the group; practice theories that could inform the students' assessment and interventions; and existing programs and community resources that may be relevant to the service user. Students report that this assignment provides them opportunity to bring in learning from a variety of courses and apply concepts and practice theories in a manner consistent with culturally informed and anti-oppressive social work.

Another assignment that provides students with opportunity to think about diversity in the context of practice is an individual presentation that MSW students deliver in a designated course on social justice, diversity, and oppression. Each student presents on a practice instrument, such as a screening or assessment tool, that has established validity or demonstrated transferability to a diversity of service-user groups. Students benefit from learning about different assessment and intervention tools and selecting them in the context of working with diverse service-user groups.

A major paper, generally due at the end of the course, serves as a final example of an assignment that enhances the students' integration of theory in practice. Students are required to discuss case example(s) from their practice or field experience. They critique the congruency of their work with culturally informed and anti-oppressive theory and practice. Students also discuss what they might now do differently. In addition, the discussion covers any implications for practice at the personal, cultural, and structural locations of oppression. Students are asked to integrate their own social location within the analysis.

Finally, we have found it important for instructors to pay attention to the institutional context where they teach. Our experience is consistent with the findings of Deepak et al. (2015), who explored educational setting and contextual factors that support or hinder the delivery of diversity and social justice content in social work education. Factors most relevant to pedagogical approaches, and that reflect our experience, include an educational program's support for delivering course content in a manner that engages students intellectually and emotionally, small class sizes with sufficient time for in-depth discussion, the inclusion of social justice and diversity content in all coursework, and the instructor having the necessary skills and abilities to discuss uncomfortable subjects and experiences (Deepak et al., 2015).

In concluding this chapter, we want to express how rewarding it is to teach about diversity and social justice. Our courses provide dedicated time for both teacher and student to explore and learn about the complexity of diversity and interacting in ways that are respectful and affirming. Undeniably, we live in a diverse society, and it is tremendously important to support and challenge students as they acquire knowledge and skills to engage in culturally informed and anti-oppressive social work. Doing this will enable them to know themselves better, understand differences more, and practice intentionally and competently as they provide service to those who may or may not look or act like them.

REFERENCES

Badwall, H. (2014). Colonial encounters: Racialized social workers negotiating professional scripts of Whiteness. *Intersectionalities: A Global Journal of Social Work Analysis, Research, Policy, and Practice, 3*(1), 1–23. http://journals.library.mun.ca/ojs/index.php/IJ/article/view/996

Baines, D. (Ed.). (2017). *Doing anti-oppressive practice: Social justice social work* (3rd ed.). Fernwood Publishing.

Bell, L. A., Love, B. J., Washington, S., & Weinstein, G. (2007). Knowing ourselves as social justice educators. In M. Adams, L. A. Bell, & P. Griffin (Eds.). *Teaching for diversity and social justice* (2nd ed., pp. 382–93). Routledge.

Bishop, A. (2015). *Becoming an ally: Breaking the cycle of oppression in people* (3rd ed.). Fernwood Publishing.

Boal, A. (1985). *Theatre of the oppressed.* Theatre Communications Group.

Cramer, E. P., Ryosho, N., & Nguyen, P. V. (2012). Using experiential exercises to teach about diversity, oppression, and social justice. *Journal of Teaching in Social Work, 32*(1), 1–13. https://doi.org/10.1080/08841233.2012.637463

Danso, A. (2018). Cultural competence and cultural humility: A critical reflection on key cultural diversity concepts. *Journal of Social Work, 18*(4), 410–30. https://doi.org/10.1177/1468017316654341

Deepak, A., Rountree, M., & Scott, J. (2015). Delivering diversity and social justice in social work education: The power of context. *Journal of Progressive Human Services, 26*(2), 107–25. https://doi.org/10.1080/10428232.2015.1017909

Fisher-Borne, M., Cain, J., & Martin, S. (2015). From mastery to accountability: Cultural humility as an alternative to cultural competence. *Social Work Education, 34*(2), 165–81. https://doi.org/10.1080/02615479.2014.977244

Heydt, M., & Sherman, N. (2005). Conscious use of self: Tuning the instrument of social work practice with cultural competence. *The Journal of Baccalaureate Social Work, 10*(2), 25–40. https://doi.org/10.18084/1084-7219.10.2.25

Hick, S., Peters, H., Corner, T., & London, T. (Eds.). (2010). *Structural social work in action, Examples from practice.* Canadian Scholars' Press.

Hook, J., Davis, D., Owen, J., Worthington, E., & Utsey, S. (2013). Cultural humility: Measuring openness to culturally diverse clients. *Journal of Counseling Psychology, 60*(3), 353–66. https://doi.org/10.1037/a0032595

Le-Doux, C., & Montalvo, F. (2008). Multicultural content in social work graduate programs. *Journal of Multicultural Social Work,* 7(1–2), 37–55. https://doi.org/10.1300/j285v07n01_03

Lundy, C. (2004). *Social work and social justice: A structural approach to practice.* Broadview Press.

Mandell, D. (Ed.). (2007). *Revisiting the use of self: Questioning professional identities.* Canadian Scholars Press.

Mullaly, B. (2007). *The new structural social work* (3rd ed.). Oxford University Press.

Mullaly, B., & West, J. (2018). *Challenging oppression and confronting privilege: A critical approach to anti-oppressive and anti-privilege theory and practice* (3rd ed.). Oxford University Press.

Olivier, C. (2010). Operationalizing structural theory: Guidelines for practice. In S. F. Hick, H. I. Peters, T. Corner, & T. London (Eds.), *Structural social work in action, Examples from practice* (pp. 26–38). Canadian Scholars' Press.

Pon, G. (2009). Cultural competency as new racism: An ontology of forgetting. *Journal of Progressive Human Services, 20,* 59–71. https://doi.org/10.1080/10428230902871173

Sisneros, J., Stakeman, C., Joyner, M. C., & Schmitz, C. L. (2008). *Critical multicultural social work.* Lyceum Books.

Sue, D. W., Rasheed, M. N., & Rasheed, J. M. (2016). *Multicultural social work practice* (2nd ed.). John Wiley & Sons.

Thompson, N. (2011). *Promoting equality, Working with diversity and difference.* (3rd ed.). Palgrave Macmillan.

Thompson, N. (2012). *Anti-discriminatory practice* (5th ed.). Palgrave Macmillan.

Young, I. (1990). *Justice and the politics of difference.* Princeton University Press.

11 Teaching Mindfulness

DIANA COHOLIC

This chapter examines rationales for including mindfulness in social work education and describes strategies to do so. While some social work programs may be able to offer stand-alone courses in mindfulness, many programs likely struggle with the reality of meeting existing program requirements. Thus, some of us, with interests in mindfulness-based interventions, likely incorporate related content and processes into appropriate existing offerings, such as practice/theory-based courses and field education. It is my aim in this chapter to offer some examples of how mindfulness concepts and practices can also be integrated into existing social work practice-based courses.

I have been researching the benefits of arts-based mindfulness interventions for approximately 10 years. I practise mindfulness and also infuse it into my clinical practice. As a result, I introduce mindfulness into my social work teaching at a variety of points in courses. Some social work educators and researchers have studied the inclusion of mindfulness into existing social work courses and programs. For example, Gockel et al. (2013) explored the inclusion of 10–15 minutes of mindfulness training in classes for master of social work (MSW) students to help them develop therapeutic alliances. They found that this training helped students manage distractions and feelings of anxiety, improved students' ability to attend and respond, and encouraged them to develop their self-awareness. Thomas (2017) also studied the inclusion of brief mindfulness training into social work practice classes and found that students perceived this learning to be helpful for managing feelings of anxiety, encouraging them to be present with service users and to become more open-minded, and promoting feelings of safety and connectedness in the class. These values are reflected in the Canadian Association of Social Work's (2005) Code of Ethics as we must refrain from imposing our personal values, views, and preferences on others through these processes.

A Brief Overview of Mindfulness

According to Germer (2009), mindfulness is an English translation of a Pali word *sati*, which means awareness, attention, and remembering. Pali was the language of Buddhist psychology approximately 2500 years ago. Mindfulness is also rooted in traditions such as contemplative Christianity, Judaism, and humanistic psychology (Burrows, 2018). Within Western helping professions, mindfulness has been secularized and it is often defined using Dr. Jon Kabat-Zinn's (1990) conceptualization: activity that encourages awareness to emerge through paying attention on purpose, non-judgmentally, in the present moment. The secularization of mindfulness has certainly facilitated its uptake within Western helping and teaching professions, which has benefited a variety of service-user populations who experience myriad challenges. However, there is debate in the field about this secularization, and people should be cautious about using mindfulness as simply another behavioural technique (Dimidjian & Linehan, 2003; Grossman, 2008). I share the viewpoint that mindfulness is much more than a set of techniques to pick up in times of stress. Rather, it is a holistic philosophy aimed at helping people see clearly and understand themselves and others better so that they can live a more fulfilling life (Weiss, 2004). It also promotes key concepts such as self-compassion and non-judgment. Kabat-Zinn (1990) identified these concepts as the attitudinal foundation of mindfulness, which includes patience, beginner's mind, trust, non-striving, acceptance, and letting go.

Mindfulness can be both a state – an experience of being mindful, and/or a trait – a more stable characteristic or way of being. This is also referred to as dispositional mindfulness (Tomlinson et al., 2018). It can be practised formally through mindful breathing exercises and meditations, and informally, through bringing mindful awareness to anything we have to do on a daily basis, such as washing dishes or eating. Short accessible mindful breathing activities can easily be included in a class. For one example, a simple 5- to 10-minute activity involves moving a finger on one hand up and down the fingers of the other hand. During this action, students focus on their breathing, becoming aware of breathing in while moving their finger up and then breathing out while moving their finger down their other hand.[1] A mindful eating activity is also quite

1 For a video demonstration of this activity, called Take 5, please see Mindfulness Exercises (2018) at https://mindfulnessexercises.com/simple-mindfulness-strategy-take-5. I also like the activity of drawing a figure 8 (infinity symbol) on a piece of paper and tracing it repeatedly. One half of the figure 8 is your breath in (through the nose), and the other half is your breath out (through the mouth).

possible to do and is often an enlightening experience for the students. Through trying to eat a small object, like a raisin, sometimes students will realize just how distracted they are when they eat.[2]

Overall, learning about mindfulness and taking part in mindfulness-based practices can help students learn to focus and pay attention to their internal and external worlds. With improved self-awareness, students can better identify what they are feeling and thinking in a given moment, make choices about these feelings/thoughts, and/or address feelings as they arise, rather than distracting themselves from what is happening in the present moment. Correspondingly, and increasingly, there are discussions about students' mental health challenges, stress, anxiety, and pressures to be perfect (Council of Ontario Universities, 2018; Curran & Hill, 2018; Matthews & Csiernik, 2019). Thus, introducing mindfulness to social work students may help them to improve both their personal and their professional coping strategies and ways of being.

While much of the research investigating the benefits of mindfulness-based interventions has emerged from health-related fields and psychology, social work can make a definite and unique contribution to studying and facilitating mindfulness-based interventions built on our knowledge. For instance, we have expertise pertaining to holistic, strengths-based, creative, and social group work practices, which are important factors and approaches to consider in learning and facilitating mindfulness-based interventions (Boone 2014; Coholic, 2019; Hick, 2009). Social work's holistic lens helps us to understand mindfulness as a way of being in the world that supports open-mindedness, curiosity, compassion, and the knowledge that we are all connected and impact one another and our environments (Coates et al., 2007). Thus, learning to be more mindful is a call to become engaged in the world and can be a force for positive change, which aligns it with social work's goals of social justice and human rights.

Arts-Based Mindfulness

Arts-based mindfulness is the intersection of mindfulness with a range of creative, artistic processes. While a broad range of non-verbal media from painting to drawing to working with clay can be employed, so can other creative approaches, such as dance, theatre, music, or a combination of these methods (Hinchey, 2018; Williams, 2014). My own work in this

2 An example of a basic mindful eating script can be found at The Mindfulness Diet website: https://www.mindfulnessdiet.com.

area has examined the effectiveness of an arts-based mindfulness group program for the development of mindfulness, resilience, and improved self-concept. Much of my work has been with marginalized children and youth, who often lack the skills required for formal mindfulness practice. This research has revealed not only that the program can improve a variety of skills and characteristics, such as self-esteem and awareness, emotion regulation, coping, and relationships, but that both youth and adult participants truly enjoy it (Coholic & Eys, 2016; Coholic et al., 2018). In addition, arts-based methods can facilitate mindfulness and make the practices and concepts accessible to and relevant for participants who may lack the interest in, and skills required for, more traditional ways of learning mindfulness, such as breathing meditations (Coholic, 2011; Hinchey, 2018). Also, the use of arts-based methods can create strong engagement as these activities are enjoyable and assist people to express themselves. They can also flatten power dynamics by letting the people/students with whom we work have more control over processes. This allows them to discuss what they want to share based upon an arts-based creation, be it visual or more dramatic. Both the research investigating the effectiveness of mindfulness-based interventions and the popular literature in this area have grown substantially over the past decade. The two best known mindfulness-based interventions for adults are mindfulness-based stress reduction (MBSR) (Kabat-Zinn, 1990), and mindfulness-based cognitive therapy (MBCT) (Segal et al., 2002). Both have been found to be effective for adults suffering from anxiety, stress, and depression (Fjorback et al., 2011; Vollestad et al., 2012). Also, both MBSR and MBCT have been adapted and applied to youth with similar results (Borquist-Conlon et al., 2017; Perry-Parrish et al., 2016; Van Vliet et al., 2017).

Introducing the Concept of Mindfulness: Thought Jar

When I introduce the concept of mindfulness to my students, I use the Thought Jar activity to illustrate our discussion. This activity can also be used as a check-in as it resonates with participants in a variety of ways (Coholic, 2019). The social work educator will need a jar that is half filled with water and has a secure lid, and another container full of a variety of small beads. Then, students should be asked to remember what they have felt and thought during the day, be encouraged to take some beads to represent these feelings and/or thoughts, and directed to drop the beads, one by one, into the jar stating out loud, if they can, what feeling/thought is represented by each bead. Once there are enough beads in the jar that different patterns can be created, and everyone has had a chance to contribute (the instructor may have to drop a few extra beads in the jar so that there are enough), students can be invited to take turns swirling and shaking the jar. The swirling beads represent our minds when we are distracted, feeling overwhelmed, or anxious. The movement makes it difficult to identify what we are feeling or thinking. Most students can relate to the feeling or state of being where their thoughts, represented by the beads, are all swirling around like a tornado, and they feel overwhelmed and distracted.

When we stop moving the jar, the feelings and thoughts settle to the bottom, which symbolizes a calmer and mindful mind. Thus, mindful people do not have fewer feelings or thoughts, but they are calm and focused enough that they can look internally and identify what they are feeling and thinking moment to moment. Thus, with improved mindful self-awareness, we can make more useful choices relating to our feelings and thoughts. The power of mindfulness is this ability to make a choice about our feelings/thoughts so that we are in control of our behaviour rather than being controlled by our feelings/thoughts and acting out or acting unconsciously.[3]

Self-Awareness and Self-Compassion Class Activities

I have been teaching a fourth-year theory for social work practice course for many years. While it is not possible to teach students all the knowledge that they will require in their future social work, we can help them build a foundation of strong critical thinking skills and self-awareness, which are crucial for all types of social work practices and for lifelong personal and professional learning and development. Indeed, if students lack self-awareness, it will be challenging for them to develop reflective practice, reflexivity, and praxis (Marlowe et al., 2015). Reflexivity is a vital process that is essential to understanding all aspects of our practices, including our use of self, our power, and how we influence our practices from conceptualization to implementation to evaluation. Reflexivity entails learning to be aware of our biases, emotional reactions, and social locations, and how these influence our understanding and analyses.

As we bring who we are to every encounter with others, therapeutic presence is a relevant concept related to mindfulness that describes our ability to be fully present with others in helping relationships (Siegel,

3 To further illustrate this point, I like to use a short video called "Why Mindfulness Is a Super Power: An Animation" by Happify at https://www.youtube.com/watch?v=w6T02g5hnT4.

2010). If we are practising mindfulness and have an ability to foster therapeutic presence, we will be less distracted, able to better tolerate emotion, and more empathic and compassionate (Fulton, 2005). If it appeals to a student, mindfulness can be a valuable approach to build and develop self-awareness. For example, Marlowe and colleagues (2015) explored the experiences of a small group of third-year social work students entering field placement who were taught mindfulness awareness practices, such as body scans and mindful breathing activities. These authors were interested in the connection between using these practices and becoming a reflective practitioner. They concluded that mindfulness practices could be an approach to support and build reflective learning.

Me as a Tree is another one of my favourite activities from our arts-based mindfulness program, and one that I often facilitate in my courses and training workshops. All that is needed to conduct this activity is paper and drawing implements, such as markers. The aim of the activity is to develop self-awareness and learn about peers. It can also be a fun and engaging "get to know you" activity. Students are encouraged to draw themselves as trees. Everyone can draw a tree, but all the trees will be different. When the drawings are completed, volunteers can share their description of their tree with the class. It is always interesting to hear the information shared, which is typically far richer than when people are asked to verbally describe themselves.[4]

At the middle point of my fourth-year social work course, I ask students to submit an assignment where they have challenged themselves to change something in their lives. The intent is to have them explore the process of professional and personal change. They are not graded on whether they were successful in the change process. This assignment is one building block in students' processes of, hopefully, becoming more self-aware and reflective in their final year of study. Indeed, most of the students take the assignment seriously and view it as an opportunity for learning and growth. This past academic year, I was surprised by the assignments in that almost all of the students discussed dealing with negative self-judgment and how this interfered in both their field practicum and academic learning. They discussed how social media and a need for perfectionism was negatively affecting them. In part, because I had earlier introduced them to the concept of mindfulness, many of

4 See "How to Effectively Use Arts-Based Activities in Youth Work" (Coholic, 2016) for a short blog post describing this: https://youthrex.com/blog/how-to-effectively-use-arts-based-activities-in-youth-work/.

them decided to engage with learning about and practising mindfulness to develop their self-awareness and increase their self-compassion. Neff (2003) explained that self-compassion includes the ideas that self-kindness helps us tolerate and understand our challenging characteristics and that mistakes are an integral part of being human. A core component of mindfulness entails not judging our pain and suffering. To practise this concept, students can engage with loving-kindness meditations, which encourage meditators to direct kind feelings towards themselves, loved ones, strangers, people we have difficulty with, and all beings (Galante et al., 2014). A few researchers have studied how learning loving-kindness impacted student counsellors and found that students experienced gains in empathy and improved mood (Leppma & Young, 2016). They also reported feeling less compassion fatigue and burnout (Beaumont et al., 2016).

Learning non-judgment and self-compassion seems especially vital in our current educational contexts, where we are witnessing increasing levels of student mental health challenges. Through the process of becoming more mindful, self-aware, and self-compassionate, students can learn to cope better with their stress or feelings of anxiety by identifying what is challenging them, interrupting rumination, challenging negative self-beliefs, and fostering positive connections with peers. Along these lines, exposure to mindfulness training has been studied with MSW students to help them deal with work-related stress and burnout (Botta et al., 2015). Also, using a survey method, Decker et al. (2015) found a positive correlation between mindfulness and compassion satisfaction, and a negative correlation between mindfulness and compassion fatigue among MSW students. They concluded that mindfulness might be a protective factor for social workers. Moreover, concepts such as mindfulness non-judgment are important to learn especially for trauma survivors. If we cannot sit with our discomfort, we cannot understand our thoughts and gain control of/heal our emotions, and negatively judging our emotions interferes with this process (Coholic, 2019).

Additional Mindfulness Concepts Relating to Social Work Values and Practices

Encouraging our students to keep an open mind and to check their assumptions is vital, and in the practice of mindfulness, it can be related to the concept of a beginner's mind. Kabat-Zinn (1990) explained beginner's mind as seeing things as they really are and not based on what we know about them. A beginner's mind is a mind "that is willing to see everything as if for the first time" (p. 35), that is, not clouded by our assumptions or opinions. One simple activity to encourage students to see something as if for the first time is to have them draw an object but from the perspective of an insect. In this activity, they have to use their imagination to contemplate what an object might look like from a completely different viewpoint. Zen Master Shunryu Suzuki (1975) explains that our minds should be "ready for anything" and "open to everything" stating that "in the beginner's mind there are many possibilities; in the expert's mind there are few" (p. 21). Those of us experienced in social work know that we must remain open to the unexpected. Attempting to keep a beginner's mind can help us remain humble and open to learning.

Finally, despite the usefulness of mindfulness, it is not a panacea for all of our challenges. It does not work for all nor does it appeal to everyone. As Burrows (2018) states, some people may feel worse as a result of mindfulness-based meditation. In her studies, she found that for students who were dealing with emotionally charged issues, meditation could bring about feelings of disconnection and of being emotionally overwhelmed, and heighten self-criticism. As we know, social work is a profession that can be appealing to students who are themselves dealing with serious personal matters. Thus, I am conscious of introducing mindfulness as a practice and philosophy that the students can try if they want to. There are many ways to practise mindfulness both informally and formally, but we need to make sure that no one feels forced to do something that may worsen a situation. There also may be students in our classes that for reasons such as religious beliefs are not comfortable engaging in a personal practice of mindfulness. However, for those students who are interested in learning and practising mindfulness, there are a plethora of available resources (see the chapter appendix).

Mindfulness-based interventions are increasingly popular and are being used across helping practices and in educational settings. A vast research literature shows the positive benefits of mindfulness-based interventions for a wide variety of service-user populations and challenges. Through exposure to the philosophy and practice of mindfulness, social work students can be helped to develop their ability to pay attention, their self-awareness, their self-compassion and empathy, their attitudes of open-mindedness, and their recognition of our interconnections. Thus, personal and professional benefits can be gained that extend far beyond the time spent in university study. Indeed, learning to live life mindfully is a lifelong endeavour. As an educator, I hope that I have exposed my students to a practice that they can build on as they progress through their careers.

REFERENCES

Beaumont, E., Durkin, M., Hollins Martin, C., & Carson, J. (2016). Measuring relationships between self-compassion, compassion fatigue, burnout and well-being in student counsellors and student cognitive behavioural psychotherapists: A quantitative survey. *Counselling and Psychotherapy Research, 16*(1), 15–23. https://doi.org/10.1002/capr.12054

Boone, M. S. (Ed.). (2014). *Mindfulness and acceptance in social work.* Context Press; New Harbinger Publications.

Borquist-Conlon, D., Maynard, B., Esposito Brendel, K., & Farina, A. (2017). Mindfulness-based interventions for youth with anxiety: A systematic review and meta-analysis. *Research on Social Work Practice,* 1–11. https://doi.org/10.1177/1049731516684961

Botta, A., Cadet, T., & Maramaldi, P. (2015). Reflections on a quantitative, group-based mindfulness study with social work students. *Social Work with Groups, 38,* 93–105. https://doi.org/10.1080/01609513.2014.975885

Burrows, L. (2018). *Safeguarding mindfulness in schools and higher education: A holistic and inclusive approach.* Routledge.

Canadian Association of Social Workers. (2005). *Code of ethics.* https://www.casw-acts.ca/sites/casw-acts.ca/files/documents/casw_code_of_ethics.pdf

Coates, J., Graham, J., Swartzentruber, B., & Ouellette, B. (Eds.). (2007). *Spirituality and social work: Selected Canadian readings.* Canadian Scholars Press.

Coholic, D. (2011). Exploring the feasibility and benefits of arts-based mindfulness-based practices with young people in need: Aiming to improve aspects of self-awareness and resilience. *Child Youth Care Forum, 40*(4), 303–17. https://doi.org/10.1007/s10566-010-9139-x

Coholic, D. (2016). How to effectively use arts-based activities in youth work. *YouthRex.* https://youthrex.com/blog/how-to-effectively-use-arts-based-activities-in-youth-work/

Coholic, D. (2019). *Facilitating mindfulness: A guide for human service professionals.* Northrose Educational Resources.

Coholic, D., & Eys, M. (2016). Benefits of an arts-based mindfulness group intervention for vulnerable children. *Child & Adolescent Social Work Journal, 33*(3), 1–13. https://doi.org/10.1007/s10560-015-0431-3

Coholic, D., Eys, M., McAlister, H., Sugeng, S., & Smith, D. (2018). A mixed method pilot study exploring the benefits of an arts-based mindfulnss group intervention with adults experiencing anxiety and depression. *Social Work in Mental Health, 16*(5), 556–72. https://doi.org/10.1080/15332985.2018.1449774

Council of Ontario Universities. (2018). *Foundations: Mental health and well-being initiatives at Ontario's universities.* https://ontariosuniversities.ca/wp-content/uploads/2017/11/Foundations-Mental-Health-and-Well-Being-Initiatives.pdf

Curran, T., & Hill, A. (2018, January 3). *How perfectionism became a hidden epidemic among young people.* The Conversation. https://theconversation.com/how-perfectionism-became-a-hidden-epidemic-among-young-people-89405

Decker, J. T., Constantine Brown, J., Ong, J., & Stiney-Ziskind, C. (2015). Mindfulness, compassion fatigue, and compassion satisfaction among social work interns. *Social Work & Christianity, 42*(1), 28–42.

Dimidjian, S., & Linehan, M. (2003). Defining an agenda for future research on the clinical application of mindfulness practice. *Clinical Psychology: Science and Practice, 10,* 166–71. https://doi.org/10.1093/clipsy.bpg019

Fjorback, L., Arendt, M., Ornbol, E., Fink, P., & Walach, H. (2011). Mindfulness-based stress reduction and mindfulness-based cognitive therapy: A systematic review of randomized controlled trials. *Acta Psychiatrica Scandinaivca, 124*(2), 102–19. https://doi.org/10.1111/j.1600-0447.2011.01704.x

Fulton, P. R. (2005). Mindfulness as clinical training. In C. Germer, R. Siegel, & P. Fulton (Eds.), *Mindfulness and psychotherapy* (pp. 55–72). Guilford Press.

Galante, J., Galante, I., Bekkers, M., & Gallacher, J. (2014). Effect of kindness-based meditation on health and well-being: A systematic review and meta-analysis. *Journal of Consulting and Clinical Psychology, 82*(6), 1101–14. https://doi.org/10.1037/a0037249

Germer, C. (2009). *The mindful path to self-compassion: Freeing yourself from destructive thoughts and emotions.* Guilford Press.

Gockel, A., Cain, T., & Malove, S. (2013). Mindfulness as clinical training: Student perspectives on the utility of mindfulness training in fostering clinical intervention skills. *Journal of Religion & Spirituality in Social Work: Social Thought, 32,* 36–59. https://doi.org/10.1080/15426432.2013.749146

Grossman, P. (2008). On measuring mindfulness in psychosomatic and psychological research. *Journal of Psychosomatic Research, 64*(4), 405–8. https://doi.org/10.1016/j.jpsychores.2008.02.001

Hick, S. (Ed.). (2009). *Mindfulness and social work.* Lyceum Books.

Hinchey, L. (2018). Mindfulness-based art therapy: A review of the literature. *Inquiries Journal, 10*(05). http://www.inquiriesjournal.com/a?id=1737

Ideapod (Producer). (2016, May 8). *In less than 3 minutes, you'll see why mindfulness is the single most powerful thing you can do for your wellbeing.* https://ideapod.com/less-3-minutes-youll-understand-practicing-mindfulness-one-single-powerful-things-can/

Kabat-Zinn, J. (1990). *Full catastrophe living: Using the wisdom of your body and mind to face stress, pain and illness.* Delta.

Leppma, M., & Young, M. (2016). Loving-kindness meditation and empathy: A wellness group intervention for counseling students. *Journal of Counseling & Development, 94,* 297–305. https://doi.org/10.1002/jcad.12086

Marlowe, J. M., Appleton, C., Chinnery, S., & Van Stratum, S. (2015). The integration of personal and professional selves: Developing students' critical awareness in social work practice. *Social Work Education: The International Journal, 34*(1), 60–73. https://doi.org/10.1080/02615479.2014.949230

Matthews, M., & Csiernik, R. (2019). A review of mental health services offered by Canada's English language universities. *Canadian Social Work, 20*(2), 31–48.

Mindfulness Exercises. (2018, May 11). Simple mindfulness strategy – Take 5. https://mindfulnessexercises.com/simple-mindfulness-strategy-take-5/

Neff, K. (2003). Self-compassion: An alternative conceptualization of a healthy attitude toward oneself. *Self and Identity, 2*(1), 85–102. https://doi.org/10.1080/15298860309032

Perry-Parrish, C., Copeland-Linder, N., Webb, L., Shields, A. H., & Sibinga, E. (2016). Improving self-regulation in adolescents: Current evidence for the role of mindfulness-based cognitive therapy. *Adolescent Health, Medicine and Therapeutics, 7,* 101–8. https://doi.org/10.2147/ahmt.s65820

Segal, Z., Williams, J., & Teasdale, J. (2002). *Mindfulness-based cognitive therapy for depression: A new approach to preventing relapse.* Guilford Press.

Siegel, D. (2010). *The mindful therapist: A clinician's guide to mindsight and neural integration.* W.W. Norton & Company.

Suzuki, S. (1975). *Zen mind, beginner's mind.* Weatherhill.

Thomas, J. T. (2017). Brief mindfulness training in the social work practice classroom. *Social Work Education, 36*(1), 102–18. https://doi.org/10.1080/02615479.2016.1250878

Tomlinson, E., Yousaf, O., Vitterso, A., & Jones, L. (2018). Dispositional mindfulness and psychological health: A systematic review. *Mindfulness, 9,* 23–43. https://doi.org/10.1007/s12671-017-0762-6

Van Vliet, K. J., Foskett, A., Williams, J., Singhal, A., Dolcos, F., & Vohra, S. (2017). Impact of a mindfulness-based stress reduction program from the perspective of adolescents with serious mental health concerns. *Child and Adolescent Mental Health, 22*(1), 16–22. https://doi.org/10.1111/camh.12170

Vollestad, J., Birkeland Nielsen, M., & Hostmark Nielsen, G. (2012). Mindfulness- and acceptance-based interventions for anxiety disorders: A systematic review and meta-analysis. *British Journal of Clinical Psychology, 51,* 239–60. https://doi.org/10.1111/j.2044-8260.2011.02024.x

Weiss, A. (2004). *Beginning mindfulness: Learning the way of awareness.* New World Library.

Williams, J. (2014). Review of mindfulness and the arts therapies: Theory and practice. *Dramatherapy, 36*(2–3), 156–7. https://doi.org/10.1080/02630672.2015.1012354

APPENDIX: ADDITIONAL RESOURCES

The website for The Foundation for a Mindful Society at http://www.mindful.org has helpful articles on a wide variety of topics, including exercises and activities to practise mindfulness.

My research team made a 12-minute video in which the concept of mindfulness is discussed and some of the student trainees discuss their experiences in learning the practices. It is available on YouTube at https://www.youtube.com/watch?v=pNPTyG20YT0.

Crystal Goh's (1997) article on mindful.org, "Your Breath Is Your Brain's Remote Control," looks at how breathing through our nose can affect our thinking: https://www.mindful.org/breath-brains-remote-control.

One of my favourite books on mindfulness is Thich Nhat Hanh's *Peace Is Every Step: The Path of Mindfulness in Everyday Life* (Bantam Books, 1991). It is manageable to read and promotes the thinking and practice of mindfulness.

The Greater Good Science Center at UC Berkeley provides a loving-kindness meditation (script and audio) at http://ggia.berkeley.edu/practice/loving_kindness_meditation.

12 Teaching Change: Navigating the Tensions in Social Change Pedagogy

KATHY HOGARTH

The idea of teaching social change to social work students is not novel. In fact, most social work educators, and students entering university to join the profession, have some expectation of engaging in social change throughout their career. For me, distinguishable patterns related to the pedagogy of social change have emerged throughout my years of teaching courses on social change to hundreds of social work students. This chapter delineates the patterns of social change that occur in academic settings. Additionally, classroom dynamics and experiences suggest that teaching social change in a way that requires students to become agents of change is challenging. The adage "be the change you want to see" has been so popularized in our profession that, in some senses, it has lost its saliency. This chapter will outline some of the challenges associated with teaching about social change. These challenges are related not only to students but also include institutional responses to students' attempts at social change, as well as the tensions teachers of change must navigate.

Conceptual Framework

Over the past few decades, greater attention has been given to ethics and social justice within social work education (Bonnycastle, 2011; Dudzik & Profitt, 2012; Hugman & Carter, 2016). This dedication to the education and practice of social justice is reflected in the educational policy, standards, and codes of ethics for bodies of social work, such as the Canadian Association for Social Work Education – l'Association canadienne pour la formation en travail social (CASWE-ACFTS), the Council on Social Work Education, the National Association of Social Work, the International Association of Schools of Social Work, and the International Federation of Social Work. Despite the greater emphasis on social justice, social work educators who want to provide guidance to students around ethics and social justice remain challenged by a lack of defining principles. The descriptions of educational policies, standards, and codes of ethics tend to be brief and lack specific theory and practical approaches. As Bonnycastle (2011) noted, "brevity, multiple meanings, and vagueness lead social workers, all under the name of social justice, to use a mishmash of concepts, theories, and approaches" (p. 268).

History of Social Justice

Examining social justice in relation to social work finds a heavy emphasis upon Kantian and/or utilitarian modes that centralize universal criteria for making judgments (Dofgoff et al., 2008; Webb & McBeath, 1989). Respect for persons, self-determination, and service-user confidentiality were original tenets of social work ethics. However, "historically, social work has often operationalized social justice in a manner that engenders exclusion, rather than inclusion, raising concerns the profession will repeat such mistakes in the future" (Hodge, 2010, p. 201). Moving beyond Kantian universality, feminist and anti-oppressive values, ethics, and theories provide a direction forward by taking into account concepts of inequality and power, social divisions, and complex intersecting personal and social relationships and identities (Bonnycastle, 2011; Hodge, 2010; Jacobson & Rugely, 2007). Clifford and Burke (2005), in advocating for the development of an anti-oppressive ethics and values module to be included in the revision of social work education in the United Kingdom, proposed the use of five principles that combine feminist and anti-oppressive ethics: taking into account social difference; using reflexivity in acknowledging that we occupy "a specific social location of social power" (p. 684); viewing people in their historical and social context; placing behaviour within a wider context of social systems; and taking power into consideration. Similarly, Hodge (2010) notes that an understanding of social justice must allow for multiple voices and conceptualizations of "a just society" (p. 202).

Social Change as Disruption

Social change refers to a disruption of the status quo. Such disruptions may involve systemic changes, institutional changes, or behavioural changes reflected in macro, mezzo, and micro levels of society. These changes are often attenuated with varying levels of anxiety, resistance, and satisfaction for those enacting change and to those on whom change is being enacted (Alinsky, 1969, 1971). Embedded within this understanding of social change is the assumption that many of our social systems and structures are skewed towards benefiting the majority population in any group or demographic of society and marginalizes minority/subordinate groups. Social movements can then be seen as a natural tool of social change as they have been defined as a

> sustained series of actions between power holders and persons successfully claiming to speak on behalf of a constituency lacking formal representation, in the course of which those persons make publicly visible demands for changes in the distribution of exercise of power, and back those with public demonstrations of support. (Tilley, 1984, p. 306)

Group Dynamics and Social Change

Social change can be viewed as both an event and a process. Social work educators have used many modalities to teach social justice, including the use of case studies, social media examples, and contemporary literature. Social change can also be understood as both an individual and a collective process, so an argument can be made that understanding group dynamics is essential. Many authors point to group work as a particularly useful way of providing skills and knowledge regarding social justice (Dudzik & Profitt, 2012; Jacobson & Rugely, 2007; Woodger & Anastacio, 2013; Woodger et al., 2019). Consequently, the emerging patterns of social change discussed here are within a framework of group work.

Thus, the use of group work as a model for social change allows students to put structural theory (Mullaly, 2007) into practice in a way that blurs the lines between micro and macro practice. Students working in groups also have the opportunity to witness how essential group work is in terms of social action and community organization. By examining social justice as an expression of human interactions, students learn that "human actors behave interactively to create our experiences" (Wiener & Rosenwald, 2008, p. 126).

Correspondingly, social work educators who assign the production of a social justice initiative for marks/towards requirements for a credit provide an opportunity for what Goffman (1986, as cited in Wiener & Rosenwald, 2008, p. 73) termed *technical redoings*, incorporating the practice and demonstration of an act or what Freire (1970) described as praxis, "reflection and action upon the world in order to transform it" (p. 38). In some ways, students are simulating the act of a social justice initiative but are, at the same time, engaging with issues in new ways. This also allows space for teaching and learning about multiple definitions of social justice and making connections between personal experiences and structural issues (Jacobson & Rugely, 2007). By researching and implementing social justice initiatives, regardless of the scope, students are able to examine issues of structure and agency within their community and in their own lives.

Studying Emerging Patterns of Social Change in an Undergraduate Environment

To assess patterns of social change, data were drawn from three sources in one bachelor of social work (BSW) program, in one Canadian school of social work. This program admits approximately 90 students each year, divided among full-time and part-time cohorts. The part-time cohort has approximately 30 students and students in the full-time cohort are randomly divided in two sections of 30 students each. The course from which data were drawn, Advance Macro Practice, is an experientially designed required BSW course. In addition to from students, data were also drawn from the three faculty members teaching the course and other institutional representatives from within the social work department, including other faculty, administrators, and field staff. Over one year, information from 90 students and input from instructors was analysed. The total student participant group was made up of primarily female identifying students, with eight male identifying students. Approximately 90 per cent of the student participants identified as White, and there was one international student among the participants.

Each class in each section of the macro practice course, during the period used for study, began with introducing the idea of social change and challenging students to see themselves as agents of social change. The first class in each section also engaged students with the concept of experiential design, which decentres the balance of learning away from the exclusivity of the classroom to the wider society. Students were instructed that the objective of experiential learning was not the experience itself but the inferences made in the process of learning that question preconceptions with critical reflection, thereby extracting lessons from actions (Kolb, 2015). At the end of the first class and every class for 12 weeks, students engaged in a daily muse in which they were asked to respond, in writing, to questions such as, "What fears or anxieties are you carrying with you about the course? What was your greatest learning from the experience you had in the course today?" or to other similar questions related to the course content and/or their experiences with the change event and process in the course itself. Students were asked to select an area of social change in which they wanted to engage and then group themselves with other students who were similarly interested. Groups were to be no larger than five members. The final decision about the change project was made by group consensus. Topics chosen included but were not limited to suicide prevention, murdered and missing Indigenous women, voting, mental health awareness, dental care for individuals with low income, and human trafficking. The first six weeks of the course centred on theory and designing a change event. The last six weeks of the course focused on implementation and reflection on the change event.

Both qualitative and quantitative data were collected through daily muses, reflexive journals, observation, and standardized student evaluations. Institutional data were gathered through formal group meetings with faculty and administrative and field staff. A total of 11 institutional representatives provided feedback on two occasions, one before the change event and one after the change event. Data from course instructors were gathered through semi-structured course instructor group meetings. Course instructors provided feedback each week for 12 weeks, followed by two post-course meetings. All course instructors adhered to the same course design and content delivery. Data were analysed using thematic analysis as described by Boyatzis (1998). Themes were generated inductively from the data, and open coding was used to condense the mass of data into categories. Data from each data source group were analysed separately and then themes were compared and matched across groups.

Findings

Four major themes emerged from the data in a progressive order and centred on the notions of resistance, rethinking, anxiety, and satisfaction. These themes were evident, in varying levels, among all three study groups, namely, students, professors/instructors, and the institutional representatives.

Resistance

Teaching courses in social work where students are required, as part of the learning process, to enter into the field and engage in social change is a novel approach to learning for some. This approach challenged the teaching/learning sensibilities for many students. From the qualitative component of the standardized course evaluations, students often noted that the experiential nature of the project was vastly different from the traditional static learning assignments (multiple choice tests, essays, theory-based group presentations) they were used to completing in their previous courses. As a result, they found this assignment to be stress provoking, and this anxiety led to resistance to the idea of engaging in a social change project. Many students seemed quite comfortable to conduct paperwork and research about a social change activity but were reluctant to take part in the experiential aspects of the course, of actually doing. In fact, in their evaluation of the course, some students in the full-time cohort, where the two professors were female and racialized, rated their professors poorly, and their rationale seemed to support their resistance to and unfamiliarity with experiential designed courses and the expectation of actually engaging in the process rather than writing about it. One student noted, "the profs only gave five lectures for 12 weeks. Seemed like a large demand for work by students, but not by profs" (anonymous, full-time cohort). It was interesting to note that the white male professor in the part-time cohort did not receive such feedback, particularly in light of the issues raised by Hillock (chapter 18) and by Yorke and Shute (chapter 19) regarding challenges in the social work classroom.

When compared against the full-time and part-time cohorts, the timing of the course in students' tenure in the program also served as an anxiety-provoking factor. The part-time student cohort was made up of students at varying stages in their degree, first course, last course, or midway in their BSW journey. For the full-time cohorts, the course came in their very first term of the three-term BSW class. As noted by one student, "the [idea] of social action scared me. It was my first introduction to it in this class. I wasn't sure if I would be successful in creating or executing change" (RH, full-time cohort).

Resistance also came as a result of having to confront their power and make sense of the dualism of saviour-oppressor, especially the unanticipated discomfort of confronting privileged positions. Although students organized around issues they were passionate about, or at the very least shared some concern with, some students expressed discomfort related to organizing against issues of which they were beneficiaries. One such case was a group of students who began organizing for "ethical clothing" and against major brands that make millions on underpaid labourers in developing countries, and then found themselves complicit in their personal support of these brands.

Resistance was also a major theme that emerged from the data gathered from instructors. As much as the instructors aimed to create an environment in which social inequities could be challenged, it became clear in the minds of the instructors that there was a limit to what would be considered "acceptable" challenges to social structure. There were concerns around whether initiatives met ethical standards, both of the profession and of the university, but also a reaction to what might be deemed too "shocking" within the university community. Small worries gave way to thoughts of "what about if this gets televised by the local news? What are the implications of this to the university, to the students, to us as untenured and sessional faculty? Had the students even considered these issues?" One main concern of the faculty was about protecting marginalized groups within the student groups. This was particularly true in one group that was working to highlight the issue of human trafficking. To visually demonstrate the concept and impact of trafficking, one group member suggested that two members of their group, one male and one female, would stand in a public space on university grounds and represent a male oppressor with a captured (rope around her neck) female victim. The imagery of this scene evoked a significant amount of anxiety for the instructor. To address this anxiety, the instructor spent time with the group exploring the idea and encouraging members to express their viewpoints. Student anxiety also emerged and, eventually, the lone male in the group, who was also of racialized status, expressed his reservations about the plan. Another member also seemed hesitant about the original idea. Over the week, group members with reservations about the original idea became more forthcoming with their concerns and the group as a whole decided to use another, less provocative, tactic to highlight the issue.

Resistance also came from the institution. Institutional resistance was most evident in the meetings with faculty and staff, who were not fully aware of the requirements of the course; after hearing of students' change proposals from various channels within and outside the university, they were both alarmed and excited about some of the change projects. Resistance from the institution was talked about in two distinct ways: upholding the social work professional values particularly related to protecting the individual, in this case, our students; and upholding the "perceived" integrity of the institution.

Rethinking

Despite the concerns directly and indirectly expressed, all the groups who were assigned social change projects completed their projects. How did they get past their own resistance and that of the instructors and institution? When instructors addressed student resistance, they took several procedural steps. First among them was seeking understanding about where the resistance was coming from and whether ethical and personal boundaries needed to be respected.

Second, a major theme in their progression was rethinking. Reimagining and redesigning emerged as necessary next steps to break through the resistance evident among students and the institutions. Instructors acted as the brokers of this rethinking process. This included brainstorming other topics and/or other types of projects with students, or finding a way to make their intervention more compatible with the context, such as by asking, for example, what was "appropriate" to present in the student union centre. In some groups, it was important to give voice to students who felt unable to express their reservations about the original idea to the larger group. Students talked about this "democratic process" and "open forum for discussion of ideas and change" as a strength of the course and highly valued what one student termed "the space-making for all voices" (full-time student cohort).

As well, instructors worked together with group members to redesign the path of the projects. A few students who had championed some of the initial ideas were somewhat resistant to change topics but did acknowledge that it was important to create consensus and to have the entire group support the ideas. After the instructors and the group members moved past the resistance, the groups each worked on planning and implementing their projects.

Eventually, the institution also began embracing the ideas of the social change projects. A few completed projects were highlighted in the weekly e-newsletter, and upcoming events began to be advertised. Over the next few months, other administrative decisions were made to provide financial support towards some of the planned events, such as offering suicide prevention training for all students.

Anxiety

Not surprisingly, students exhibited the greatest level of anxiety and for longer compared to the instructors, faculty and administrators, and other institutional representatives. The greatest levels of student anxiety were seen close to the start of the course when the idea of social change was introduced. There was a consistent spike in anxiety levels across all study participants around the time of preparing for the change event. However, students' anxiety levels remained fairly high throughout the change events and in assessing the impact of change. The institution displayed no evidence of concern regarding the assignment until the point of students preparing to engage in the change activities they had planned. This point in the process also coincided with the rethinking theme. After the rethinking and reframing processes were completed, institutional anxieties were sharply reduced as the extent of the activities became evident and less controversial. Instructors' anxiety levels were also elevated at this time, and while they were somewhat reduced, they remained at a moderate level until the very end of the course, when they dipped sharply.

Satisfaction

The final theme in the progression was satisfaction. All study groups exhibited satisfaction of varying degrees throughout the course. Among the student cohorts, each student group had an opportunity to present its social change project to the rest of the class to highlight the challenges and successes of the project. Each student section was able to learn about five to six different social change projects conducted during the term and students were very vocal in their excitement about what had been accomplished: "I do not typically feel passionate about community organizing but that has changed!" (anonymous full-time student).

Discussion

We live in an age of *click, click, download.* With a consumerist mentality to education, students expect that in return for their payment to the institution, they will receive a box of goodies transferred to them by their instructors. This is the traditional "sage on the stage" classroom design. Stepping outside the conventional box is anxiety provoking for both students and the institution. One of the ways we have found of mitigating these challenges is in investing the time, very early in the course, to orient students to experiential designs and offer constant reminders, evidence, and affirmations of the validity of other ways of learning. This helped in redefining the role of professors as facilitators of learning opportunities rather than just providers of information through lecturing.

Requiring students to think of themselves as change agents was another factor that created a great deal of personal and group anxiety. These reactions often led to what we have identified as resistance to the process. The confrontational aspect of change can be a frightening alternative to student-constructed narratives of social workers as "reconcilers" and "peacemakers." To think of conflict as inevitable or even desirable in the change process seems to provoke significant levels of anxiety, particularly when students are challenged to choose an area for advocacy and intervention. However, after "champions" arose in the groups, there seemed to be less resistance to ideas concerning social change, and enthusiasm grew about the proposed intervention.

The notion of sending students out into the community to advocate for change may be quite an appealing one for faculty members who see "doing social justice" on a macro scale as an imperative for the profession. Requiring students to brainstorm ideas of social change, however, can be anxiety provoking for all stakeholders. Faculty, and sometimes members of the larger institution, can be faced with questions concerning the nature of social justice activities on campus and in the community. Concerns about repercussions from the community and the university may govern a faculty member's excitement over students' ideas. By expressing overt or covert concerns about the appropriateness of the initiative to student groups, we, as faculty, were demonstrating a counter-narrative that was antithetical to what was being taught during the lectures of the class. Thus, a number of questions emerged needing further reflection:

1 What would the impact have been if the more "risky" approaches had been taken?
2 Some groups received less intervention from the instructors than others did. On what was that based? Our level of discomfort? Our predictions of the institutional response versus the actual response?
3 What is the impact of teaching a course on social justice but demonstrating fear of repercussions?

One of the ironies noted in the process was the perceived need, in a few cases, for instructors to "water down" students' social justice initiatives. Instructors have an obligation to teach students in a safe environment. However, does this really support students in pursuing true social change? As we teach them social change, are we also teaching them that they need safeguards, a type of "social change within the boxes" to avoid real risk, which in turn don't truly challenge the status quo? Can we truly accomplish change with this model? While we think this is possible, the change initiatives were moderate at best, most remaining at the level of raising awareness but not actually challenging systems or changing structures of injustice.

Despite these concerns, a discernable transformation occurred in the minds of the students, the instructors, and the institution administrator after students began to understand themselves to be agents of change. For some students, this change in their view of self signalled the beginning of many other larger scale social change initiatives. One example is the group of students who started off to change the institution's policy around suicide prevention training for BSW students. Through this group's continued and sustained actions, well beyond the course, this issue is now a national agenda item that has garnered significant media attention and forms a part of the discussion in many schools of social work across the country. It has also been part of the discussion of the CASWE-ACFTS.

Instructors learned more about assisting students to find ways to be activists while balancing their positions as agents of the institution. Despite the notions of academic freedom, there is still a sense that professors remain the agents of institutions that pay their salaries. Protecting the integrity of the institution and its community partners while not written in our job descriptions, is somehow an unwritten code, and one that, particularly untenured, faculty abide by. Yet we must balance student learning outcomes, particularly when these outcomes seem to be in tension with the image of the institution. Finding a good middle ground between social provocation and social action provides a softer landing, especially for faculty members and the institution, without necessarily compromising student learning. There is also rich learning embedded in that tension between the institution and instructors that can be passed on to students. Without a full appreciation of the learning embedded in the tension, we inadvertently end up teaching students values that are contradictory to what we set out to teach. And in so doing, we become part of the problem.

Conclusion

From this experience, it was evident that institutional responses are open to change. The question is, how do we facilitate this change in teaching methods? Changing the institutional mindset towards supporting the social change projects in which students were engaged came as a result of both pushing back against the institution and strengthening relationships with it. While an unnerving question remains about how much more the institution should have been pushed, or how much more it could have pushed back, our collective efforts in advocating for students, in students advocating for themselves, and in maintaining good relationships between instructors and institution eventually materialized into the institution supporting these student and faculty social change initiatives.

REFERENCES

Alinsky, S. D. (1971). *Rules for radicals: A pragmatic primer for realistic radicals.* Vintage Books.

Alinsky, S. D. (1969). *Reveille for radicals.* Vintage Books.

Bonnycastle, C. R. (2011). Social justice along a continuum: A relational illustrative model. *Social Service Review, 85*(2), 267–95. https://doi.org/10.1086/660703

Boyatzis, R. (1998). *Transforming qualitative information: Thematic analysis and code development.* Sage Publication Inc.

Clifford, D., & Burke, B. (2005). Developing anti-oppressive ethics in the new curriculum. *Social Work Education, 24*(6), 677–92. https://doi.org/10.1080/02615470500185101

Dofgoff, R., Loewenberg, F., & Harrington, D. (2008). *Ethical decisions for social work practice* (8th ed.). Brooks/Cole.

Dudzik, S., & Profitt, N. J. (2012). Group work and social justice: Designing pedagogy for social change. *Social Work with Groups, 35*(3), 235–52. https://doi.org/10.1080/01609513.2011.624370

Hodge, D. R. (2010). Social justice as a unifying theme in social work education: Principles to realize the promise of a new pedagogical model. *Journal of Comparative Social Welfare, 26*(2–3), 201–13. https://doi.org/10.1080/17486831003687600

Hugman, R., & Carter, J. (2016). *Rethinking values and ethics in social work.* Palgrave Macmillan.

Jacobson, M., & Rugely, C. (2007.) Community-based participatory research: Group work for social justice and community change. *Social Work with Groups, 30*(4), 21–39. https://doi.org/10.1300/j009v30n04_03

Kolb, D. (2015). *Experiential learning: Experience as the source of learning and development* (2nd ed.). Pearson Education.

Mullaly, B. (2007). *The new structural social work* (3rd ed.). Oxford University Press.

Tilley, C. (1984). *Big structures, large processes, huge comparisons.* Russell Sage Foundation.

Webb, S., & McBeath, G. (1989). A political critique of Kantian ethics in social work. *The British Journal of Social Work, 19*(1), 491–506. https://doi.org/10.1093/bjsw/19.6.491

Wiener, D. R., & Rosenwald, M. (2008). Unlocking doors: Providing MSW programs and students with educational "keys" to social justice. *Journal of Progressive Human Services, 19*(2), 125–39. https://doi.org/10.1080/10428230802475422

Woodger, D., & Anastacio, J. (2013). Groupwork: Training for social justice. *Groupwork, 23,* 26–47. https://doi.org/10.1921/5001230204

Woodger, D., Thompson, N., & Anastacio, J. (2019). Learning does not reside in a place called comfortable": Exploring identity and social justice through experiential group work. In M. Seal (Ed.), *Teaching youth work in higher education: Tensions, connections, continuities and contradictions* (pp. 152–9). University of Tartu; Newman University; Humak University of Applied Sciences; Estonian Association of Youth Workers.

13 Horses and Baseball: Social Work's Cultivation of the Third Eye

JAN YORKE, SCOTT GRANT, AND RICK CSIERNIK

Active self-reflection between social workers and service users requires the ability to observe our professional self and the service users while simultaneously participating in the interaction with all that occurs, as it occurs. It is a sophisticated and subtle multilayered process that includes more than monitoring our reaction to the effect we have on others and others have on us. Schon (1983) identifies this as a "response-in-action" and a "response-to-action": the ability to perpetually review our actions and strategically change them in response to the situation at hand. We might compare this to the role of individual players in sports. In baseball, this is the pitcher's job, watching for the opposing team's players attempts to steal a base while all the time strategically planning what pitch to throw to the hitter, depending upon the batter's particular strength. Swift (1985), a noted equestrian, calls this using a soft eye: focusing upon performing a task while taking in and observing all that occurs around it. These analogies provide a visual example of how to successfully cultivate the ability to self-reflect in undergraduate social work students' learning.

The development of a generalist approach to social work practice should prepare students with a well-rounded understanding of community work, social policy and advocacy, theory, and direct practice techniques. In Canada, competencies identified by the Canadian Council of Social Work Regulators (2012) expect bachelor of social work students to graduate with a generalist set of skills regardless of their area of interest. There has been some controversy about these recommendations. Although many of the competencies are necessary to entry-level social work positions, students do not always graduate equipped in this way (Yorke, 2005). Further, many of the competencies demand subject expertise that can only be acquired through specific direct experience and mentoring over time. Licensing in many jurisdictions in the United States requires a two-year mentorship, followed by a pass or fail in state exams, to obtain the professional licence required to perform many of these competencies. Accurate methods of developing and measuring these competencies require standardized approaches that can address the complexity of the task. Critical social work scholars argue that a focus on teaching technique obscures the recognition of the power imbalance between social workers and service users that is perpetuated in their role as professionals (Macias, 2012). Macias (2012) proposed that ethically, a type of double self-detachment from the desire that emerges from dominant power/knowledge is required, "a process of internal transformation and disentanglement from ... the discourse and traditions of social work" (p. 13). Establishing mechanisms for students to grasp these essential skills is at the heart of this discussion.

This chapter explores the importance of developing the capacity for communicating meaningfully and collaboratively using the third eye or critical self-reflection practice for undergraduate social work students. This is not unlike the skills one might use in team sports like baseball or handling a team of eight horses in close quarters. Baseball and horses: what do they have to do with communication in social work? In baseball, verbal and non-verbal cues are essential to strategic play, inning to inning, as is the coaching of a mentor who has experienced the range of possibilities and can assist in anticipating possible outcomes. Basic communication with your horse and the fundamentals of interaction are important to successful and safe team work. Without these, a person courts disaster. Ask a rider who ignores injuries or cues of frustration in a horse as they pick themselves up after getting bucked off or the baseball player who is struck by a ball or who misses the coach's sign, allowing the winning run to be stranded on the base path. More importantly, grasping the nature of the power relationship and its relationship to success is essential to comprehending the notion of the third eye.

The Third Eye

An experience with a relative in intensive care involved a physician who had recently lost his own grandmother. That physician wanted to impose this experience upon the decisions being made regarding life or death in another patient. The physician was oblivious to the impact that his subjective experience was having upon his professional judgment. No amount of discussion on the part of family or allied health professionals could dissuade him. This physician clearly had difficulty separating his professional self from his subjective self, with all that it implied.

In social work, a clinician's *first eye* is objective and theoretically informed. Our ability to watch ourselves, analyse, and proceed with a professional response to the circumstance is essential for our practice. It requires the capacity to separate our professional narrative in a situation from our personal narrative. The personal narrative is the professional's *second eye*: their personal reactions, anxieties, and/or responses. Monitoring these two perspectives requires the ability to objectively sort and process our thoughts, feelings, and actions in the moment. When fully developed, it constitutes the capacity to use a *third eye*: an additional view of our interaction with others that continually converts subjective responses to objective reactions, allowing the inner dialogue to be monitored, analysed, and reframed while actively participating in day-to-day practice. This requires more than passive self-reflection after the fact; it is a dynamic, evolving process of converting thought processes into professional action. It is often described as an objective versus a subjective stance in counselling or reflexivity (Schon, 1983). It is a skill that some social workers have great difficulty honing. It can be conceptualized as the capacity for insight with foresight.

This ability to use the third eye allows a social worker to disconnect and appraise practice, perspective, and inner dialogue from a suspended vantage point. For example, if a student's first practicum is working in a drop-in centre for homeless individuals with mental health and addiction problems, a new environment with a new population, the social work intern might initially respond to interactions with a particular service user in the following way. The intern's developing professional self might assess a service user's abrasiveness as a coping strategy. With the help of clinical supervision, the intern may identify the need for an assessment resulting from talking with the individual, the capacity the service user has in that moment to respond, and the person's ability to interact socially in the environment. This may also relate to whether the individual has a mental illness, for example, or is part of the dominant group or a marginalized/oppressed one. The developed personal self might feel threatened or angry; may find the person's hygiene wanting, leading to difficulty in engaging the person; or might cause the intern to respond instinctively to an insult by walking away, setting boundaries, or even calling the police. The intern may not be able to disentangle the self from the unconscious biases of class, race, age, ableism, or gender.

With the introduction of the concept of the third eye, social work interns may be better able to identify subjective internal dialogue and learn to process their personal feelings with their supervisors. Our personal selves may bring a host of issues to bear upon the decision-making process, unrelated to service users or their behaviour. A profound lesson from a riding coach still resonates; when accused of pulling on a horse's mouth during a gallop, one of the authors denied that she was doing so and said it was the horse that was pulling. The coach said, "Drop the reins." When the gallop was maintained at the same pace, the coach responded by saying, "Who changed?" Who changed indeed! This is what we would call an emotionally significant experience: a profound shift in thought and perspective resulting from the interaction with the other. Accurate self-perception and honest self-appraisal can be fostered while learning active, critical self-reflection in undergraduate social work education, and it underscores the importance of direct supervision and mentoring in both the classroom and field settings.

Literature Review

Social Work and the Third Eye

Although many professions may find the critical self-reflective notion of the third eye helpful, social work in particular relies upon this approach to work with service users, such as the homeless individual described above. O'Sullivan (2005) describes this as a process of interpreting and synthesizing information from our environment and framing it. Information is refined through a degree of critical control in which a frame is filtered of "ambiguous and fallible" interpretations (p. 8). Reframing of the information is then constructed from a service-user-centred perspective and not the social worker's lens. This degree of critical control, according to Schon (1983), requires workers to step back from reflection-in-action to a reflection-on-action approach. The third eye refers to the stepping back process and the reframing of subjective information as professional information simultaneously, in the now, thus incorporating O'Sullivan (2005) and Schon's (1983) concepts into one. It should also include the use of a power and an anti-oppression lens, as described by Macias (2012). To develop this skill, students must have emotionally significant experiences, just as in the galloping horse example. Emotionally significant experiences are moments of transformational change, *aha* moments that foster empathy for the service user and an understanding of the need for awareness and change of self. Students indicate that hands-on tactical approaches provide useful ways of having those aha moments (Bogo et al., 2011).

Overall, the use of the third eye as a form of constant critical self-reflection is vital to the development of competence in social workers. It involves holding at once a complex constellation of related issues that requires the use of that soft eye. Swift (1985) describes taking in all that surrounds the rider when on a horse as a way of determining action.

The rider's capacity to respond appropriately determines the horse's reaction. Pitchers are pulled from games in crucial situations not only because of fatigue but because their capacity for self-reflection is no longer helpful. Similarly, the third eye can be used with social work students to address vigilance in self-reflection in the learning context; it is safe enough to allow for feedback and provides experiences that elicit recognition of blind spots. The ability to recognize when and how our own behaviour contributes to a problem is essential.

Some experienced students may want to discuss challenging situations while less experienced students struggle to grasp basic concepts. This is further complicated by the balance between theory and practice that undergraduate social work programs have to find. Students may become consumed with doing social work and may be less inclined to critically self-reflect and detach, especially when grappling with how to practise collaboratively within anti-oppressive and critical frames (Macias, 2012). Using the concept of the third eye helps students to visualize theory in a broader context. Theory in social work provides awareness into why strategies are valuable, allowing students to continue to improve through their undergraduate experience and beyond.

THE ROLE OF SOCIAL WORK THEORY

The relationship between self-reflection, the impact of the environment, and competency is underwritten by classic social work epistemology. Social work literature has long supported the link between nature and nurture within historical holistic approaches, such as the ecological, person-in-environment (PIE) perspectives, and system's theory (Berkes et al., 2008; Germain, 1973, 1979; Germain & Gitterman 1980). More contemporary theoretical approaches, such as structural and critical social work (Lundy, 2008; Macias, 2012; Mullaly, 2007), strength-based approaches (Guo & Tsui, 2010; Saleebey, 2002), and mindfulness (Kabat-Zinn, 2003; Shier & Graham, 2010) challenge workers to be contemplative about how they see themselves, their biases, the individuals they work with, and, therefore, how they might choose consequently to interact with service users. All these approaches inform the social worker's ability to practise within the broader framework of the social, ideological, economic, and political context. They also contribute to the development of a therapeutic alliance while building upon strengths with attunement and thoughtfulness. The use of the third-eye concept fits well with the goals undergraduate social work educators have to link theory to practice and develop competency, though this certainly can benefit graduate social work students as well.

THE ROLE OF LEARNING THEORY

Andragogy proposes broad conceptual guidelines in adult learning. Kolb (2014) asserts that experiential learning involves the constant adaptation and engagement with our environment, and growth and development are enhanced when students have an opportunity to directly engage with the studied phenomena. Contained in the experience are disagreements and differences that cultivate reflection, feeling, and thinking. This is what Kolb calls *transformational learning*: a process that includes concrete experience, reflective observation, abstract conceptualization, and active experimentation. Cheung and Delavega (2014) describe how the four stages of transformational learning in Kolb's learning cycle are important to competency development. They allow the learner to gain experience from concrete activities and reflect on the experience while using the experience to conceptualize knowledge and understand how to apply abstract knowledge to active experimentation (Askeland, 2003; Kolb & Kolb, 2009, as cited in Cheung & Delavega, 2014). It involves a transformational change that both is tacit and evolves awareness.

Competency Development

Urdang (2010) describes the arduous course that most helping profession students must follow to develop competency and points out the impact that the evidence-informed approach appears to be having on social work's shift away from the building of a "professional self" (p. 524). Most importantly, she indicates that evidence-based approaches to social work focus solely on outcome rather than on processes.

The helping professions of psychology, nursing, psychiatry, and social work identify the ability to look inward in a frank and unobstructed way as fundamental to good practice. Problems with competency often arise in those who are considered to be "wounded healers," students or professionals whose personal challenges stem from physiological illness/disability, family dysfunction, mental health issues, trauma experiences, or grief and loss issues (Bogo et al., 2012; Didham et al., 2011; Yip, 2006).

Social workers must be prepared for vented anger, withdrawal, or, in crisis situations, shock, psychoses, or dissociation, while keeping their personal response, the second eye, in check. Timing and accuracy are often imperative. They may be asked to play active social control roles in policing, managing, or oppressing service users against their code of ethics and personal convictions. Keeping the Canadian Association of Social Workers Code of Ethics (2005) and social justice values in the forefront is part of using the third eye. Field placements and the introduction to intervention skill classes are not always an adequate means of addressing these experiences; these teaching mediums are inconsistent across cohorts at best (Bogo et al., 2012). They may arm the student with techniques of interaction but often do not include standardized approaches that measure competency development, power relationships, or identification of decisions that are the result of the student's own unresolved issues. Competency requires a sense of suspended subjectiveness that also implies a double detachment from oppressive interactions that can be implied in many social work settings (Macias, 2012).

DEVELOPMENT AND MEASUREMENT OF COMPETENCY SKILLS

Competency development of communication skills in social work and other health care professions is now a curriculum priority. Medicine has created a standardized approach to therapeutic communication skills development with courses and oral exams that are mandatory for licensing. Barrows and Abrahamson (1964) were leaders in the field in their research on the use of a programmed patient for teaching and evaluating students. In the mid-1970s, Harden Stevenson, Downie, and Wilson (1975) designed the first objective structured clinical exam (OSCE) in human medicine, which Bogo discussed in greater detail in chapter 9. The OSCE comprises a number of stations; at each station, an examiner evaluates students on a specific skill. Following the interview with the simulated client (SC), the student engages in a reflective dialogue with the examiner and SC. Researchers and academics in many allied health professions now regard this tool as evidence based.

The Calgary Cambridge Guide (CCG) (Kurtz et al., 2005) provides templates for the therapeutic interview learning process and has been researched by medical and veterinary schools worldwide (Adams & Kurtz, 2006; Adams & Ladner, 2004; Adams et al., 2003; Harden et al., 1975; Shaw et al., 2006). It is used with simulated patient practice labs to hone therapeutic communications skills that contribute to more accurate assessments. It also suggests that these skills can be taught and learned because, for many, they are not innate (Kurtz et al., 2003). Service users who work with professional helpers who have good therapeutic communication skills are more satisfied, more engaged, and less likely to terminate the therapeutic relationship before attaining agreed upon goals (Ley, 1988). To go back to our analogy, some jockeys are more successful at coaxing a horse to work harder and successful baseball coaches have mastered the art of mentorship. Similarly, social work is compelled to look closely at how it develops competencies in one-on-one interaction.

Cheung and Delavega (2014) have adapted a four-stage model of teaching competency based on Kolb's (1984) four-stage learning model that incorporates a fifth stage of integration. They reiterate that engaging communication happens in a "spiral fashion," using the helical model, revisiting and repeating issues and concerns so that rapport and engagement grows through the interaction (Carkhuff, 2000). All these approaches employ the use of SC. Further discussion of the relevancy of their use to development of the BSW student's active self-reflection process or third eye is warranted.

Simulated Clients in Social Work Education

Studies have explored the use of SCs to develop mastery in therapeutic communication skill techniques in both undergraduate and graduate cohorts, and the results indicate that they provide an authentic, internally valid learning experience (Asakura et al., 2018; Badger & MacNeil, 2002; Bogo et al., 2017; Bogo et al., 2011, 2013; Miller, 2002, 2004; Mooradian, 2008; Petracchi & Collins, 2006; Rogers & Welch, 2009). The use of SCs differs from role-play in the sense that actors are trained to portray a particular service-user case in a replicable fashion. The array of emotions when engaging with a "friendly-stranger" are new to the social work student and provide a learning opportunity that can rarely be experienced otherwise inside the classroom. The experience of anxiety and excitement, among other subjective emotions, cultivates an authentic learning opportunity that is located as internally in the body as it is externally in the experience (Jordi, 2011).

Qualitative data suggest that social work supervisors struggle with failing underperforming social work interns in field placement experiences, losing opportunities to provide transformational learning for students (Tupling, 2015). Despite the use of mandatory skills training in a number of helping professions, little follow-up data exist that measure the accurate use of therapeutic communication skills in practice (Shaw et al., 2006). This led to the creation of a standardized approach to developing therapeutic communication practice in a small satellite campus in southern Ontario.

Case in Point: Introduction of a Simulated Client Program

One way to cultivate BSW students' capacity to use their third eye is to provide opportunities to practise in a safe environment with service users who can step in and out of the roles they portray. Structured interactions provide students with immediate feedback from faculty or peer observers, as well as the SC. SCs are trained to give specific feedback regarding students' tone, verbal and non-verbal behaviour, body language, and demeanour. This has been useful, students report, for improving their skills, promoting self-reflection, and incorporating theory into practice. How this is accomplished relies heavily on the faculty-student interaction as well. As with the subtle three-way interaction between coach, horse, and rider, subtle feel or practice wisdom is fundamental to good habits. Harsh, disrespectful, or bullying approaches towards the horse or rider by coaches can undermine the risk-taking required to achieve self-awareness. Being open to that experience means the horse and rider must both be open to making mistakes. Likewise in professional baseball, rookies, new practitioners, are not suddenly introduced into situations where they play in front of thousands of spectators but are slowly mentored through the minor leagues, enhancing their skills until ready to perform – and even then they practise before every game under the supervision of multiple coaches, each specializing in a different part of the game. This same principle applies to introducing students to working with simulated service users and mentors. Taking risks to develop skills comes with the creation of trust, positive reinforcement, and the building of the student's confidence to be reflective.

The Program

In fall 2012, the School of Social Work at Laurentian University in Barrie, Ontario, began to pilot the use of SCs in a second-year BSW basic intervention skills' course. The program uses a structural approach (Lundy, 2008; Mullaly, 2007), viewing social work through a systemic lens of social justice and inequity. The specific course focuses on an outline for human-to-human interaction (context, sequence of an interaction over time) and process (developing rapport, building a relationship, establishing trust, dealing with ethical considerations, probing, and challenging). The SCs were trained using biographical profiles that would become apparent to students only if they used their skills effectively. In the classroom, students were divided into small groups or pods, and each student rotated through the role of counsellor in the pod, to experience and observe the interaction with the SC, with class size limited to 15 students. In the course, students are provided with a copy of the CCG (Kurtz et al., 2017) to learn how to structure the interview and a lab manual (Yorke, 2005) that scaffolds skills and exercises across 13 three-hour units over the 26-week semester that includes readings, two videos, and self-reflective assignments. Self-critiques of videos provide additional opportunities for self-reflection. Students processed each interaction with their group members and, where possible, a facilitator (faculty, agency social worker) using the wrap-around model (Yorke, 2005), which focuses on the learning goals of each student counsellor in the five-person pods.

The feedback to the student counsellor is meant to facilitate objective self-analysis and acceptance of constructive feedback, and facilitate bringing the unconscious to the conscious, thus provoking an emotionally significant experience for the recipient. The combination of the lab manual exercises, videos, work with the simulated clients, and biweekly small-group experiences is designed to increase active self-monitoring and help students feel comfortable with feedback and their observation by others.

The Study

This small, ethically approved pilot project, with four individual interviews and three focus groups, collected qualitative feedback from 29 students. The qualitative data were coded and suggested that students working with SC felt it was like working with a real service user and that the program helped develop their self-awareness, confidence, and competency. The observational data were different.

Using the CCG (Kurtz et al., 2003) template to review subsequent final video assignments of random students in the pilot cohort, researchers did not identify an expected increase in student competency conducting clinical interviews (Yorke et al., 2012).

These pilot results suggested that the CCG template was measuring the structure and sequence of a clinical interview but was not measuring the emotionally significant experience and student reflexivity, despite the feedback from students to the contrary. Students reported that the SC, videos, and small-group experiences combined were useful for developing reflexivity and use of their third eye. However, the CCG does incorporate ways of measuring behaviour and how to conduct an interview. The researchers concluded the use of a tool that better captures the relationship between competency and the use of the third eye or active reflexivity would be useful.

Conclusion

This chapter was intended to make a case for exploring the use of practice labs with SCs to assist adult students to have transformational, emotionally significant experiences designed to contribute to the development of their third eye. This includes the student's experience of conscious and unconscious *aha* moments that move learning from the external development of techniques, devoid of internal understanding of self, power, and structural social implications and consequences, to the internal development of double detachment, empathy, and ultimately, critically self-aware, anti-oppressive practice.

Like the horse and rider, or the pitcher and the batter facing each other on a baseball diamond, development of the third eye requires the ability to watch ourselves from outside the interaction to determine strategically how to be successful. The cultivation of the third eye cannot be pedagogically instilled because it requires an emotionally significant experience on the part of the learner. Finding unique and engaging ways to create that experience means embracing experiential and transformative teaching in social work education.

REFERENCES

Adams, C., & Kurtz, S. (2006). Building on existing models from human medical education to develop a communication curriculum in veterinary medicine. *Journal of Veterinary Medical Education, 33*(1), 28–37. https://doi.org/10.3138/jvme.33.1.28

Adams, C. L., & Ladner, L. (2004). Implementing a simulated client program: Bridging the gap between theory and practice. *Journal of Veterinary Medical Education, 31*(2), 138–45. https://doi.org/10.3138/jvme.31.2.138

Adams, C., Nestel, D., & Wolf, P. (2003). Reflection: A critical proficiency essential to the effective development of a high competence in communication. *Journal of Veterinary Medical Education, 33*(1), 58–64. https://doi.org/10.3138/jvme.33.1.58

Asakura, K., Bogo, M., Good, B., & Power, R. (2018). Social work serial: Using video-recorded simulated client sessions to teach social work practice. *Journal of Social Work Education, 54*(2), 397–404. https://doi.org/10.1080/10437797.2017.1404525

Askeland, G. (2003). Reality-play – Experiential learning in social work training. *Social Work Education, 22*(4), 351–62.

Badger, L. W., & MacNeil, G. (2002). Standardized clients in the classroom: A novel instructional technique for social work educators. *Research on Social Work Practice, 12*(3), 364–74. https://doi.org/10.1177/104973150201200300

Barrows, H., & Abrahamson, S. (1964). The programed patient: A teaching technique for appraising student performance in clinical neurology. *Journal of Medical Education, 39*(8), 802–5.

Berkes, F., Colding, J., & Folke, C. (Eds.). (2008). *Navigating social-ecological systems: Building resilience for complexity and change.* Cambridge University Press.

Bogo, M., Katz, E., Regehr, C., Logie, C., Mylopoulos, M., & Tufford, L. (2013). Toward understanding meta-competence: An analysis of students' reflection on their simulated interviews. *Social Work Education, 32*(2), 259–73. https://doi.org/10.1080/02615479.2012.738662

Bogo, M., Lee, B., McKee, E., Ramjattan, R., & Baird, S. L. (2017). Bridging class and field: Field instructors' and liaisons' reactions to information about students' baseline performance derived from simulated interviews. *Journal of*

Social Work Education, 53(4), 580–94. https://doi.org/10.1080/10437797.2017.1283269

Bogo, M., Regehr, C., Katz, K., Logie, L., Tufford, L., & Litvack, A. (2012). Evaluating an objective structured clinical examination (OSCE) adapted for social work. *Research on Social Work Practice, 22*(4), 428–36. https://doi.org/10.1177/1049731512437557

Bogo, M., Regehr, C., Logie, C., Katz, E., Mylopoulos, M., & Regehr, G. (2011). Adapting objective structured clinical examinations to assess social work student's performance and reflections. *Journal of Social Work Education, 47*(1), 5–18. https://doi.org/10.5175/jswe.2011.200900036

Canadian Association of Social Workers. (2005). *Code of ethics.*

Canadian Council of Social Work Regulators. (2017). *Entry-level competency profile for the social work profession in Canada.* http://www.ccswr-ccorts.ca/wp-content/uploads/2017/03/Competency-Profile-FINAL-Eng-PG-1-51.pdf

Carkhuff, R. (2000). *The art of helping in the 21st century.* Human Resource Development Press.

Cheung, M., & Delavega, E. (2014). Five-way experiential learning model for social work education. *Social Work Education, 33*(8), 1070–87. https://doi.org/10.1080/02615479.2014.925538

Didham, S., Dromgole, L., Csiernik, R., Karley, M. L., & Hurley, D. (2011). Trauma exposure and the social work practicum. *Journal of Teaching in Social Work, 31*(5), 523–37. https://doi.org/10.1080/08841233.2011.615261

Germain, C. (1973). An ecological perspective in casework practice. *Social Casework, 54*(6), 323–30. https://doi.org/10.1177/104438947305400601

Germain, C. (1979). *Social work practice, people and environments.* Columbia University Press.

Germain, C. B., & Gitterman, A. (1980). *The life model of social work practice.* Columbia University Press.

Guo, W., & Tsui, M. (2010). From resilience to resistance: A reconstruction of the strengths-based perspective in social work practice. *International Social Work, 53*(2), 233–45. https://doi.org/10.1177/0020872809355391

Harden, R., Stevenson, M., Downie, W., & Wilson. (1975). Assessment of clinical competence using objective structured examination. *British Medical Journal, 1*(5955), 447–51. https://doi.org/10.1136/bmj.1.5955.447

Jordi, R. (2011). Reframing the concept of reflection: Consciousness, experiential learning, and reflective learning practices. *Adult Education Quarterly, 61*(2), 181–97. https://doi.org/10.1177/0741713610380439

Kabat-Zinn, J. (2003). Mindfulness-based interventions in context: Past, present and future. *Clinical Psychology: Science and Practice, 10*(2), 144–56. https://doi.org/10.1093/clipsy.bpg016

Kolb, D. A. (2014). *Experiential learning: Experience as the source of learning and development* (2nd ed.). FT Press.

Kurtz, S., Draper, J., & Silverman, J. (2017). *Teaching and learning communication skills in medicine* (2nd ed.). CRC Press.

Kurtz, S., Silverman, J., Benson, J., & Draper, J. (2003). Marrying content and process in clinical method teaching: Enhancing the Calgary Cambridge guides. *Academic Medicine, 78*(8), 802–8. https://doi.org/10.1097/00001888-200308000-00011

Ley, P. (1988). *Communicating with patients: Improving communication, satisfaction and compliance.* Croom Helm.

Lundy, C. (2008). *Social work and social justice: A structural approach to practice.* University of Toronto Press.

Macias, T. (2012). "In the world": Toward a Foucauldian ethic of reading in social work. *Intersectionalities: A Global Journal of Social Work Analysis Research Polity and Practice, 1*(1), 1–19.

Miller, M. (2002). Standardized clients: An innovative approach to practice learning. *Social Work Education, 21*(6), 663–70. https://doi.org/10.1080/0261547022000026373

Miller, M. (2004). Implementing standardized client education in a combined BSW and MSW program. *Journal of Social Work Education, 40*(1), 87–102. https://doi.org/10.1080/10437797.2004.10778481

Mooradian, J. K. (2008). Using simulated session to enhance clinical social work education. *Journal of Social Work Education, 44*(1), 21–35. https://doi.org/10.5175/jswe.2008.200700026

Mullaly, R. P. (2007). *The new structural social work.* Oxford University Press.

O'Sullivan, T. (2005). Some theoretical propositions on the nature of practice wisdom. *Journal of Social Work, 5*(2), 221–42. https://doi.org/10.1177/1468017305054977

Petracchi, H. E., & Collins, K. S. (2006). Utilizing actors to simulate clients in social work student role plays: Does this approach have a place in social work education? *Journal of Teaching in Social Work, 26*(1/2), 223–33. https://doi.org/10.1300/j067v26n01_13

Rogers, A., & Welch, B. (2009). Using standardized clients in the classroom: An evaluation of a training module to teach active listening skills to social work students. *Journal of Teaching in Social Work, 29*(2), 153–68. https://doi.org/10.1080/08841230802238203

Saleebey, D. (2002). *The strengths perspective in social work practice.* Allyn & Bacon.

Schon, D. (1983). *The reflective practitioner: How professionals think in action.* Basic Books.

Shaw, J., Bonnett, B., Adams, C., & Roter, D. (2006). Veterinary-client-patient communication patterns used during clinical appointments in companion animal practice. *Journal of the American Veterinary Medical Association, 28*(5), 714–21. https://doi.org/10.2460/javma.228.5.714

Shier, M., & Graham, J. (2010). Mindfulness, subjective well-being, and social work: Insight into their interconnection from social work practitioners. *Social Work Education, 30*(1), 29–44. https://doi.org/10.1080/02615471003763188

Swift, S. (1985). *Centered riding.* Ebury Press.

Tupling, P. (2015). *Gatekeeping and social work: Failing students in field placements* [Unpublished master's thesis]. School of Social Work, Laurentian University.

Urdang, E. (2010). Awareness of self: A critical tool. *Social Work Education, 29*(5), 523–38. https://doi.org/10.1080/02615470903164950

Yip, K. (2006). Self-reflection in a reflective practice: A note of caution. *British Journal of Social Work, 36*(5), 777–88. https://doi.org/10.1093/bjsw/bch323

Yorke, J. (2005). *Lab manual for social work students* [Unpublished manuscript]. School of Social Work, Laurentian University.

Yorke, J., Grant, S., & Craggs, M. (2012). *A mixed method pilot study of the use of simulated clients as a teaching tool with social work students* [Unpublished manuscript]. School of Social Work, Laurentian University.

14 Bridging the Micro-Macro Divide: Making Policy Relevant to Social Work Students

TRACY SMITH CARRIER AND BHARATI SETHI

While the social work profession is quick to acknowledge the importance of macro-level practice, students and instructors in schools of social work continue to be wary of a growing micro-macro divide. To combat this binary thinking, this chapter adopts a social justice approach to the practice of social policy. Although students recognize that social justice is one of the core tenets of the profession, they struggle to understand the profound connection between social policy, social work, and social justice. Bridging the micro-macro divide and strengthening the integration of policy in direct practice education are essential to equipping social work graduates with the skills and tools necessary for practice with oppressed and marginalized populations. Having heard from students that social policy courses can be branded as dry or abstract, we discuss how direct practice at the macro level can be reimagined and revitalized, not as ancillary knowledge for social workers but as a quintessential expression of the profession. Reflecting on our own experiences as instructors in the academe, we provide examples and make suggestions on how to implement social policy objectives in social work curricula to better prepare students for meaningful and equitable social work practice.

Reflexivity: Positions of the Authors

As social work educators, we recognize that we must be part of the solution in addressing the tension between micro and macro practice in social work curricula. It is important to situate ourselves by providing insight into our social locations, how we bring intersections of our

---

The two authors' contributions to the chapter were equal, leading to a different presentation in the table of contents and introduction to this section.

identity into our teaching, and why these matter for us and for our students. Both authors have been teaching social policy courses in social work postsecondary educational institutes for approximately eight years, at both the undergraduate and the graduate levels. Four years ago, we came together as new academics at a small liberal arts college in southwestern Ontario. We confess that although we do not have practice wisdom amassed over decades, in our relatively short time as instructors, we have experimented with multiple strategies to improve our social policy courses to make them transformative sites where critical thinking, reflection, and active learning can readily take place.

We are women and have personally encountered racism, specifically Bharati, who is of Southeast Asian descent. In addition, Tracy has faced discrimination, challenges, and inequities based on class, gender, and family status as she has raised three children, with her partner, over her academic career. These intersections help us talk about oppression and social justice, not from a seemingly aloof abstract standpoint but from an all too familiar and personal one. For example, when we discuss income security programs, we typically employ a case study approach, including personal reflections on how such programs have fallen short in our own lives. Being an immigrant, without legal immigration status, provided little access to important health and income benefits for Bharati; having a child during her doctoral studies meant that Tracy had insufficient work hours to qualify for Employment Insurance. It is because of our lived experiences that we can spell out the direct impact public policies can have on people. As Breton et al. (2003) aptly argue, "social injustices cannot be dealt with in any significant way without dealing with the policies that create or exacerbate them, nor can social justice be pursued effectively without promoting social policies" (p. 4).

Critical Themes

A substantial literature base has emerged discussing the merits of policy education in social work. Concomitantly, a smaller amount of scholarship has amassed on how to equip social work graduates with the interest, knowledge, and skills to successfully engage in policy practice. Below, we discuss three critical themes in this regard.

The Ostensible Micro-Macro Divide

The tension and divisiveness related to the micro-macro divide, social workers' role as direct practitioners (social work as a cause), and their role as policy advocates (social work as a function) that came to the fore in the late 1920s still persists (Austin et al., 2016). From our perspective, there is currently a penchant among large swathes of social work students to pursue micro-level work that is directed towards the individual, couple, or family. The present *specialization era* and the migration of the profession towards practice specialties and therapeutic modalities have further solidified the ostensible micro-macro divide. This leaves less space for students to appreciate, and aim to practise, across the multiplicity of social work practice roles and settings (Sherraden et al., 2015; Weiss et al., 2006; Wyers, 1991), particularly those taking indirect practice form in examining community, policy, and organizational issues. Sadly, and incorrectly, some direct practice students do not consider policy practice as a key part of their role. In turn, policy-oriented social work educators become concerned regarding the lack of policy content in social work curricula, the lack of integration of policy content within social work practice courses, and the proclivity of some clinical social workers to see policy issues as ancillary to the intrapersonal or interpersonal dilemmas of their service users (Strier & Feldman, 2018; Wyers, 1991).

How does policy practice fit within direct practice social work? This unanswered question intricately connects to the ongoing generalist-specialist debate (Breton et al., 2003). For instance, we have found that students tend to prefer micro-level field placements rather than policy-oriented ones, believing that they are more likely to secure paid employment in direct practice settings (Mendes, 2003). The partitioning of micro- and macro-level courses in social work curricula (Weiss et al., 2006), together with the romanticization of highly specialized therapeutic training, contributes to what we see as the growing micro-level orientation of students. Yet this bifurcation leads to the inability of some students to comprehend that casework and social policy are not distinct fields of expertise (Fisher & Karger, 1997), and that the integration of policy in direct practice and field education is essential, not only to increase social work students' understanding of social, economic, and political social justice issues, but to link these issues within the specific context of their service users' lives. In other words, the personal is indeed political. One way that educators can aid students to make the connection between social work practice and social policy is by continually integrating social policy and its implications within non-policy social work courses and field practice (Weiss et al., 2006). If social work educators do not unify "the bifurcated structure of social work, it would be difficult to adequately address issues of social justice, power, and oppression" (Vodde & Gallant, 2002, p. 439).

The micro-macro divide is, in fact, contrived and socially constructed. This division situates these domains as "binary opposites" that pose "artificial boundaries and hierarchies" (Vodde & Gallant, 2002, p. 440).

Examining this schism through a postmodern lens, Vodde and Gallant (2002) offer a narrative deconstructive model that reveals the bifurcation of micro-macro practice as myth and seeks to unify direct practice with larger goals of social change and social justice. Through this lens, the authors demonstrate how discourses internalized by individuals can be identified and dispelled, and new preferred narratives can be created. Lock et al. (2005), for example, elucidate how the discourses surrounding anorexia and bulimia shape the construction of these eating disorders, and how resistance can be mobilized to unsettle them. Here, internalizing and pathologizing problems are externalized and defined as distinct from the individual, recognizing that "the person is not the problem, the problem is the problem" (Lock et al., 2005, p. 322). In this way, harmful narratives are unmasked and made visible, releasing or loosening the shame that typically accompanies them (Vodde & Gallant, 2002). In each case, issues that the service user is experiencing at the individual level, such as a job loss, or a housing eviction, are understood through a structural lens. This lens clearly identifies how related policies interact and come to bear on the service user's life and what can be done to advocate for change. The difficulty associated with securing safe and affordable child care, for instance, is not an individual problem of the service user but one that many parents experience in the face of lengthy and protracted wait-lists, ever-rising costs, and inadequate facility hours for people working in jobs outside the standard workday. Here, the decision of policymakers to introduce affordable daycare programs, augment childcare benefits, or to simply do nothing in response really matters, effecting direct practice options.

Praxis, the synthesis of reflection and action, is about not only recognizing the externalities of personal narratives but also doing something about them! Indeed, as Vodde and Gallant (2002) point out, Epston's (1993) work was not only about locating the structural roots of individual "problems" and envisioning new narratives to replace them, but also about linking service users with others sharing similar narratives, to build their social support networks and to foster activism and social change. A social-justice-oriented perspective honours the agency of service users, assisting them to transform their consciousness from victims to agents so that they can participate in their own liberation (Baines, 2011). This focus appears amiss in some direct practice courses. Preferring to work with the individual or family's presenting problems, some students are not always cognizant of how direct practice translates into action to remedy the discursive relations, broader structures, and immediate environment from which these problems actually arise. The limits of micro-level clinical social work are visible at this juncture. In leaving the therapeutic session, service users must re-engage in the same familial, school, work, and societal environments from which their problem(s) emerge. Without plans to remedy these structures and relations, social work practice has limited impact. Direct practice must therefore move beyond "fixing the client" to treat the social relations and broken systems within which they interact. The integration of macro realities into micro-level instruction is thus essential.

Students' Apprehension of Policy Practice

Students perceive policy practice to be vital to the social work profession while often believing social policy courses to be boring (Henman, 2012), abstract (Sherraden et al., 2015), or inapplicable to direct social work practice (Weiss et al., 2006). Several reasons have been posited to account for students' lack of interest in social policy (Henman, 2012) with a dominant, though faulty, theme being: "I won't ever have to use this" (Sherraden et al., 2015, p. 310). Misperceptions about the profession proliferate, as students, perhaps unintentionally, mirror a neo-liberal individualist perspective, resulting in policy practice taking "a backseat to clinical practice" (Sherraden et al., 2015, p. 309). Not surprisingly, then, students may find it difficult to make sense of a structural social policy perspective, specifically the link between how social policies play out in individuals' daily lives (Henman, 2012). Students can also often believe that policy practice is "too big" and "intimidating" (Sherraden et al., 2015, p. 315). Personal agency in policy practice may therefore appear overwhelming, idealistic, and, ultimately, impractical. Moreover, there is often marginal, if any, social policy content in direct practice subjects or field education practicums (Csiernik, 2001; Csiernik & Karley, 2004; Pawar, 2004). Indeed, as Mendes (2003) notes, "most social policy subjects are taught separately from social work theory and practice subjects. This distinction appears to leave social work students with the impression that social policy is simply about theoretical knowledge, without any need for practical application" (p. 220). Additionally, the separation of social policy from social work theory and practice subjects and the subordinate position of policy within social work curricula make the teaching of social policy far less successful.

Effective Teaching Approaches in Policy Social Work Education

A common yet overly simplistic assumption is that students must first acquire knowledge to effectively apply it. However, Gregory and Holloway (2005) contend that even when students appear to have acquired the requisite knowledge related to a specific concept or phenomenon, they will not fully comprehend it until they have put it into practice. Consequently, a purely didactic instructional approach may work well with motivated students who can personally relate to the course content, yet it would be a poor way to engage learners who palpably feel disconnected from it. Strategies that promote learning by doing are part of an effective pedagogical approach that uses both real and simulated practice situations (Doel & Shardlow, 2005).

Active learning, experiential learning, service learning, and *hands-on learning* or *high-impact practices,* terms that have, erroneously, been used interchangeably, have recently emerged in the literature to depict signature pedagogical approaches shown to be "more effective" in deepening student learning (Weiss et al., 2006, p. 797). Consequently, Weiss et al. (2006) argue that traditional instructor-centred methods, involving lectures or didactic instruction, are not as effective as student-centred approaches involving, for example, open-group discussions, problem-based learning, simulation games, and case analyses. These findings are echoed in relation to social policy courses specifically. Evaluations of policy practice courses that incorporate experiential learning components have shown more favourable attitudes among students towards policy practice, an increase in confidence in their ability to carry it out (Keller et al., 2001), and consequently, a higher likelihood of engagement to redress policy failings (Saulnier, 2000). However, because of growing class sizes and reductions in teacher support resources, some policy teachers have found it more practical to integrate teacher-centred learning with student-centred learning models (Pawar, 2004).

Active learning approaches can involve the use of field trips (Henman, 2012; Pawar, 2004), simulation games (Pawar, 2004), small-group discussions (Henman, 2012), or free group discussions of "hot policy topics" (Henman, 2012, p. 341). The structured debate has also been shown to be effective in enhancing students' critical thinking skills and social policy learning and confidence in public speaking, all of which are necessary to pursue policy-oriented activities and influence social policy. Through such debates, students gain the skills necessary to effectively critique the opposing group's policy position and defend their policy stance (Keller et al., 2001). Weiss-Gal (2016) notes that through the integration of policy-related activities, including policy analyses, the use of popular or mass media, and legislative advocacy, students' perceived efficacy in policy practice improves. The author found that these activities were vital in creating the awareness that policy practice "is relevant to all social workers, that social workers can contribute to policy processes and that they should be key players in policy change" (Weiss-Gal, 2016, p. 298).

Henman (2012) suggests that policy practice educators must aim to make the link between social policy and students' individual and professional lives transparent and clear. Further, the courses must demonstrate the ways in which students, as future social workers, can participate and contribute to the policy process. The social work educator's passion should be apparent and be used to ignite students' own enthusiasm for social policy. We would argue that while the social work educator's passion and enthusiasm for policy class is important to student learning and comprehension, it is not sufficient to make social policy courses attractive. In fact, from our experience, and as affirmed in social work pedagogical literature (Henman, 2012), students may perform well in policy courses, even when they are disinterested in the subject. It is imperative that social work faculty "renew their efforts in this era of specialization to collaboratively teach micro and macro practice in teaching teams" (Austin et al., 2016, p. 270). To clarify, we are not only referring to instructors who teach macro-level courses. For us, meaningful collaboration, in the interest of the profession's goal of social justice, means infusing policy courses into micro social work curricula and finding spaces for direct practice and policy-oriented social work educators to work together and instill the importance of social policy at all levels of practice. Furthermore, social work leaders must recognize the significance of policy practice and be accountable to the profession's historic social justice and social action goals that have been weakened and "replaced by individualism and therapeutic interventions" (Mattocks, 2018, p. 7).

Teaching Social Policy: What We Have Learned

We entered social work to promote social justice and social change through our research and education. We hoped that, through modelling our passion for policy practice and providing real-life stories from our field work and professional lives, we could draw students' attention to the significance of policy in social work. For example, Bharati uses findings from her arts-based research (Sethi, 2014) in her classroom to inform students about the integration issues that immigrants and refugees recurrently experience in Canada. Tracy frequently conducts a poverty simulation in her classes to debunk poverty myths, build empathy, and prompt social action among her students (Smith-Carrier et al., 2018). Through our commitment to the teacher-scholar model, where research informs teaching and teaching informs research, we aim to enhance our teaching and stimulate student learning by providing students with the knowledge base to build their own evidence-informed processes (Thyer & Pignotti, 2011) and change strategies.

Although social work education research points to several reasons why students may lack interest in policy practice, obscured in the literature is clarity related to how to educate students to explicate the meaning of social policy and its many applications in everyday life. Often, policy courses invoke fear in students; many equate policy with politics, matters that they feel ill-prepared to consider. Thus, questions asking, "What is policy? How do students understand it? What aspects of life are governed by policy?" are at the forefront of our policy curriculum design, and we aim to work cooperatively to ensure a seamless integration of course materials and concepts. In a required course, during their first year of undergraduate social work education, students learn the basics of social policy with Bharati, and in a future course with Tracy, they review and apply concepts in more depth. Even though we provide students with many case examples, we have still found that students' dislike of policy stems in part from their lack of understanding of what policy is. Students also struggle with the relevance of policy and how it matters, not only to service users but to them personally.

Interestingly, in a class taught by Tracy, most students, when asked to reflect on their thoughts and feelings in relation to social policy, suggested that fear and anxiety came to the forefront of their minds and bodies. Sitting with these emotions, students were asked why social policy courses seem to be associated with such reactions. Some suggested that social policy is branded in a way that gives them the impression that, like other mandatory courses such as statistics or research methods, they "won't like it but need to take it" as part of the professional program. Delving into a discussion of where these ideas come from, students were asked if they felt it was important that social workers learn about policy; they all indicated with hands raised that indeed it was. Yet when asked if they personally were interested in learning about social policy, only a few hands stayed up. As a class, we reflected on this apparent disconnect. Students were then asked to think of any part of their life and/or some aspect of human functioning not governed in some way by social policy. Few, if any, instances appear to exist. Discussions such as these concretely link the conditions of everyday life to policy and its varied manifestations.

Recommendations for Teaching Policy

We employ several strategies to engage and educate students on the importance of policy practice in social work. Tracy begins every course with a What's New in the News story. Students are asked to share their own news clips, and the class collectively considers controversial or "juicy" topics, using video clips. In this way, students are encouraged to keep abreast of local news stories, take an active role in critically analysing the way current events are framed, and discuss ways to get involved for change.

Bharati uses a Face of Policy reflection exercise in which students work in dyads to reflect upon their own oppression and the relationships and circumstances in their lives that have positively influenced them. Using sticky notes, students write the key factors that have influenced their life, both positively and negatively. As they go deeper into each factor, they come to a place where formerly abstract policies come alive; they recognize the face of policy and how it directly impacts their lives. Following this reflection exercise, students submit a written assignment where they focus on a policy that has impacted them personally. They are encouraged to link the concepts they have learned in class to their past experiences, thereby integrating policy with their real-life examples.

In the Flower of Power exercise (Barry & Greencorn, n.d.), students are invited to visualize how their multiple and intersecting social locations, such as age, class, gender, race, and ability, marginalize or privilege them. Specifically, they are encouraged to reflect on these social locations vis-à-vis the policies that have been advantageous or disadvantageous to them. A fundamental concept that runs through and solidifies the courses is the person-environment fit or lack of fit in relation to policy practice. This framework is also brought to life through social media, videos, arts-based methods, case studies, and guest lectures.

Conclusion

In the age of intense globalization, increased migration, and political and economic unrest, it is time for the social work community to come together and engage in essential conversations about how to rectify the imbalance between micro and macro social work in our educational curricula and social work practice. Such an "effort reflects and reinforces the understanding that social problems require complex and sustained intervention at all levels of social work practice" (Rothman & Mizrahi, 2014, p. 91). Re-envisioning future social work education means not conceding to a neo-liberal agenda of individualism; rather, it problematizes the contrived boundary between direct practice and policy work and engages in critical reflection of the person-in-environment. If this fit is critical to social work thinking, then students require a solid foundation that enables them to challenge the artificial boundaries of macro and micro practice and prepares them to proficiently redress the policy failures that create problems for service users (Weiss-Gal, 2016).

REFERENCES

Austin, M. J., Anthony, E. K, Knee, R. T., & Mathias, J. (2016). Revisiting the relationship between micro and macro social work practice. *Families in Society: The Journal of Contemporary Social Services, 97*(4), 270–7. https://doi.org/10.1606/1044-3894.2016.97.33

Baines, D. (Ed.). (2011). *Doing anti-oppressive practice: Social justice social work* (2nd ed.). Fernwood Publishing.

Barry, P., & Greencorn, M. (n.d.). *Power Flower: Exploring notions of diversity, power, and privilege.* Mount Saint Vincent University. http://www.msvu.ca/site/media/msvu/Documents/POWER_flower.pdf

Breton, M., Cox, E. O., & Taylor, S. (2003). Social justice, social policy, and social work: Securing the connection. *The Social Policy Journal, 2*(1), 3–20. https://doi.org/10.1300/j185v02n01_02

Csiernik, R. (2001). The practice of field work: What social work students actually do in the field. *Canadian Social Work,* 3(2), 9–20.

Csiernik, R., & Karley, M. L. (2004). The experience of social work practicum: Activities in the field. *Currents: New Scholarship in the Human Services,* 3(2), 1–24.

Doel, M., & Shardlow, S. M. (2005). *Modern social work practice: Teaching and learning in practice settings.* Routledge.

Epston, D. (1993, October). *A narrative therapy with eating disorders: The work of the Anti-anorexia/Bulimia League* [therapy training workshop]. The Gallant Center, Atlanta, GA, United States.

Fisher, R., & Karger, H. J. (1997). *Social work and community in a private world.* Longman.

Gregory, M., & Holloway, M. (2005). The debate as a pedagogic tool in social policy for social work students. *Social Work Education, 24*(6), 617–37. https://doi.org/10.1080/02615470500182132

Henman, P. (2012). Making social policy "sexy": Evaluating a teaching innovation. *Australian Social Work, 65*(3), 341–54. https://doi.org/10.1080/0312407x.2011.652139

Keller, T., Whittaker, J., & Burke, T. (2001). Student debates in policy courses: Promoting policy practice skills and knowledge through active learning. *Journal of Social Work Education, 37*(2), 343–55. https://doi.org/10.1080/10437797.2001.10779059

Lock, A., Epston, D., Maisel, R., & Faria, N. D. (2005). Resisting anorexia/bulimia: Foucauldian perspectives in narrative therapy. *British Journal of Guidance & Counselling, 33*(3), 315–32. https://doi.org/10.1080/03069880500179459

Mattocks, N. (2018). Social action among social work practitioners: Examining the micro–macro divide. *Social Work, 63*(1), 7–16. https://doi.org/10.1093/sw/swx057

Mendes, P. (2003). Teaching social policy to social work students: A critical reflection. *Australian Social Work, 56*(3), 230–3. https://doi.org/10.1046/j.0312-407x.2003.00079.x

Pawar, M. (2004). Social policy curricula for training social workers: Towards a model. *Australian Social Work, 57*(1), 3–18. https://doi.org/10.1111/j.0312-407x.2003.00110.x

Rothman, J., & Mizrahi, T. (2014). Balancing micro and macro practice: A challenge for social work [Commentary]. *Social Work, 59*(1), 91–3. https://doi.org/10.1093/sw/swt067

Saulnier, C. F. (2000). Policy practice: Training direct service social workers to get involved. *Journal of Teaching in Social Work, 20*(1/2), 121–44. https://doi.org/10.1300/j067v20n01_08

Sethi, B. (2014). *Intersectional exposures: Exploring the health effect of employment with KAAJAL immigrant/refugee women in Grand Erie through Photovoice* (Paper 1659) [Doctoral dissertation. Wilfrid Laurier University]. Scholars Commons @ Laurier. http://scholars.wlu.ca/cgi/viewcontent.cgi?article=2737&context=etd

Sherraden, M., Guo, B., & Umbertino, C. (2015). Solving current social challenges: Engaging undergraduates in policy practice. *Journal of Policy Practice, 14*(3/4), 308–32. https://doi.org/10.1080/15588742.2014.956972

Smith-Carrier, T., Leacy, K., Sangster Bouck, M., Justrabo, J., & Decker Pierce, B. (2018). Living with poverty: A simulation. *Journal of Social Work.* https://doi.org/10.1177/1468017318766429

Strier, R., & Feldman, G. (2018). Reengineering social work's political passion: Policy practice and neo-liberalism, *The British Journal of Social Work, 48*(3), 751–68. https://doi.org/10.1093/bjsw/bcx064

Thyer, B. A., & Pignotti, M. (2011). Evidence-based practices do not exist. *Clinical Social Work Journal, 39*(4), 328. https://doi.org/10.1007/s10615-011-0358-x

Vodde, R., & Gallant, J. P. (2002). Bridging the gap between micro and macro practice: Large scale change and a unified model of narrative-deconstructive practice. *Journal of Social Work Education, 38*(3), 439–59. https://doi.org/10.1080/10437797.2002.10779109

Weiss, I., Gal, J., & Katan, J. (2006). Social policy for social work: A teaching agenda. *British Journal of Social Work, 36*(5), 789–806. https://doi.org/10.1093/bjsw/bch324

Weiss-Gal, I. (2016). Policy practice in social work education: A literature review. *International Journal of Social Welfare, 25*(3), 290–303. https://doi.org/10.1111/ijsw.12203

Wyers, N. L. (1991). Policy-practice in social work: Models and issues. *Journal of Social Work Education, 27*(3), 241–50. https://doi.org/10.1080/10437797.1991.10672196

15 Navigating Real-World Research Steps: Behind the Scenes

RACHEL BIRNBAUM

Research is a journey. Along the way are a number of steps that begin with thinking about what you want to explore, where you want to go, what you need to know about how to get there, what you need to take with you, and what you may learn. Real-world research, that is, research done outside the classroom, is the same process. The research journey begins with planning the tasks – research ethics review, budgeting and logistics, how and where to obtain the sample, data collection, type of data analysis, report writing, and knowledge translation – to facilitate your journey and reach the goal. After the journey is over, the mistakes made and lessons learned along the way become clear, and the process is complete. What also becomes clear while travelling in the real world of research, the world where social workers practise their profession with people and organizations, is that what students learn in theory about research and how they apply what they have learned are often very different experiences.

All students are exposed to research studies, which are typically well planned, designed, and presented. Each study has a beginning that explains and explores the research question, the sample size, and the data analysis and implications from quantitative, qualitative, or mixed methods approaches. Additionally, voluminous research textbooks written about methodology, design, and sampling provide students with the "how to" of research (Creswell, 1998; Csiernik & Birnbaum, 2016; Grinnell & Unrau, 2011; Neuman, 2014; Rubin & Babbie, 2017). Yet there is a paucity of literature about the context of the research activities (Gray, 2014; Robson & McCartan, 2016). By context, I refer to the actual doing of research activities and the behind the scenes events that make or break the research study. In addition, little is written about the issues raised by the participants as a result of their involvement in and with the researchers' journey. This makes it appear as if the research activities/context can be separated from the process and participants.

Using a case vignette, this chapter explores the context of the research process that can be seen as either a contributory or a challenging factor in carrying out real-world research outside the classroom versus the mechanics of learning the research steps alone. The case vignette illustrates one of the author's research projects about, and for, children involved in separation/divorce. The goal is to illustrate the value of teaching social work students that real-world research is not solely about knowing and understanding the methodology and design of any research project; knowing and understanding the context can be a learning experience all on its own.

Context

Children's participatory rights in separation and divorce has been a topic of debate by academics and policymakers for years. Rodham (1973) stated more than 40 years ago that "the phrase 'children's right's' is a slogan in search of a definition" (p. 487). Despite the recognition of the rights of children, which is supported by the adoption of the United Nations Convention on the Rights of the Child that guarantees children the right to express views on matters that affect them (Article 12), children have largely remained absent from the decision-making process following parental separation (Birnbaum, 2017; Birnbaum & Bala, 2017; Holt, 2016; Smith et al., 2003). As Butler et al. (2002) have argued:

> Children do not experience their parents' divorce passively. Their involvement is an active, creative and resourceful one. Recognizing children as competent (as well as relevant) witnesses to the process of family dissolution may further assist the process whereby their accounts are attended to and valued. (p. 99)

Interest is growing in hearing directly from children as part of the research process to understand their views and perspectives about parental separation (Birnbaum, 2017; Birnbaum & Saini, 2012a, 2012b; Campbell, 2008; Graham & Fitzgerald, 2010; Punch, 2002; Simpson, 2003).

Case Vignette

The research question involved children's views about and experiences with family justice professionals in Ontario and in Ohio, United States, during parental separation (Birnbaum & Bala, 2010; Birnbaum et al., 2011).

Specifically, the objectives of the research were to examine how children felt about their involvement with different family justice professionals, whether their voices were heard, and what lessons could be learned from them to assist other children whose parents are involved in disputing custody and access in family courts. The study was guided by an inductive qualitative design using grounded theory strategies (Creswell, 1998; Csiernik & Birnbaum, 2016; Cutcliffe, 2005).

The research process began by negotiating with the site manager at the courthouse who provided the family court files containing the names and telephone numbers of the children for possible recruitment (i.e., the sample). In this case, children were recruited from closed family court files where trials or hearings took place between 2000 and 2010 in three Ontario court jurisdictions (different levels of court) and four Ohio court jurisdictions. In negotiating the recruitment of the sample, the question became, how do you practically obtain closed family court files and then get the permission of the family court to review them?

In Ontario, Section 137 of the Courts of Justice Act provides for public access to family court documents. Moreover, members of the public are entitled to see any current list maintained by the court of family cases being disputed, any documents filed in a family case, or any orders signed unless a statutory provision, common law rule, or court order restricts access. In Ohio, the judge had jurisdiction over the court files and provided permission to the researcher. A related matter in the recruitment of the sample is, who is allowed to access the court files and remove them from their shelves to be reviewed? The public cannot just walk into courts and access court files. A court clerk has to remove the files from their shelves and thus specific knowledge of family court file numbers is required. To access potential participants, the court clerk has to find custody and access cases from the given year in the computer database to be able to retrieve the files. That process takes time, as the clerks are busy with the daily operations of court and research is not a priority. In addition, all court files may not be on site, and some files may have to be ordered from a storage location. Who pays for the related transfer fees? Have they been budgeted for in the research? Another issue is having available space in the courthouse to review the files. Typically, courthouses have limited space for the public, let alone for a researcher, to sit in court and review files. All these behind the scene steps must be carefully planned as part of the operational tasks required for sample recruitment. Careful planning and execution of these steps builds towards establishing clear and respectful communications with the court manager and court staff throughout data collection.

The next step in the design of the research project is completing an ethics review application to obtain approval from a university's research ethics committee or institutional review board. The ethics committee needs to know exactly what is involved in the research, including what steps will be carried out and if they are doable and feasible. In other words, is it ethical to carry out a study that may not be doable? While it may seem straight forward, given that legislation exists about viewing court records and space can be arranged for viewing files, other concerns may also arise in the ethics process. University ethics committees are made up of many academics from different departments. Some social science committee members may conduct applied research; others, such as historians, may only review documents and manuscripts while others may never have conducted any type of community-based research. It is likely that the vast majority have never interviewed children about their views and preferences about parental separation. Moreover, each academic on these committees comes to the ethics review process with their own frame of reference based on their life history, values, and biases. The researcher must be attuned to these issues and be clear in the ethics application about how each step will unfold so that no child is put at risk. It also assists committees if researchers report on their clinical experiences with interviewing children of separation/divorce and whether mental health professionals will be made available for children if necessary.

In this case, children were to be provided with a $25 honorarium for their time and participation. The research ethics committee expressed several concerns. First, they had concerns about children being interviewed and the potential emotional harm that may result from being asked questions about their views and experiences of the parental separation. Second, they were concerned about children being paid for their time and that it could bias their participation by being rewarded for talking. Third, they wondered amount of money was too much for a child. Fourth, they wanted to know how children would be receiving the money or if it would be used by custodial parents. All these ethical concerns were legitimate and needed to be addressed. The children recruited across Ontario and Ohio for this study were from 7 to 16 years of age. They did not have their own bank accounts and the cheques were being written to the custodial parents' attention. Therefore, there was no way of knowing if parents were going to give the money to the child or keep it. Providing honorariums to adults involved in medical research and to psychology students participating in experiments has been done for years. Therefore, it was this author's position that providing an honorarium to children should not be any different. It would certainly be noted in any scholarly publication that the participants were provided with an honorarium. However, this alone does not mean it is a limitation in the design of the research methodology (Csiernik & Birnbaum, 2016).

As the proposal made its way through the research ethics committee, they did approve the research, with the understanding that the Information to Participants form would clearly document that the $25 was to be given to the named child and that this would be clearly expressed again to the parents during the audio-recorded interviews.

After research ethics approval was provided and the site agreed upon, the next step in the research journey was to review the court files and screen for participants. This step, while seemingly straightforward often is not; that is the difference between classroom learning of research and real-world, community-based, research practice. Court files are not always complete or up to date. For example, if there is an address and a telephone number for parents, they may be outdated and no longer valid. Additionally, both parents received a letter requesting an interview with the child, which had the potential to open the door to a parent who had no contact and wanted another chance to explain their views about the family breakdown and obtain information about the location of the child. Therefore, in this context, it is extremely important that the researcher has not only knowledge of the methodology and design of the research but also significant clinical experience in separation/divorce, as these cases can be emotionally charged. Indeed, the research process may dredge up old feelings and experiences of separation that can be overwhelming for some parents and children, particularly if intimate partner violence was involved.

One question often asked in qualitative research about sampling is, how much is "enough" for a sample size? Harry Wolcott (as cited in Baker & Edwards, 2009, p. 3), one of the pioneers in qualitative research, states,

> That is, of course, a perennial question if not a great one. The answer, as with all things qualitative, is "it depends." It depends on your resources, how important the question is to the research, and even to how many respondents are enough to satisfy committee members for a dissertation. For many qualitative studies one respondent is all you need – your person of interest. But, in general, the old rule seems to hold that you keep asking as long as you are getting different answers, and that is a reminder that with our little samples we can't establish frequencies, but we should be able to find the RANGE of responses. (pp. 3–4)

The sample in this study was based on purposive sampling: seeking children to interview based on the research question. In this case, they were children whose parents were disputing parenting arrangements post-separation/

divorce. The methodology was based on qualitative interviews with children that would capture the breadth and depth of their views and experiences with family justice professionals in Ontario and Ohio. Qualitative research is not about generalizing results; rather, it draws out the complexities and tensions that are inherent in the real world, in this case, the varied experiences the children had with different family justice professionals. In other words, children are interviewed until there is maximum variation and saturation among the themes being heard.

The next step in the operational tasks was the selection and training of a student as a research assistant to conduct follow-up telephone calls with the parents where telephone numbers were included. The training required some education about separation and divorce issues as the student was not familiar with the topic and had little to no clinical experience in the area. The research student had to understand that a parent may be very unhappy about receiving the telephone call, may ask how she, in this case, obtained the telephone number, and what authority she had in asking personal questions, particularly about the child who was selected for the study. However, no amount of preparatory training is enough to fully prepare the research student to conduct this type of research as each parent may react differently. The training process also required engaging the student in training to explain to each parent how the research process unfolds, to address issues of confidentiality of the interviews, to obtain written consent from one or both parents if there was joint decision making, and to obtain written consent from the child to participate. From a research training perspective, how well this process goes in relation to sample recruitment, which is really about establishing a relationship with each parent, determines how well the next phase of the research process will go: the interviews with the children and young adults.

The research literature is clear: children want to be heard during separation and divorce, and they understand the difference between having a voice and having a choice (Campbell, 2008; Cashmore & Parkinson, 2008, 2009; Graham et al., 2009). However, from a research perspective, interviewing children adds more protocols that need to be established at the beginning and throughout the interview stage. That is, parents need to know that the interview with the child is confidential. In this case, all the interviews were conducted by telephone as the children lived all over Ontario and Ohio. The researcher had to be clear that the child needed space in the house to be able to speak freely and not be overheard by the parent(s). While children may want to speak about their views and experiences, one or both parents may change their minds or decide to listen in on the interview. If any parent or child decided not to go through with the interview before or during the interview, then it was cancelled, and the child still received the honorarium. Having significant clinical experience as a researcher is essential to be able to pick up any type of stress or risk that the child may experience during the interview.

Exiting the research interview with children also requires careful planning. That is, children must be thanked for the interview but that does not end the process as the parent must also be thanked for allowing the child to participate in the study. This process served two important purposes. The first was to obtain a sense of whether or not the parent had been listening, determined by how long it took for the parent to get back on the phone; the second was to assure each parent that the child was very thoughtful and doing well, and to express gratitude for the permission to interview the child.

The next stage in the research was the data analysis. In grounded theory, the researcher begins with open coding (reading through the data and creating tentative categories), then moves to axial coding (identifying relationships among the categories and interrelationships), and then moves to selective coding (the core storyline) (Charmez, 2006; Sandelowski et al., 1997). How to choose which participant quotes are included or excluded is all part of the data analysis and writing stage. If the research is to be published in a peer-reviewed journal, those journals have strict word limits, and although all the data that have been generated are important, much has to be left out.

Last, but certainly not least, is knowledge translation and lessons learned. What results can be provided that contribute to the knowledge base for social work practitioners, lawyers representing children, judges, and the family justice system? Research must inform and be part of any ongoing knowledge translation in the field. This means that while the goal for the academic may be writing in peer-reviewed journals about the research study, children deserve knowledge translation into practice and policy change at a broader level.[1]

Implications

All too often in teaching research to students, too much emphasis is placed on teaching the *right* methodology for the *right question*, the *right* design, the *right theory*, the *right* analysis, and the *right* discussion

1 The results of this study can be found in Birnbaum et al. (2011). Since this study was published, judicial interviewing across Canada has increased, albeit slowly (Birnbaum & Bala, 2014; Birnbaum et al., 2013). Moreover, the research study led to more work on children's participation in the family justice system and policy change in Ontario (see Birnbaum, 2017; Birnbaum & Bala, 2017).

and limitations to the study. Little, if any, focus is placed on the practical aspects of the practice of doing the research. Whether the sample recruitment takes place in a courthouse, a hospital, an agency, or the community, detailing every aspect of the practicalities of making it happen must be part of the research activities and planning. Furthermore, engaging with children, adults, or the elderly, engaging with any vulnerable population, requires some degree of clinical expertise as well as research knowledge. If the researcher has no clinical background, then it is important to work with another colleague who has the specific, necessary clinical expertise. Applied research is working with people, and people act and react in many ways that can contribute to or challenge even seasoned researchers.

While many studies do unfold as they are laid out in the methodology and design, there will also be many times when the process does not unfold as intended for all the reasons discussed above. In fact, it is often when the study does not work out as intended that is the most fruitful and lasts over a lifetime of doing research. Learning from mistakes cannot always be taught, but unintended outcomes certainly become etched in memory about what not to do.

Conclusion

Doing research in the real world can be exciting, rewarding, and challenging as it often engages with different disciplines, different government or agency mandates and expectations, and funders who may have different agendas. Participants may or may not always cooperate and professionals may or may not always follow research protocols that are prescribed to enhance the reliability and validity of the study. Each stage of the research journey needs to be carefully planned, have options available for backup, and, most importantly, be doable and feasible. That is, whether it is a quantitative, a qualitative, or a mixed method design, access to participants in health, schools, community, or government must be established before any other research-related task can begin.

No research project is immune from challenges, but it is important to learn from them so that the next research project factors these into the design and execution. While research textbooks about methods, sampling, statistics, and related methodological processes are important in understanding basic research methods, actually carrying out the design and implementing it moves abstract theory to the real world of research outside the classroom. It is vital to include in teaching.

REFERENCES

Baker, S., & Edwards, R. (2009). How many qualitative interviews is enough? Expert voices and early career reflections on sampling and cases in qualitative research. *National Center for Research Methods Review.* http://eprints.ncrm.ac.uk/2273/4/how_many_interviews.pdf

Birnbaum, R. (2017). Views of the child reports: Hearing directly from children involved in post separation disputes. *Social Inclusion, 5*(3), 148–54. https://doi.org/10.17645/si.v5i3.922

Birnbaum, R., & Bala, N. (2010). Judicial interviewing with children in custody and access cases: Comparing experiences in Ontario and Ohio. *International Journal of Law, Policy and the Family, 24*(3), 300–37.

Birnbaum, R., & Bala, N. (2014). A survey of Canadian judges about their meetings with children: Becoming more common but still contentious. *Canadian Bar Review, 91*, 637–55.

Birnbaum, R., & Bala, N. (2017). Views of the child reports: The Ontario pilot project. *International Journal of Law, Policy and the Family, 31*(3), 344–62. https://doi.org/10.1093/lawfam/ebx008

Birnbaum, R., Bala, N., & Bertrand, L. (2013). Judicial interviews with children: Attitudes and practices of Canadian lawyers for children. *New Zealand Law Review, 3*(4), 465–82.

Birnbaum, R., Bala, N., & Cyr, F. (2011). Children's experiences with family justice professionals and judges in Ontario and Ohio. *International Journal of Law, Policy and the Family, 25*(3), 398–422. https://doi.org/10.1093/lawfam/ebr014

Birnbaum, R., & Saini, M. (2012a). A scoping review of qualitative studies on the voice of the child in child custody disputes. *Childhood, 20*(2), 260–82. https://doi.org/10.1177/0907568212454148

Birnbaum, R., & Saini, M. (2012b). A qualitative synthesis of children's participation in custody disputes. *Journal of Social Work Research Practice, 22*(4), 400–9. https://doi.org/10.1177/1049731512442985

Butler, I., Scanlon, L., Robinson, M., Douglas, G., & Murch, M. (2002). Children's involvement in their parents' divorce: implications for practice. *Children and Society, 16*(2), 89–102. https://doi.org/10.1002/chi.702

Campbell, A. (2008). The right to be heard: Australian children's views about their involvement in decision-making following parental separation. *Child Care in Practice, 14*(3), 237–55. https://doi.org/10.1080/13575270802042496

Cashmore, J., & Parkinson, P. (2008). Children's and parents' perceptions on children's participation in decision making after parental separation and divorce. *Family Court Review, 46*(1), 91–104. https://doi.org/10.1111/j.1744-1617.2007.00185.x

Cashmore, J., & Parkinson, P. (2009). Children's participation in family law disputes: The views of children, parents, lawyers and counsellors. *Family Matters, 82,* 15–21. https://aifs.gov.au/sites/default/files/jc.pdf

Charmez, K. (2006). *Constructing grounded theory: A practical guide through qualitative analysis*(Introducing qualitative methods series). Sage.

Creswell, J. (1998). *Qualitative inquiry and research design: Choosing among five traditions.* Sage.

Csiernik, R., & Birnbaum, R. (2016). *Practicing social work research: Case studies for learning* (2nd ed.). University of Toronto Press.

Cutcliffe, J. (2005). Adapt or adopt: developing and transgressing the methodological boundaries of grounded theory. *Journal of Advanced Nursing 51*(4), 421–8. https://doi.org/10.1111/j.1365-2648.2005.03514.x

Graham, A., & Fitzgerald, R. (2010). Exploring the promises and possibilities for children's participation in Family Relationship Centres. *Australian Institute of Family Matters, 84*(1), 53–60.

Graham, A., Fitzgerald, R., & Phelps. R. (2009). *The changing landscape of family law: Exploring the promises and possibilities for children's participation in Australian Family Relationship Centres.* Southern Cross University.

Gray, D. (2014). *Doing research in the real world* (3rd ed.). Sage.

Grinnell, R., & Unrau, Y. (2011). *Social work research and evaluation: Foundations of evidence-based practice* (9th ed.). Oxford University Press.

Holt, S. (2016). The voice of the child in family law: A discussion paper. *Children and Youth Services Review, 68*(2), 139–45. https://doi.org/10.1016/j.childyouth.2016.07.007

Neuman, W. (2014). *Research methods: Quantitative and qualitative approaches.* Pearson Education.

Punch, S. (2002). Research with children: The same or different from research with adults? *Childhood, 9*(3), 321–41. https://doi.org/10.1177/0907568202009003005

Robson, C., & McCartan, K. (2016). *Real-world research: A resource for users of social research in applied setting* (4th ed.). John Wiley & Sons.

Rodham, H. (1973). Children under the law. *Harvard Educational Review, 43*(4), 487–514. https://doi.org/10.17763/haer.43.4.e14676283875773k

Rubin, A., & Babbie, E. (2017). *Research methods for social work.* Thompson Higher Education.

Sandelowski, M., Docherty, S., & Emden, C. (1997). Focus on qualitative methods, qualitative metasynthesis: Issues and techniques. *Research in Nursing & Health, 20*(3), 365–71. https://doi.org/10.1002/(sici)1098-240x(199708)20:4%3C365::aid-nur9%3E3.0.co;2-e

Simpson, C. (2003). Children and research participation: Who makes what decisions. *Health Law Review, 11*(2), 20–9.

Smith, A., Taylor, N., & Tapp, P. (2003). Rethinking children's involvement in decision-making after parental separation, *Childhood 10*(2), 201–16. https://doi.org/10.1177/0907568203010002006

16 Charting a New Course for Community-University Partnership for Teaching Child Welfare Social Work: Learning by Lived Experience

NANCY FREYMOND, GISSELE DAMIANI-TARABA, SHERRI-LYNN MANTO, SARAH ROBERTSON, LEIGH SAVAGE, MARILEE SHERRY, AND ANDREW KOSTER

In bachelor of social work (BSW) programs across Canada, learning about child welfare is a curriculum staple. As the truth regarding the legacy of systems of child welfare and the complicity of Canada's social work educators in colonial practices settles into our consciousness, our approach to teaching and learning about this issue must change. Some questions have evolved that need to be explored. What is the responsibility of the social work academy in preparing students for child welfare practice? What are the best ways to teach about child welfare social work practice? Besides academics, who from the child welfare community should be involved?

To explore these questions, we, the authors, have formed a learning partnership that involves stakeholders from social work education and the child welfare community. The purpose of our partnership is to critically examine what it means to "help" as a child welfare social worker, tackling key questions such as those posed above. Through collective discussion, we analyse child welfare and educational structures with a view to transforming research, teaching, and practice. As a concrete example of how to teach child welfare, this chapter will discuss how we planned and delivered curriculum for an introductory child welfare course in a new BSW program and what we learned along the way in aiding students to practise in this area.

New Managerialism

Our BSW program welcomes students, many of them fresh graduates from high school, who tend to enter the discipline of social work because of a perceived need to "help" others and desire to learn the technologies of helping. Sometimes students refer to these technologies as tools for their "helping toolkits" that, upon graduation, will purportedly give them an advantage in the competitive job market. These ideas are not surprising. They reflect neo-liberal ideology and specifically the tenets of new managerialism, a term used to refer to the public sector's broad adoption of values and practices associated with private business (Deem, 1998; Vito, 2016). We see this in social work education, where there are mounting pressures to serve the market by developing a competitive, economic, entrepreneurial citizen/social worker (Brown, 2016; Lynch, 2014).

One of the most disturbing aspects of new managerialism for the social work profession is the subtle ways in which the bureaucratic social worker, alienated from a caring, relational self, is gaining credibility. The flexibility and autonomy of front-line child welfare work have largely been replaced with standardized, competency-based procedures that happen regardless of the nature of the concern or the idiosyncratic needs of families, communities, or young people. Performing checklist audits and documenting every interaction is now the norm (Harlow, 2008). Assessments are constrained and scripted with the language of risk (Featherstone et al., 2018). Some would argue that paperwork accountability, which diminishes worker time for relationship building, support, and advocacy, is designed to quantify, measure, and control the work in a system intent on decreasing risks to the state (Baines, 2004; Carniol, 2010; Swift & Parada, 2004). There are worries that standardization contributes to the deskilling and de-professionalization of social service jobs (Carey, 2009; Ferguson & Lavalette, 2006; Healy, 2009). Accompanying these conditions is an ongoing debate in the literature about the extent to which child welfare social workers are able to rely on professional expertise rather than regulation in decision making (Gillingham, 2006; Gillingham & Humphreys, 2010; Goddard et al., 1999; Heggdalsvik et al., 2018; Parton, 1998).

The Complicity of Social Work Education

What is largely missing from these critiques is the role of social work education in maintaining and perpetuating the colonial status quo of child welfare systems. The work of the Truth and Reconciliation Commission of Canada (TRC, 2015a) details the devastating impacts, both past and present, of child welfare systems on Indigenous communities. The current over-representation of Indigenous children in child welfare systems is reminiscent of residential school systems where children were systematically removed from their families and community. The TRC report draws attention to the shared complicity of education and child welfare. Of its 94 calls to action, the first 12 are directed at the systems of child welfare and education (TRC, 2015b). In response, social work educators need to ask how learning is occurring and who determines what should be learned.

Correspondingly, there are social workers and educators who work from within the systems of education and child welfare in an effort to resist and transform their practices. For example, over the past decade, our local child welfare agency has continued to make collaboration and prevention central to its mandate. It focuses on walking alongside families through a community-based approach to child welfare social work (Cameron et al., 2012; Freymond & SmitQuosai, 2011; Robertson, 2011). The community-based model co-locates child protection offices within various neighbourhoods, enabling workers to build ongoing formal and informal relationships with people who live in the community they are supporting. The agency also makes routine use of the principles and practices of family group conferencing (American Humane Association & the FGDM Guidelines Committee, 2010; George Hull Centre, 2011) in situations where the immediate and long-term safety of a young person must be addressed. In our current climate, the survival of these transformative initiatives showcases the fortitude and creativity of people who want child welfare social work practices to be different.

Child Welfare Learning Partnership: Core Elements

Our partnership comprises 15 core members who are service users, social work faculty, child welfare social workers, and students. Our learning partners represent more than one group. For example, one is a BSW student with 10 years of experience as a foster parent, and another is a worker who grew up in foster care. Cultural diversity among members is an imperative. Our circle includes Indigenous, Black, and other racialized voices. Our partnership commitment represents a considerable investment of time and energy. We rely on the organizational leadership, in both child welfare and the social work faculty and the university, to endorse this collaboration and support our work with creative solutions to organizational cultural barriers when they arise.

We strive to teach and learn by making central the multiple voices of those who participate in the system, both service providers and service users. Indeed, along with those who work to resist and transform child welfare systems are those who truly need and want child welfare social workers to help them. In addition, we do not focus on the claims of child welfare, that is, what the system declares as its intentions. Rather, our analysis focuses on system outcomes. that is, what people say who have experienced, or are experiencing, its effects. Through this interactive examination, we piece together ideas about ethical child welfare social work practices.

We want to emphasize the journeying nature of our work. We do not write this chapter from a place of having arrived at a destination and now imparting wisdom. Every time we meet together, we are confronted with the limits of our understanding. Perhaps our only certainty is that we continually seek to move from awareness and towards more ethical practices and pedagogies. Over time, we have been able to establish a framework that reflects our values and ideas. The core elements follow:

1 Valuing the lives, identities, and embodied experiences of each other and drawing on our experience of the child welfare system as a valid source of knowledge (Bellefeuille, 2006; Bhattacharjee, 2015)
2 Sharing stories spoken from the heart to help us to appreciate each other and our shared purpose
3 Dismantling the silos between the institutions of education and systems of child welfare, situating our learning in the classroom and child welfare settings
4 Taking steps to equalize the relationships of power among service users, professors, students, and service providers (Giroux, 1994; Hillock, 2011; Mackay et al., 2009)
5 Drawing on principles from critical feminist pedagogy, experimenting with the process of teaching and learning, with a goal of reaching new levels of awareness
6 Engaging with multiple stories of child welfare experiences and growing in our consciousness about the operations of oppression and the imperative for change (Friere, 1970; hooks, 1994, 2003; Navia et al., 2018; Shrewsbury, 1987)
7 Remaining consciously hopeful about change

The Introductory Child Welfare Course

The introductory child welfare course we collaboratively developed has been offered three times to second-year BSW students. Students and course facilitators have generously provided written feedback about their teaching and learning experiences. Additionally, a focus group was conducted with nine students at the conclusion of the second course offering.[1] Here is what we have learned.

1 Human subjects approval was obtained from Wilfrid Laurier University's Research Ethics Board (#4571).

Teaching and Learning through Lived Experience

In our course, we ask young people in the child welfare system or raised in the system and now living independently, as well as parents, front-line workers, administrators, and community developers, to share their experiences. Most often these storytellers are recruited informally; they learn of our work and express interest in sharing their stories. This focus on lived experience is powerful in that it surfaces diverse perspectives about child welfare and the operation of markers such as class, race, gender, culture, and sexual orientation. In addition to lived experience storytellers, who attend the classroom, students are invited to intentional dialogue workshops with people who hold particular perspectives about child welfare. For example, a Muslim woman who has been a worker and a foster parent of Muslim children speaks about Islamic law, her identities in the context of the child welfare system, and racism while inviting questions about her Muslim identity and experience.

BSW students join this course with a preliminary understanding of the legacy of residential schools through required Indigenous studies courses from their first year of undergraduate studies. Students hear the stories told by Indigenous young people about their experience of growing up disconnected from land in the system of child welfare. In response, Indigenous child welfare workers discuss culturally appropriate practices. We have also been guests of the local Indigenous child welfare agency, where we were introduced to alternative approaches to practice in this field of social work.

Curriculum Content: Exposure Experiences

Students enter the course with stigmatized perceptions of parents and young people who receive child welfare services. This is worrisome. They tend to hold primarily negative stereotypical views of child welfare families, particularly the mothers, who occupy some of the most marginalized and oppressed positions in our society (Freymond, 2013). Generally, students expect to meet "bad mothers" who neglect their children and "fail to protect them" from circumstances such as poverty, violence, mental health challenges, and addictions (Strega, 2013). Some students make comparisons to their own "good mothers" who are lauded for being self-sacrificing and continually attending to the needs of their children. Often, students imagine that their future job as a child welfare worker will be to help mothers take responsibility for their actions and to rescue their children through child placement when mothers fail. Largely missing is an awareness of how the binary of "good" and "bad" mother is operating; the multiple, intersecting oppressions fuelled by various *-isms* including, but not limited to, racism, classism, and sexism (Dunkerley, 2017); as well as the ways in which fathers and fathering are rendered invisible (Brown et al., 2009). A feminist analysis directs us to a contextualized and nuanced understanding of mothers' environments, including how patriarchal systems reinforce men's dominance, a focus on caring rather than blaming, the feminization of poverty, and a reformulated view of the role of the child welfare worker who resists institutionalized responses that render mothers powerless (Dunkerley, 2017; Swift, 1991; Zeman, 2008).

The exposure experiences we offer in our course are particularly powerful. Sometimes they enable students to reformulate their preconceived negative images of these mothers, recognizing them as people trying to do their best for their families:

> Before I thought "oh they must have done something wrong, their kids aren't safe." But really, they're ... just trying to make money and survive and have a healthy family like everyone else ... I learned that because we went on the community tours ... Like the mothers would come and bake together, and they could bring their kids ... I learned they're just like us and they're people too. (Focus Group Participant S4)

Seeing families who might be involved with a child welfare social worker challenges students' distorted images but also awakens them to the realities of their everyday living circumstances. Focus Group Participant S2 said, "I grew up in this town. I had no idea about poverty. The only thing I knew is that my mom told me I was not allowed to be in this part of town." And yet another student reflected:

> After taking this course, you learn ... it's not even necessarily just the parents, like it could be the circumstantial ... we talked about housing, and like an area where there's a lot of factories and the kids are getting sick. Like that's out of the parents' control, but is that still child abuse? So, it made me think a lot more critically about ... what child abuse is in terms of social and structural barriers that are out of the parents' control. (Focus Group Participant S1)

Thus, we have found that the learning that occurs in the real-life context of child welfare community-based settings where students, in encountering the people who have, to date, been accessible to them only through negative societal stereotypes, can critically question their previous views helps to dispel misogynistic, classist, and racist myths and distortions.

This work is vital, as we know that stereotypes, either consciously or unconsciously, will affect these future child welfare workers' decision making and behaviours towards these families.

Situated Biography

In our work, we have become increasingly focused on students' turning inward, becoming introspective, so that they may develop a deep understanding of themselves and their beliefs. Our knowledge of our selves embodies our biography and our history. Students are invited to create an auto-ethnographic account that situates them in relation to their unique history. Their methodology is to gather and analyse significant stories told and retold in their families. They cultivate key themes from these stories and trace these over a 100+ year time span. A primary goal of this particular assignment is to awaken student awareness that they do not come to the work of child welfare neutral or empty, in other words, the classic state of tabula rasa (Locke, 1959). Instead, they bring values, beliefs, and attitudes shaped over time by their own histories of privilege, blessing, abuse, injustice, and prejudice. Their situatedness also informs what they will think and do in their child welfare practice with young people, families, and communities.

We are particular about students drawing explicit connections between their autobiographical themes and perceptions of families, young people, community, child welfare, and social work helping. The situated biography acquaints us with the facts of our history and gives rise to a wholeness through claiming our history in the context of our present and future reality. It has been a significant tool for students and for many of us in the learning partnership who search for deeper understanding:

> The situated biography is an important assignment that the students are given, and I wanted to highlight why having that exercise is important and relevant to child welfare practice. Understanding my family's history of colonization and evangelism has fueled my desire to work towards changing how Indigenous families experience child welfare. It was the first time that I openly shared within such a large group my family history of colonizing the Blackfoot and Cree Peoples in Western Canada. That is my history. And I work in child welfare. I decided to share how I manage the conflicting feelings knowing that I work within a system where there is a disproportionate number of Indigenous children in care while knowing that my ancestor took Indigenous children from their lands, communities, and families and put them in the residential school that he developed and led. Am I re-creating history because I work in the period of what I have been told is the Millennial Scoop? What

> came afterwards was something that I never anticipated. I owned my story and suddenly Truth and Reconciliation had a new meaning for me. A fire was ignited within my spirit of wanting to right the wrongs that my family had contributed to. I was held accountable in a new way. So, while I shared my experiences with young and impressionable minds, I ended up gaining more than I was expecting. It made me more aware and held me more accountable of how I work with and interact with Indigenous families, children and community partners. It has become an experience and a moment in my life that I am forever grateful for. (Storyteller Reflection SR1)

Readings

Along with developing curriculum, the learning partners challenged the tendency of these social work professors to rely on peer-reviewed journal articles as the source of the most legitimate knowledge for learning about child welfare practices. Why, they reason, when reliance on lived experience is a core pedagogy, would we privilege academic journal articles as the primary resources?

> It has been a humbling process to let go of the stronghold of academic writing as the primary assigned reading for students and lecturing from PowerPoint slides as the main pedagogy. These are the ways I have learned. I was nervous that students were not getting "enough" of what they "should" learn. I kept inserting comments from the literature, asking storytellers particular questions to try to illustrate points that I thought useful. Sometime during the second iteration of this course, I realized that I knew little of what it really means to let go of the need to control content in favour of listening and learning from lived experience. I am still learning about how to withdraw from using power in the classroom in ways I now recognize as undermining and unhelpful. Students and members of the learning partnership have been gracious and encouraging. (Professor Reflection PR1)

If a text needs to be used in your teaching, we suggest *Three Little Words* by author Ashley Rhodes-Courter (2009), an internationally recognized child and human rights advocate, who writes about her life as a young person growing up in multiple foster homes. It has become the primary text for this course and a constant reference point for illustration. A consistent theme across the focus group data and the reflection pieces is that students find value in the non-academic reading resources:

> Another experience that touched me was Three Little Words, by Ashley Rhodes-Courter (2009). To think that she had experienced 19 different

> foster parents before finally feeling a place of belonging is heartbreaking. I felt many emotions while reading this book, including infuriated and powerless, however by the end of the book I felt inspired. Ashley's story is one that I will carry with me throughout my career. (Student Reflection RP1)

In one class, students reacted strongly to Rhodes-Courter's description of moving her possessions in garbage bags from one foster home to another. Child welfare workers confirmed that this is a reality in our community. Students then took action by mounting a successful campaign to locate new and gently used luggage for young people in foster care.

Storytelling and Listening

Storytelling is deeply personal. It brings us together in community and it promotes healing and transformation for listeners and tellers. The involvement of people who have used social work services in the delivery of social work education is complex, particularly with the risks that their involvement will be experienced as tokenistic (Burrows, 2011; Sadd, 2011). Service users and child welfare social workers find their way to our classroom because they are part of our learning partnership or have connections to one of its members. Careful explanations and written materials about our intentions, what to expect, permission to withdraw at any point, what to do if a traumatic reaction arises, and how to refuse unwanted questions are necessary. The following is an example of feedback offered:

> There was something empowering about talking about my experience. It's like it started to take some shame away and it was also nice that, parts of my story, I could lighten with humour. I spent 11 years of my childhood dealing with the child welfare system, including two instances of placement in a foster home. I wanted to ask these young hopefuls a few questions: Are they willing to simply remember that past their job checklists, there's a *human being* in front of them? Are they willing to let go of their preconceived notions and see the potential for success, *despite* circumstance? Are they going to be the one to encourage a child or a teenager to defeat the odds? Young people will always know what kind of worker you were and how you made them feel. Will they remember that help is sometimes letting go, or directing them to the appropriate resource? As much as you want to save them all, it truly takes a village. I wanted to ask them these questions because even ten years ago, when my personal case file was being closed even though I still needed help, I would've never guessed my life would be the way it is now – or that the child social work field would have evolved in

> such a way. I was and I am very blessed. I wanted them to know, there are workers that I attribute my once "rebel without a cause" attitude to, and there are workers who made me believe I could be better. They are the ones I want to celebrate my success with. I wanted them to think about how much power they will have to make an impact on a kid's life. (Storyteller Reflection SR2)

We also learned that it is critically important to prepare students as listeners. During our first course offering, students sometimes felt overwhelmed by lived experience stories and were unsure of how to respond. In some instances, when students did not engage with questions, lived experience storytellers felt disrespected. Now, we invite students, in advance, to brainstorm their curiosities. We talk about how to bring not just our minds to the storytelling encounter, but our hearts and spirits. Afterwards, while storytellers are privately debriefing with facilitators in an adjoining room, students prepare gratitude notes. Our encounter concludes with students presenting these notes to storytellers. This practice is an attempt to move away from the university norm of presenting guest speakers with university swag or monetary tokens.

Adapting the Principles of Circle Learning

When our learning partnership was struggling to move forward, a member suggested that we stop hosting our meetings at boardroom style tables and start sitting in a circle facing each other. We were immediately impressed with the increased vulnerability and authentic storytelling among us. This experience, the writings of Palmer (1993, 2004), and the learning in circle we have experienced from Indigenous professors and Elders, led us to experiment with circle pedagogy the third time we taught this course. Learning circles have been used in Indigenous community–university partnerships to indigenize curriculum (Ragoonaden & Mueller, 2017), as well as in feminist classrooms, as discussed by Hillock earlier in chapter 3.

Students were wonderfully gracious and cooperative as we sought to infuse the principles of circle pedagogy into our work. Protocols for circle pedagogy required that students be active participants and authentically engaged, demonstrating respect for others and processes. We asked that they arrive to class consistently on time, speak from their heart, respect silence, display humility, and keep a journal of their learning/circle experience from week to week.

We underestimated how frightening circle learning would be for students who have spent all of their education sitting at desks. Some reported that, over time, they grew more confident with expressing their views. They were learning to be with each other, to sit with vulnerability without the desk acting as a shield. We would be remiss if we did not acknowledge that there were struggles and tensions as students and facilitators attempted to embrace circle learning. Some students never saw value in the process; others seemed to thrive. Our beginning experience affirmed that circle learning creates vulnerability and inspires authentic sharing and deeper learning.

Conclusion: We Are in This Together!

> One of the greatest gifts of this journey together has been the opportunity to unpack authenticity, accept vulnerability, and appreciate deeply the profound impact of hearing and holding the stories of others close to my heart. There have been many areas of growth for me personally in my understanding of these concepts. I struggle, at times, to accept vulnerability as part of this process – letting my own biases and judgments fill my garden with weeds. I am conflicted about having challenged and resisted the involvement of the child welfare system in my family life. As a survivor of domestic violence, I bumped up against a variety of systems and was left feeling unsupported, stigmatized, and shamed. Yet each day, in my work life, I acted as an ambassador of this same system, finding new soil to hoe, planting new seeds to try to squeeze out the pesky weeds. Being a member of this learning partnership has afforded me the benefits of reflective and reciprocal learning with a compassionate circle of people. Our stories help us help ourselves and our students to learn and grow. With authenticity, kindness, compassion, and gratitude, we reclaim our own humanity and have these as our touchstones, our alignment of heart and mind, when challenging the oppressive practices of the child welfare system. (Storyteller Reflection SR3)

These are not easy times. As we grapple with unsettling our entrenched patterns of thinking about child welfare social work, we do so inside child welfare and university systems founded on the principles of elitism, exclusion, and colonization. If no changes are made in BSW teaching of child welfare, people encountering systems of child welfare, who are most often the most marginalized, poor, and oppressed, will continue to be the subjects of bureaucratic processes. In the case of Indigenous people, bureaucratic practices can even displace them from their lands. This is why, in our opinion, this course experience is so important. It provides future practitioners with a framework of lived experiences that can elicit empathy, caring, and the importance of engagement on a human level. We believe that the discussions and narratives found in the BSW course will significantly shape how these tools are applied. These may not be the technological tools that our present neo-liberal society enshrines, but they are the foundations for authentic relationship building, support, and advocacy. We would contend that BSW students must become conscious of their social responsibilities. They need to embrace change, value reconciliation, and engage as allies when requested. For this to be a reality, they cannot simply be taught to engage in social work education as consumers of helping technologies; their role models must be educators and practitioners engaged in their own work of decolonization.

Together, we are learning about ourselves, our teaching and learning, and our child welfare practices. It is hard to disentangle ourselves from our entrenched ways of being and thinking and doing but we continue to be committed to deeply and critically questioning our ideas and considering what it means to engage with and respond to the stories of lived experience.

REFERENCES

American Humane Association & the FGDM Guidelines Committee. (2010). *Guidelines for family group decision making in child welfare.* http://www.fgdm.org

Baines, D. (2004). Caring for nothing: Work organization and unwaged labour in social services. *Work, Employment and Society, 18*(2), 267–95. https://doi.org/10.1177/0950017200404277O

Bellefeuille, G. L. (2006). Rethinking reflective practice education in social work education: A blended constructivist and objectivist instructional design strategy for a web-based child welfare practice course. *Journal of Social Work Education, 42*(1), 85–103. https://doi.org/10.5175/jswe.2006.200303153

Bhattacharjee, J. (2015). Constructivist approach to learning: An effective approach of teaching learning. *International Research Journal of Interdisciplinary & Multidisciplinary Studies, 1*(6), 65–74.

Brown, C. (2016). The constraints of neo-liberal new managerialism in social work education. *Canadian Social Work Review, 33*(1), 115–23. https://doi.org/10.7202/1037094ar

Brown, L., Callahan, M., Strega, S., Walmsley, C., & Dominelli, L. (2009). Manufacturing ghost fathers: The paradox of father presence and absence in child welfare. *Child and Family Social Work, 14*(1), 25–34. https://doi.org/10.1111/j.1365-2206.2008.00578.x

Burrows, H. M. (2011). Evaluation of the involvement of service users in post-qualifying social work education. *Social Work and Social Sciences Review, 15*(3), 44–56. https://doi.org/10.1921/095352212x655339

Cameron, G., Frensch, K., Quosai, T.M., DeGeer, I., & Freymond, N. (2012). Employment experiences of frontline child protection service providers in accessible and central delivery settings. *Journal of Public Child Welfare, 6*, 590–613. https://doi.org/10.1080/15548732.2012.723967

Carey, M. (2009). It's a bit like being a robot or working in a factory: Does Braverman help explain the experiences of state social workers in Britain since 1971? *Organization, 16*(4), 505–27. https://doi.org/10.1177/1350508409104506

Carniol, B. (2010). *Case critical: Social services and social justice in Canada* (6th ed.). Between the Lines Publishing.

Deem, R. (1998). "New managerialism" and higher education: the management of performances and cultures in universities in the United Kingdom. *International Studies in Sociology of Education, 8*(1), 47–70. https://doi.org/10.1080/0962021980020014

Dunkerley, S. (2017). Mothers matter: A feminist perspective on child welfare-involved women. *Journal of Family Social Work, 20*(3), 251–65.

Featherstone, B., Gupta, A., Morris, K., & Warner, J. (2018). Let's stop feeding the risk monster: Towards a social model of "child protection." *Families, Relationships and Societies, 7*(1), 7–22. https://doi.org/10.1332/204674316x14552878034622

Ferguson, I., & Lavalette, M. (2006). Globalisation and global justice: Towards a social work of resistance. *International Social Work, 49*(3), 309–18. https://doi.org/10.1177/0020872806063401

Freymond, N. (2013). Mothers of children in placement. In G. Cameron, M. Fine, S. Maiter, K. Frensch, & N. Freymond (Eds.), *Creating positive systems of child and family welfare: Congruence with the everyday lives of children and parents* (pp. 94–114). University of Toronto Press.

Freymond, N., & SmitQuosai, T. (2011). "Working with families where they're at": Front-line child welfare in neighbourhood settings. *Ontario Association of Children's Aid Societies Journal, 56*(2), 24–30.

Friere, P. (1970). *Pedagogy of the oppressed.* Herder and Herder.

George Hull Centre. (2011). *Family group conferencing/family group decision making coordinator manual for Ontario: Family group conferencing Ontario provincial resource.* http://www.georgehullcentre.on.ca/Family-Group-Conferencing-Ontario-Provincial-Resource

Gillingham, P. (2006). Risk assessment in child protection: problem rather than solution? *Australian Social Work, 59*(1), 86–98. https://doi.org/10.1080/03124070500449804

Gillingham, P., & Humphreys, C. (2010). Child protection practitioners and decision making tools: Observations and reflections from the front line. *British Journal of Social Work, 40*(8), 2598–616. https://doi.org/10.1093/bjsw/bcp155

Giroux, H. (1994). Toward a pedagogy of critical thinking. In K. S. Walters (Ed.), *Re-thinking reason: New perspectives on critical thinking* (pp. 199–204). State University of New York Press.

Goddard, C., Saunders, B., Stanley. J., & Tucci. J. (1999). Structured risk assessment procedures: Instruments of abuse? *Child Abuse Review, 8*(4), 251–63. https://doi.org/10.1002/(sici)1099-0852(199907/08)8:4%3C251::aid-car543%3E3.0.co;2-m

Harlow, E. (2008). New managerialism, social service departments and social work practice today. *Practice: Social Work in Action, 15*(2), 29–44. https://doi.org/10.1080/09503150308416917

Healy, K. (2009). A case of mistaken identity: The social welfare professions and new public management. *Journal of Sociology, 45*(4), 401–18. https://doi.org/10.1177/1440783309346476

Heggdalsvik, I., Rød, P., & Heggen, K. (2018). Decision-making in child welfare services: Professional discretion versus standardized templates. *Child & Family Social Work, 23*(3), 522–9. https://doi.org/10.1111/cfs.12444

Hillock, S. (2011). *Conceptualizing oppression: Resistance narratives for social work* [Unpublished doctoral dissertation]. Memorial University of Newfoundland.

hooks, b. (1994). *Teaching to transgress: Education as the practice of freedom.* Routledge.

hooks, b. (2003). *Teaching community: A pedagogy of hope.* Routledge.

Locke, J. (1959). *Essay concerning human understanding.* Dover Publications.

Lynch, K. (2014). *"New managerialism" in education: The organisational form of neoliberalism.* Open Democracy. https://www.opendemocracy.net/en/new-managerialism-in-education-organisational-form-of-neoliberalism/

Mackay, R., Fairclough, M., & Coull, M. (2009). Service users and carers as co-educators of social work students. *Journal of Practice Teaching & Learning, 9*(1), 95–112. https://doi.org/10.1921/175951509x481484

Navia, D., Henderson, R., & Charger, L. (2018). Uncovering colonial legacies: Voices of Indigenous youth on child welfare (dis)placements. *Anthropology & Education Quarterly, 49*(2), 146–64. https://doi.org/10.1111/aeq.12245

Palmer, P. J. (1993). *To know as we are known: Education as a spiritual journey.* HarperCollins.

Palmer, P. J. (2004). *A hidden wholeness: The journey toward an undivided life.* Jossey-Bass.

Parton, N. (1998). Risk, advanced liberalism and child welfare: The need to rediscover uncertainty and ambiguity. *British Journal of Social Work, 28*(1), 5–27. https://doi.org/10.1093/oxfordjournals.bjsw.a011317

Ragoonaden, K., & Mueller, L. (2017). Culturally responsive pedagogy: Indigenizing curriculum. *Canadian Journal of Higher Education, 47*(2), 22–46.

Rhodes-Courter, A. (2009). *Three little words: A memoir.* Atheneum.

Robertson, S. (2011). *"Warden" or "neighbour": Can power be shared in child welfare?* [Unpublished master's thesis]. McMaster University.

Sadd, J. (2011). *"We are more than our story": Service user and carer participation in social work education* (Report No. 42). Social Care Institute for Excellence.

Shrewsbury, C. M. (1987). What is feminist pedagogy? *Women's Studies Quarterly, 15*(3 & 4), 6–14.

Strega, S. (2013). Whose failure to protect? Child welfare interventions when men abuse mothers. In R. Alaggia & C. Vine (Eds.), *Cruel but not unusual: Violence in Canadian families* (2nd ed.). Wilfrid Laurier University Press.

Swift, K. (1991). Contradictions in child welfare: Neglect and responsibility. In C. Baines, P. Evans, & S. Neysmith (Eds.), *Women's caring: Feminist perspectives on social welfare* (pp. 234–71). Toronto, Canada: McClellan & Stewart, Inc.

Swift, K., & Parada, H. (2004). Child welfare reform: Protecting children or policing the poor. *Journal of Law and Social Policy, 19,* 1–17.

Truth and Reconciliation Commission. (2015a).*Honouring the truth, reconciling for the future: Summary of the final report of the Truth and Reconciliation Commission of Canada.*

Truth and Reconciliation Commission. (2015b). *Truth and Reconciliation Commission of Canada: Calls to action.*

Vito, R. E. (2016). *Leadership practice, organizational culture and new managerialism: strengths, challenges, variations and contradictions in three children's service agencies* (Publication No. 1843) [Doctoral dissertation, Wilfrid Laurier University]. Scholar Commons @ Laurier. http://scholars.wlu.ca/etd/1843

Zeman, L. D. (2008). Feminism, child protection, and mothers with psychiatric disabilities in the United States. *Journal of the Association for Research on Mothering, 10*(1), 161–70.

PART THREE

Issues in Teaching

In the opening chapter, the question was asked about what effective teaching entails in postsecondary institutions, and a definition of the word *effective* was offered that led social work educators from across Canada to provide their insights on their approaches to pedagogy and practice. This last section offers three final reflections on critical areas outside those two domains. These concluding chapters examine how to do what social work educators are expected to do: recognize our own standpoints, identities, and positions of privilege; engage students; develop leadership skills and critical, ethical, and intersectional thinking; prepare students for field and practice; manage difficult moments in the classroom; provide a space to celebrate diversity and foster inclusion; implement recommendations from the Truth and Reconciliation Commission of Canada (2015); support our field communities and marginalized groups; encourage social justice and social action initiatives; evaluate student learning and field performance; and, in the end, act as gatekeepers to protect future service users. Moreover, we are expected to do all of these despite not typically receiving any training, education, guidelines, or instructions on how to best do so. The content in this teaching section is directed at examining these gaps.

Thus, this final section begins with an examination of a critical matter not only for social work education at the postsecondary level but also for engaging with students in general. Stephanie L. Baird discusses "Understanding and Responding to the Complexities of Student Anxiety." Colleges and universities have become increasingly concerned about the high anxiety experienced by students and the resulting related behaviours. In social work programs, where students are being prepared to work in a complex and demanding profession, student anxiety is of particular concern. For this reason, it is imperative that social work educators have a full understanding of how to best support students who are coping with anxiety. From considering situational and contextual contributors to anxiety, such as the specific characteristics and demands of university programs, courses, and field practicums, to respecting the individual experiences and needs of each student, this chapter outlines the complexities educators need to understand so they can then identify and implement valuable support strategies.

One of the book's co-editors, Susan Hillock, follows with her chapter on "Teaching from the Margins: No Good Deed Goes Unpunished." Hillock, a White, queer-identified, cisgender, female social work educator teaching courses to mostly White, straight, middle-class students, applies her social work experiences and understandings of oppression and resistance to the social work classroom and field, as well as to curriculum and program development, through feminist perspectives. Hillock argues that feminist education and teaching function as resistance to social, political, and cultural oppression, patriarchy, domination, and misogyny. Earlier, in chapter 3, she articulated a new perspective in teaching that she describes as femagogy. As social work remains a predominantly female profession, and many female service users and social workers have experienced violence, harassment, oppression, trauma, poverty, and inequality, femagogy is a particularly important social work educational perspective.

For Hillock, the classroom can be viewed as a consciousness-raising and social change laboratory where social work educators can choose to either perpetuate or disrupt cultural norms. Some have referred to this situated location as teaching from the margins, which is difficult for both educators and students, who can be caught in the crossfire when they attempt to introduce and apply feminist analyses, ideas, critiques, and practices to traditional agencies, conservative classrooms, and conventional social work colleagues. Teaching from this perspective, though consistent with feminist and social work values and principles – what Hillock considers as good deeds – can be met with negative reactions, in the form of backlash and even punishment. Hostile student reactions, harassment, resistance to critical ideas, and gendered, heterosexist, cisgendered, and racist educational workplaces/classrooms are common and have been described as creating a "chilly climate" for faculty who teach from the margins, as well as students who learn from that location. This chapter builds on Hillock's earlier contribution on femagogy, sharing personal and professional academic experiences and examples, to illustrate some of the challenges inherent in applying femagogy and discuss major challenges social work educators face when they teach from the margins.

The closing chapter reflects on one of the fundamental reasons this book was developed: to aid social work educators to navigate the skill, art, and politics of teaching in postsecondary institutions at both undergraduate and graduate levels. This makes Jan Yorke and Tanya Shute's chapter one that all educators should read, regardless of their pedagogical orientation or their areas of practice knowledge and wisdom, and whether they teach at the undergraduate or graduate level. "Incivility or Bullying? Challenges in the Social Work Classroom" is premised on the belief that confrontations relating to teaching at the postsecondary level are on the rise. Corporatization of education has transformed students into academic consumers. Faculty are identifying, in journals and conference discussions, that student behaviours can make meaningful classroom interaction difficult. Students complain that professors need to be more tech-savvy and understand their unique demographic better. Disruptive student behaviour can be challenging for other students in the classroom, as well as for professors. Many students come to the postsecondary classroom from secondary school settings where expectations are quite different from those of college and university environments. Employment opportunities, growing up experiencing active mental health and/or substance abuse problems, chronic health problems, or experiences of trauma can underpin particular student behaviours and vulnerabilities to course material, as well as draw students towards certain vocational education programs. Literacy issues aside, students can have a steep learning curve within a context where retention has become a pressing priority for university administrators. What draws students to the field of social work in the twenty-first century may be different from the past. Learning useful therapeutic communication skills, having integrity, and using skilled non-judgmental interaction are imperatives in social work, yet both students and faculty complain about plagiarism, difficulty with participation in group work or shared assignments, pervasive social media distractions, or assignments produced from dubious material from the internet. Faculty face such distractions, as well as bullying and abusive, threatening, ablest, racist, homophobic, and ageist behaviours, comments, and misconceptions. Yorke and Shute conclude this insightful chapter with recommendations regarding how to address these issues in our current context of higher education.

REFERENCE

Truth and Reconciliation Commission of Canada. (2015). *Calls to action, education.* http://trc.ca/assets/pdf/Calls_to_Action_English2.pdf

17 Understanding and Responding to the Complexities of Student Anxiety

STEPHANIE L. BAIRD

Student anxiety is an issue of growing concern among postsecondary institutions, with increasing attention placed on how to best support students coping with anxiety (Day et al., 2013; Matthews & Csiernik, 2019; Reiss et al., 2017). While many students register for anxiety-related accommodations for further support, it is important for instructors to develop a baseline of knowledge for how they will address student anxiety. Within social work academic programs, addressing student anxiety is particularly important to adequately prepare students for a complex and stressful profession (Baird, 2016; Lloyd et al., 2002). The stress of learning how to perform the role of a social worker during practicums may also contribute to student anxiety in unique ways (Baird, 2016; Boath et al., 2017). Drawing on research from social work and other academic fields, this chapter provides an overview of key concepts in understanding and responding to student anxiety. From reviewing contributors to anxiety, such as the specific characteristics and demands of programs, courses, field practicums, and/or teaching styles, to considering the individual experiences and needs of each student, this chapter outlines the complexities educators need to understand in order to identify appropriate support strategies (Baird, 2016).

Understanding Anxiety

Anxiety, which is broadly defined by Amstadter (2008) as "a state of diffuse arousal following the perception of a real or imagined threat," (p. 213) is an issue that is increasingly being recognized. Anxiety can impact students in different ways and has many different meanings, which are all relevant when teaching social work. Student anxiety is often described in terms of its detrimental impacts on students, such as its effects on academic success, sleep, substance use, and student relationships (Eisenberg et al., 2007). However, there are additional concepts to consider related to anxiety to fully understand the complexity of its potential impacts on students (Eisenberg et al., 2007).

Within the social work literature, the term *anxiety* is often used interchangeably with words such as *stress*, *worry*, or *concern* (Baird, 2016). Students' worries and concerns, specifically related to their field placements, have been investigated in several studies (Didham, Dromgole, et al., 2011; Rompf et al., 1993; Rosenthal Gelman, 2004). Rompf et al. (1993), who were among the first to investigate anxiety among social work students, identified that both undergraduate and graduate students felt anxious before starting practicums, with students reporting that they felt worried about making mistakes. The links between stress and student anxiety have been highlighted by other social work studies as well (Carello & Butler, 2015; Collins, 2006; Didham et al., 2011).

However, in addition to thinking about the stress caused by anxiety, instructors may want to consider the possible helpful or motivating aspects of anxiety for some students (Baird, 2016). Previous researchers have noted the positive role that anxiety can play in encouraging student growth (Shulman, 2005; Wayne et al., 2010). First discussed by Atherton (1974), the concept of anxiety as adaptive or helpful for social work students was further articulated by Shulman (2005), who emphasized the essential role of educators in both helping students to cope with anxiety and highlighting anxiety's capacity to enhance learning. This concept has also been discussed by Collins (2006), who described how a certain amount of anxiety can be helpful in motivating students to complete academic assignments.

This concept of anxiety as potentially adaptive in the context of educational settings was tested by Alpert and Haber (1960) with the Achievement Anxiety Test (AAT), which measured both adaptive and debilitating aspects of anxiety, such as whether it helped students to perform better when writing exams or led to poor results on exams. Their scales are still used to measure test anxiety and have been lauded for creating a more in-depth picture of the complexity of anxiety (Cheng et al., 2009; Wong, 2008). For social work instructors, integrating both debilitating and facilitating aspects of anxiety into discussions with students may ensure a more balanced approach to addressing anxiety. This balanced approach provides an opportunity to focus on the negative impacts that anxiety can have on learning, as well as the potentially motivating and helpful aspects of anxiety (Baird, 2016).

Another relevant concept to consider is the role of performance anxiety in academic settings, with previous researchers drawing parallels between the concepts of performance anxiety and academic anxiety

(Hopko et al., 2001; McGinnis & Milling, 2005). *Performance anxiety* is defined as anxiety specific to the context of performing, which may be related to giving class presentations, writing tests or exams, or performing the social work role in practicum settings (Baird, 2016; Hopko et al., 2001). Rather than stemming from not having the skills needed to complete a task, performance anxiety is linked to difficulties in performing these skills (Hopko et al., 2001). The concept of performance anxiety is relevant in understanding how students begin to act as new social work practitioners and attend to the needs of service users, and how anxiety may impact their abilities to perform these developing skills (Baird, 2016; Hopko et al., 2001).

Performance anxiety has been specifically investigated within other academic fields, such as in music education (McGinnis & Milling, 2005; Taborsky, 2007) where it has been linked to health problems and the abandonment of music careers (Wolfe, 1989), an implication which must be considered for social work where there is already a risk of early career burnout (Baird, 2016; Lloyd et al., 2002). However, among musicians experiencing performance anxiety, in addition to the negative aspects of performance anxiety, there were positive aspects, such as increased attention and intensity, and with additional performance experience, these positive aspects increased and the negative aspects decreased (Wolfe, 1989).

Program Characteristics

Institutional and program characteristics might also specifically impact the anxiety experienced by social work students. Key structural and design considerations of social work programs are whether programs are part time, full time, distance based, or structured with block courses or placements, and how these elements affect anxiety. Other considerations are related to the institutional values and context within which programs operate, how the design of programs fit with students' expectations and previous educational experiences, and whether there is a potential for any increased anxiety if programs do not match expectations.

Stanley and Mettilda Bhuvaneswari (2016) discussed the need to consider how the focus of social work programs, as well as their external environments, affect students' experiences of stress and anxiety. They stated that in India, "while the theoretical content is similar to what is taught in the west, the emphasis on reflective practice ... is not something which undergraduate students in India are well acquainted with," (p. 79) illustrating the need to consider how the focus of social work programs can differ, which can in turn impact students differently. The authors also described an emphasis on evaluation of student knowledge through examinations, as well as an overall lack of societal recognition of social workers, as unique program and contextual characteristics influencing student anxiety and stress. This study illustrates the importance of considering not only how the design of social work programs relates to experiences of anxiety, but also how broad societal and cultural contexts differently affect students. Similarly, Rosenthal Gelman and Baum's (2010) international comparison of pre-practicum anxiety of social work students showed differences between students in the United States and Israel. American students were significantly more anxious than their Israeli counterparts, even though the American students reported having more practicum-related experience.

Course Characteristics

Certain courses, such as those focused on research and statistics, seem to create particularly high levels of anxiety for social work students (Einbinder, 2014; Quinn, 2006; Royse & Rompf, 1992; Tonsing, 2018). Anxiety related to math and statistics has been investigated, with one study identifying that social work students had higher levels of math-related anxiety than did those from other social sciences. These high rates of anxiety have been attributed to social work students choosing an educational path that they believe will not include math or science (Royse & Rompf, 1992). Anxiety specifically related to statistics has also been found to negatively impact students' performance in their social work courses (Wilson & Rosenthal, 1993) to the point that some schools of social work no longer require a statistics course for admission. Other researchers found that anxiety about research-focused courses was linked to students lacking confidence in their skills in math and computers, and an overall concern about doing well (Gustavsson & MacEachron, 2001).

Given the higher levels of anxiety associated with research and statistics courses, instructors may wish to develop courses and teaching strategies with this information in mind. Student-centred teaching methods are suggested to reduce statistics-related anxiety among social work students, allowing students to become as engaged in the course material as possible, using approaches such as group presentations and journal writing (Davis, 2004; Quinn, 2006). To reduce anxiety in research courses, Maschi and colleagues (2007) recommend that instructors encourage positive experiences in conducting research, such as finding ways for students to gain satisfaction from seeing the potential impacts of their research. A case study approach to learning also provides a way to engage students in research by applying research concepts to social-work-specific case studies, building comfort with research methods, and illustrating ways to apply the concepts in social work settings (Csiernik & Birnbaum, 2017). Student engagement can also be enhanced by arranging the class into small groups to work together on case studies, by assigning small groups to conduct research projects, and by moving away from using exams to evaluate students (R. Csiernik, personal communication, May 27, 2018). Other recommended teaching techniques include building supportive relationships with students, incorporating relaxation exercises and fun activities into classes, and ensuring lessons are paced appropriately (Maschi et al., 2013).

A recent study by Tonsing (2018) found that, in an undergraduate research methods course, instructor immediacy behaviours were related to reductions in statistics-related anxiety among social work students. Immediacy behaviours, such as smiling, showing concern for how students were feeling, and being available for students, helped instructors to illustrate their awareness of students' feelings of anxiety and showed students "that their teacher is genuinely humane, and students are thereby less likely to feel fear" (Tonsing, 2018, p. 231). As Tonsing explains, higher levels of instructor immediacy behaviours identified by students "such as engaging students in dialogue about their fears and anxiety, and letting students know that they are available, can significantly reduce students' statistics anxiety" (p. 230). Immediacy behaviours, then, show important areas for instructors to emphasize, particularly when teaching research or statistics courses.

Practicum Characteristics

The practicum experience can be a major source of anxiety for social work students. Given that instructors are usually teaching students as they either prepare for their practicums or during their practicums, it is essential to be aware of the potential anxiety-producing elements of practicums. Considerable research has focused on anxiety among social work students before entering practicums (Rompf et al., 1993; Rosenthal Gelman, 2004; Rosenthal Gelman & Lloyd, 2008; Tompsett et al., 2017). Rosenthal Gelman (2004) investigated the worries of students before beginning field placements, and then later specifically investigated students' pre-practicum anxiety (Rosenthal Gelman & Lloyd, 2008). As identified by Tompsett and colleagues (2017), anxiety has been associated with students learning new skills when entering practicums, with anxiety specifically linked to students feeling "exposed and out of their comfort zone" (p. 20). As well, performance anxiety may be exacerbated in practicum settings (Baird, 2016). However, if performance anxiety lowers with increased experience, as Wolfe (1989) found with musicians, it may be helpful to encourage increased role-play and simulated practice experience before entering social work practicums (Baird, 2016). While increased practice experience may result in increased performance anxiety in the interim for students, more research is needed to determine if this additional experience results in overall decreases in longer-term anxiety. More research is needed to understand the most useful strategies to support students with anxiety related to entering their practicums.

Practicum-related anxiety can also arise from students' relationships with their field instructors (Baird, 2016). Research conducted by Ellis (2001, 2010), within the field of psychology, determined that high anxiety was linked to poor working relationships with clinical supervisors, and low anxiety was linked to positive relationships with clinical supervisors. Litvack et al. (2010) found that when field instructors responded to students by normalizing their anxiety, this in turn helped to reduce negative emotions among students. Field instructors can help to normalize anxiety by discussing feelings of worry, fear, and anxiety as common and expected experiences during practicums, and by making sure that students receive the message that making mistakes is part of the learning process. These findings suggest that field instructors play an important role in helping to mitigate anxiety in social work students (Litvack et al., 2010).

Outside of practicums, social work educators provide empathy to uncertain students, provide detailed information about practicum settings, devote time to discussing time-management strategies before entering practicums, and discuss the ways practicum experiences can be emotionally challenging and anxiety provoking (Didham et al., 2011; Rompf et al., 1993). Educators can also ensure that students are aware of on-campus counselling services to help with anxiety and continue in the classroom to discuss both helpful and unhelpful aspects of anxiety. In addition, a recent pilot study by Boath and colleagues (2017), using emotional freedom techniques (EFT) (Craig, 2011) to reduce anxiety among social work students pre-practicum, offers a concept that social work programs could consider adapting. EFT is a four-stage therapeutic intervention involving repeating affirmations while tapping acupressure points (Boath et al., 2017; Craig, 2011). EFT was found to significantly reduce performance anxiety when social work students practised it before completing a practice-based skills assessment (Boath et al., 2017). Qualitative results also indicated that EFT was "calming, relaxing and helpful," as well as "a transferable skill," suggesting that the addition of EFT training into curricula may help prepare students to cope with anxiety, as well as providing them with practice skills (Boath et al., 2017, p. 722).

Teaching Style

Another important consideration is how teaching style impacts students' experiences of anxiety. A study by McMillan and colleagues (2007) found that the use of adult learning techniques with nursing students, particularly focusing on self-directed learning, while providing clear goals and structure and building on the life experiences of students, helped reduce anxiety in science and theory courses. Teaching styles have also been linked to student anxiety in English as a foreign language courses, with facilitating and supportive teaching styles linked to lower anxiety among students, compared to expert or formal teaching styles (Briesmaster & Briesmaster-Paredes, 2015). This study also found twice the rate of anxiety among female participants as among male participants, with female participants describing how they sought out instructors they perceived as supportive and flexible as a way to cope with anxiety.

The manner in which an instructor's teaching style relates to the context of the institutional culture, or relates to the teaching style of students' previous instructors, can produce or reduce anxiety. For instance, if students have had previous courses with instructors who teach from a formal structured or authoritative stance, they may feel increased anxiety when encountering an instructor teaching from a more collaborative or relational-based pedagogy emphasizing student choice. In response, instructors may need to spend additional time discussing their teaching approach with students at the beginning of each course to help students adjust to their different teaching style. This phenomenon also calls for instructors to continue to reflect on their teaching style and its effect on students, and to check in with students not only about the content of courses, but also about how their teaching techniques are fitting with students' learning needs. More research is needed to examine links between teaching styles and student anxiety within the field of social work.

Understanding Differing Student Needs

Important in responding to student anxiety is recognizing different student needs. Didham and colleagues' (2011) study drew attention to differences between undergraduate and graduate social work student experiences of anxiety, finding that graduate students were less anxious than undergraduates about their field practicums. Another study of undergraduate and graduate social work students' perceptions of their pre-practicum skills found that they also had different learning preferences (Tompsett et al., 2017). The study found that graduate students "valued multi-source feedback, particularly from authoritative, independent and credible sources, while undergraduates valued peer support in group work" (Tompsett et al., 2017, p. 22). These findings suggest the need to tailor support strategies for anxiety to the differing needs and levels of education of students.

Other studies have identified differences in anxiety related to students' position or year within social work programs. For instance, anxiety related to graduate foundational year students entering practicums has been identified as an issue (Rosenthal Gelman, 2004; Rosenthal Gelman & Lloyd, 2008). However, Stanley and Mettilda Bhuvaneswari's (2016) study revealed that, in a three-year undergraduate program, students in the first and third years had high levels of anxiety, with the third-year students' levels rating the highest. Again, this finding shows the need for educators to recognize differences among stages of social work programs and to develop strategies, to support students coping with anxiety, that correspond to stressors at particular points of the programs. For first-year students, recommendations include using orientation to "brief students about the nature of the course, the institutional ethos, the subjects that they will be taught and aspects relating to assignments, examinations, evaluation and other academic requirements" (p. 87). Further, Stanley and Mettilda Bhuvaneswari recommend ensuring that first-year students are told how to access supports, as well as devoting resources to allow for an academic lead to meet with students monthly to discuss any concerns they might have or answer any questions. In contrast, third-year students' anxieties were often related to completing programs successfully and preparing for what happens after graduation. Stanley and Mettilda Bhuvaneswari recommend instituting support systems, such as study groups and cohort meetings to help alleviate anxiety among third-year students. They state that "anxieties usually revolve around clearing their final examination and any arrears (examinations not passed in the previous years) that add to their academic baggage, anxieties relating to whether to pursue a postgraduate degree or to explore vocational options" (p. 86).

Recent discussions about differences in anxiety between generations of students are also important to recognize. For instance, some claim that millennial students, born between 1982 and 2003, may show more anxiety that other generations of students (Wilson & Gerber, 2008). Others have suggested that millennial social work students prefer safe and structured environments, which in turn can create anxiety when dealing with the many unknowns that occur during field practicums (Moore, 2012). However, others suggest that millennials in particular may not be as different from other generations as previously suggested (DiLullo et al., 2011). While it is crucial to be aware of different needs among students, including aspects of their identities, such as their age, generalizations based on age or generation must be avoided as all students have unique needs as individuals.

Another difference among students to consider may be related to emotional regulation skills. Given previous links made between emotional regulation and anxiety (Amstadter, 2008), this is an area that social work educators may want to address during orientations to both undergraduate and graduate social work programs, as well as within social work curricula. Emotional regulation has been described as an important skill for social work students to develop to manage anxiety (Birnbaum, 2008; Katz et al., 2014). In a study that investigated social work students' responses to their simulated interviews of suicidal service users, students who rated themselves as having low confidence in their risk assessment and interview skills also described having difficulties with anxiety. Students themselves linked these difficulties with anxiety to problems regulating emotions (Bogo et al., 2017; Regehr et al., 2016).

Because no set response to student anxiety can be recommended based solely on a student's age, gender identity, race, culture, country of origin, ability, or sexual orientation, it is important for instructors to recognize that all students have unique needs. A study by Chi-pun Liu (2017) investigated the impact of intersectional identities within social work programs. In particular, the study found that "the intersections between race, gender and learning difficulty has moderated the academic performance of some students" (p. 235), suggesting the need to further explore how some students may have more difficulty because of intersections of racism, oppression, and other forms of discrimination. Further investigation is needed to understand how this relates to students' experiences of anxiety, as well as the most helpful responses for instructors.

Different mental health needs among students are also important to recognize. Mental health difficulties, such as depression, anxiety, trauma, and suicidal ideation, have been identified by social work students (Didham et al., 2011; Horton et al., 2009). More broadly, there is a growing awareness of mental health issues among all university students, with a Canadian study reporting dramatically increasing rates of depression, eating disorders, and psychotic symptoms among students in the last few decades (Matthews & Csiernik, 2019). Students struggling with mental health issues can also be at risk for substance misuse (Eisenberg et al., 2007). Although it is suggested that substance misuse is underreported among university students (Matthews & Csiernik, 2019; Robinson et al., 2016), it is important, as one social work study found (Didham et al.,

2011), for instructors to be aware that students may increase their substance use as a way to cope with worsening anxiety. This is a concern because mental health and substance use issues can impact students' academic success, their relationships, and their overall well-being (Eisenberg et al., 2007). Thus, given the prevalence of many mental health issues that can co-occur with anxiety, it is essential that instructors consider students' overall mental health when teaching social work (Baird, 2016).

Trauma is a particularly concerning issue affecting social work students, with a Canadian study finding that a majority of undergraduate and graduate social work students had experienced one or more traumatic events before entering their social work program (Didham et al., 2011). Given the links between characteristics of anxiety and trauma, this is an important issue for instructors (American Psychiatric Association, 2013; Cisler & Olatunji, 2012). Also of concern is the potential for students' past traumatic experiences to be exacerbated by further distressing and/or traumatic experiences with instructors, with classmates, or during practicums (Didham et al., 2011). Among student populations that are often largely female, as in social work, the high rates of previous exposure to trauma may be related to higher rates of gender-based violence and oppression among women, with one in three women worldwide reporting experiencing sexual or intimate partner violence in their lifetime (World Health Organization, 2017).

Consequently, in response to increasing concern about mental health difficulties such as anxiety among university students, most Canadian universities have developed comprehensive plans to help support students. A review of mental health strategies among Canadian universities found that individual counselling was the most commonly offered mental health service. As well, the study identified that services such as stress-reduction programs were frequently offered to support students coping with anxiety and other mental health concerns, and that almost half (47 per cent) of English-language Canadian universities offered specialized counselling services for anxiety (Matthews & Csiernik, 2019). Social work educators, therefore, need to ensure students are aware of, and referred to, these mental health services. However, in addition to referring students to on-campus mental health services, social work programs are in a unique position to offer further supports to students experiencing anxiety, such as by teaching skills in mindfulness or cognitive-behavioural therapy (CBT), as these interventions have been found to reduce anxiety among students (Katz et al., 2014; Regehr et al., 2013).

Implementing Useful Support Strategies

When considering how best to support students coping with anxiety, and also to help anxiety to be optimized as a motivating influence in learning when appropriate, strategies can be implemented in several areas of social work programs, as suggested below.

PROGRAM STRATEGIES

- Ensure adequate resources and referrals for individual supports and student mental health and counselling services (Matthews & Csiernik, 2019; Stanley & Mettilda Bhuvaneswari, 2016).
- Provide training/workshops and techniques in mindfulness and CBT (Katz et al., 2014; Regehr et al., 2013).
- Tailor support strategies to recognize changing needs and differences in anxiety related to the structure of the program and at different points in the program (Rosenthal Gelman & Lloyd, 2008; Stanley & Mettilda Bhuvaneswari, 2016).
- Ensure adequate orientation to program philosophies and available supports at the beginning of programs and cohort check-in meetings (Stanley & Mettilda Bhuvaneswari, 2016).

PRACTICUM STRATEGIES

- Understand the unique stressors and potential for anxiety related to practicums (Didham et al., 2011; Tompsett et al., 2017).
- Normalize possibilities for increased performance-based anxiety during practicums (Baird, 2016).
- Support students by normalizing and addressing potential anxiety-provoking situations, such as difficulties with supervisory relationships (Baird, 2016; Didham et al., 2011; Litvack et al., 2010).
- Refer students to university mental health programs for further support (Matthews & Csiernik, 2019).

TEACHING STRATEGIES

- Consider including mindfulness, journal writing, and EFT into courses, if appropriate Baird, 2016; Boath et al., 2017; Katz et al., 2014).
- Recognize the potential for certain course material to be anxiety provoking and plan accordingly (Einbinder, 2014; Maschi et al., 2013).
- Discuss anxiety in ways that connects it to broader societal events and forms of oppression (e.g., traumatic events, shared trauma, current events) (Chi-pun Liu, 2017; Didham et al., 2011, Tosone, 2003).

- Check in with students about anxiety and on how they are doing in courses.
- Reflect on the impact of teaching style on student anxiety and adjust accordingly.
- Reflect on the use of instructor immediacy behaviours and how to include more of them (Tonsing, 2018).
- Consider presenting and discussing anxiety in the classroom in a normalizing, balanced way (potentially overwhelming and/or potentially motivating) (Baird, 2016).
- Refer students to university mental health programs for further support (Matthews & Csiernik, 2019).

Conclusion

Anxiety is an issue of growing concern among postsecondary educators. During recent years, universities have become increasingly aware of, and concerned about, high levels of anxiety experienced by students and about how to best support students (Bayram & Bilgel, 2008; Matthews & Csiernik, 2019). For social work educators, this is important to consider in preparing students to work in an occupation that is described as both rewarding and highly stressful (Collins, 2008). In response, this chapter has provided concepts integral to understanding anxiety among social work students, as well as strategies to implement to support social work students with this anxiety.

REFERENCES

Alpert, R., & Haber, R. N. (1960). Anxiety in academic achievement situations. *The Journal of Abnormal and Social Psychology, 61*(2), 207–15. https://doi.org/10.1037/h0045464

American Psychiatric Association. (2013). *Diagnostic and statistical manual of mental disorders: DSM-5* (5th ed.).

Amstadter, A. (2008). Emotion regulation and anxiety disorders. *Journal of Anxiety Disorders, 22*(2), 211–21. https://doi.org/10.1016/j.janxdis.2007.02.004

Atherton, C. R. (1974). The effect of work experience on the self-concept and anxiety level of the social work graduate student. *British Journal of Social Work, 4*(4), 435–44. https://doi.org/10.1093/oxfordjournals.bjsw.a056524

Baird, S. L. (2016). Conceptualizing anxiety among social work students: Implications for social work education. *Social Work Education, 35*(6), 719–32. https://doi.org/10.1080/02615479.2016.1184639

Bayram, N., & Bilgel, N. (2008). The prevalence and socio-demographic correlations of depression, anxiety and stress among a group of university students. *Social Psychiatry and Psychiatric Epidemiology, 43*(8), 667–72. https://doi.org/10.1007/s00127-008-0345-x

Birnbaum, L. (2008). The use of mindfulness training to create an "Accompanying place" for social work students. *Social Work Education, 27*(8), 837–52. https://doi.org/10.1080/02615470701538330

Boath, E., Good, R., Tsaroucha, A., Stewart, T., Pitch, S., & Boughey, A. J. (2017). Tapping your way to success: Using emotional freedom techniques (EFT) to reduce anxiety and improve communication skills in social work students. *Social Work Education, 36*(6), 715–30. https://doi.org/10.1080/02615479.2017.1297394

Bogo, M., Regehr, C., Baird, S. L., Paterson, J., & LeBlanc, V. (2017). Cognitive and affective elements of practice confidence in social work students and practitioners. *The British Journal of Social Work, 47*(3), 701–18. https://doi.org/10.1093/bjsw/bcw026

Briesmaster, M., & Briesmaster-Paredes, J. (2015). The relationship between teaching styles and NNPSETs' anxiety levels. *System: An International Journal of Educational Technology and Applied Linguistics, 49*, 145–56. https://doi.org/10.1016/j.system.2015.01.012

Carello, J., & Butler, L. (2015). Practicing what we teach: Trauma-informed educational practice. *Journal of Teaching in Social Work, 35*(3), 262–8. https://doi.org/10.1080/08841233.2015.1030059

Cheng, W. K., Hardy, L., & Markland, D. (2009). Toward a three-dimensional conceptualization of performance anxiety: Rationale and initial measurement development. *Psychology of Sport & Exercise, 10*(2), 271–8. https://doi.org/10.1016/j.psychsport.2008.08.001

Chi-pun Liu, B. (2017). Intersectional impact of multiple identities on social work education in the UK. *Journal of Social Work, 17*(2), 226–42. https://doi.org/10.1177/1468017316637220

Cisler, J. M., & Olatunji, B. O. (2012). Emotion regulation and anxiety disorders. *Current Psychiatry Reports, 14*(3), 182–7. https://doi.org/10.1007/s11920-012-0262-2

Collins, S. (2006). Mental health difficulties and the support needs of social work students: Dilemmas, tensions and contradictions. *Social Work Education, 25*(5), 446–60. https://doi.org/10.1080/02615470600738809

Collins, S. (2008). Statutory social workers: Stress, job satisfaction, coping, social support and individual differences. *The British Journal of Social Work, 38*(6), 1173–93. https://doi.org/10.1093/bjsw/bcm047

Craig, G. (2011). *The EFT manual* (2nd ed.). Energy Psychology Press.

Csiernik, R., & Birnbaum, R. (2017). *Practicing social work research: Case studies for learning* (2nd ed.). University of Toronto Press.

Davis, S. (2004). Statistics anxiety among female African American graduate-level social work students. *Journal of Teaching in Social Work, 23*(3–4), 143–58. https://doi.org/10.1300/j067v23n03_12

Day, V., McGrath, P. J., & Wojtowicz, M. (2013). Internet-based guided self-help for university students with anxiety, depression and stress: A randomized controlled clinical trial. *Behaviour Research and Therapy, 51*(7), 344–51. https://doi.org/10.1016/j.brat.2013.03.003

Didham, S., Dromgole, L., Csiernik, R., Karley, M. L., & Hurley, D. (2011). Trauma exposure and the social work practicum. *Journal of Teaching in Social Work, 31*(5), 523–37. https://doi.org/10.1080/08841233.2011.615261

DiLullo, C., McGee, P., & Kriebel, R. M. (2011). Demystifying the millennial student: A reassessment in measures of character and engagement in professional education. *Anatomical Sciences Education, 4*(4), 214. https://doi.org/10.1002/ase.240

Einbinder, S. D. (2014). Reducing research anxiety among MSW students. *Journal of Teaching in Social Work, 34*(1), 2–16. https://doi.org/10.1080/08841233.2013.863263

Eisenberg, D., Gollust, S. E., Golberstein, E., & Hefner, J. L. (2007). Prevalence and correlates of depression, anxiety, and suicidality among university students. *American Journal of Orthopsychiatry, 77*(4), 534–42. https://doi.org/10.1037/0002-9432.77.4.534

Ellis, M. V. (2001). Harmful supervision, a cause for alarm: Comment on Gray et al. (2001) and Nelson and Friedlander (2001). *Journal of Counseling Psychology, 48*(4), 401–6. https://doi.org/10.1037/0022-0167.48.4.401

Ellis, M. V. (2010). Bridging the science and practice of clinical supervision: Some discoveries, some misconceptions. *The Clinical Supervisor, 29*(1), 95–116. https://doi.org/10.1080/07325221003741910

Gustavsson, N. S., & MacEachron, A. E. (2001). Perspectives on research-related anxiety among BSW students: An exploratory study. *Journal of Baccalaureate Social Work,* 7(1), 111. https://doi.org/10.18084/1084-7219.7.1.111

Hopko, D. R., McNeil, D. W., Zvolensky, M. J., & Eifert, G. H. (2001). The relation between anxiety and skill in performance-based anxiety disorders: A behavioral formulation of social phobia. *Behavior Therapy, 32*(1), 185–207. https://doi.org/10.1016/s0005-7894(01)80052-6

Horton, E. G., Diaz, N., & Green, D. (2009). Mental health characteristics of social work students: Implications for social work education. *Social Work in Mental Health,* 7(5), 458–75. https://doi.org/10.1080/15332980802467696

Katz, E., Tufford, L., Bogo, M., & Regehr, C. (2014). Illuminating students' pre-practicum conceptual and emotional states: Implications for field education. *Journal of Teaching in Social Work, 34*(1), 96–108. https://doi.org/10.1080/08841233.2013.868391

Litvack, A., Bogo, M., & Mishna, F. (2010). Emotional reactions of students in field education: An exploratory study. *Journal of Social Work Education, 46*(2), 227–43. https://doi.org/10.5175/jswe.2010.200900007

Lloyd, C., King, R., & Chenoweth, L. (2002). Social work, stress and burnout: A review. *Journal of Mental Health, 11*(3), 255–65. https://doi.org/10.1080/09638230020023642

Maschi, T., Bradley, C., Youdin, R., Killian, M. L., Cleaveland, C., & Barbera, R. A. (2007). Social work students and the research process: Exploring the thinking, feeling, and doing of research. *The Journal of Baccalaureate Social Work, 13*(1), 1–12. https://doi.org/10.18084/1084-7219.13.1.1

Maschi, T., Wells, M., Yoder Slater, G., MacMillan, T., & Ristow, J. (2013). Social work students' research-related anxiety and self-efficacy: Research instructors' perceptions and teaching innovations. *Social Work Education, 32*(6), 800–17. https://doi.org/10.1080/02615479.2012.695343

Matthews, M., & Csiernik, R. (2019). A review of mental health services offered by Canada's English language universities. *Canadian Social Work, 20*(2), 31–48.

McGinnis, A. M., & Milling, L. S. (2005). Psychological treatment of musical performance anxiety: Current status and future directions. *Psychotherapy: Theory/Research/Practice/Training, 42*(3), 357–73. https://doi.org/10.1037/0033-3204.42.3.357

McMillan, D., Bell, S., Benson, E. E., Mandzuk, L., Matias, D. M., McIvor, M. J., Robertson, J. E., & Wilkins, K. L. (2007). From anxiety to enthusiasm: Facilitating graduate nursing students' knowledge development in science and theory. *Journal of Nursing Education, 46*(2), 88–91. https://doi.org/10.3928/01484834-20070201-10

Moore, L. (2012). Millennials in social work field education. *Field Educator, 2*(2). http://www2.simmons.edu/ssw/fe/i/Moore.pdf

Quinn, A. (2006). Reducing social work students' statistics anxiety. *Academic Exchange Quarterly, 10*(2), 167.

Regehr, C., Bogo, M., LeBlanc, V. L, Baird, S., Paterson, J., & Birze, A. (2016). Suicide risk assessment: Clinicians' confidence in their professional judgment. *Journal of Loss and Trauma, 21*(1), 30–46. https://doi.org/10.1080/15325024.2015.1072012

Regehr, C., Glancy, D., & Pitts, A. (2013). Interventions to reduce stress in university students: A review and meta-analysis. *Journal of Affective Disorders, 148*(1), 1–11. https://doi.org/10.1016/j.jad.2012.11.026

Reiss, N., Warnecke, I., Tolgou, T., Krampena, D., Luka-Krausgrillb, U., & Rohrmann, S. (2017). Effects of cognitive behavioral therapy with relaxation vs. imagery rescripting on test anxiety: A randomized controlled trial. *Journal of Affective Disorders, 208*, 483–9. https://doi.org/10.1016/j.jad.2016.10.039

Robinson, Am. M., Jubenville, T. M., Renny, K., & Cairns, S. (2016). Academic and mental health needs of students on a Canadian campus. *Canadian Journal of Counselling and Psychotherapy, 50*(2), 108–23.

Rompf, E. L., Royse, D., & Dhooper, S. S. (1993). Anxiety preceding field work: What students worry about. *Journal of Teaching in Social Work, 7*(2), 81–95. https://doi.org/10.1300/j067v07n02_07

Rosenthal Gelman, C. (2004). Anxiety experienced by foundation-year MSW students entering field placement: Implications for admissions, curriculum, and field education. *Journal of Social Work Education, 40*(1), 39–54. https://doi.org/10.1080/10437797.2004.10778478

Rosenthal Gelman, C., & Baum, N. (2010). Social work students' pre-placement anxiety: An international comparison. *Social Work Education, 29*(4), 427–40. https://doi.org/10.1080/02615470903009007

Rosenthal Gelman, C., & Lloyd, C. M. (2008). Pre-placement anxiety among foundation-year MSW students: A follow-up study. *Journal of Social Work Education, 44*(1), 173–83. https://doi.org/10.5175/jswe.2008.200600102

Royse, D., & Rompf, E. L. (1992). Math anxiety: A comparison of social work and non-social work students. *Journal of Social Work Education, 28*(3), 270–7. https://doi.org/10.1080/10437797.1992.10778780

Shulman, L. S. (2005). Signature pedagogies in the professions. *Daedalus, 134*(3), 52–9. https://doi.org/10.1162/0011526054622015

Stanley, S., & Mettilda Bhuvaneswari, G. (2016). Stress, anxiety, resilience and coping in social work students (a study from India). *Social Work Education, 35*(1), 78–88. https://doi.org/10.1080/02615479.2015.1118451

Taborsky, C. (2007). Musical performance anxiety: A review of literature. *Update: Applications of Research in Music Education, 26*(1), 15–25. https://doi.org/10.1177/87551233070260010103

Tompsett, H., Henderson, K., Mathew Byrne, J., Gaskell Mew, E., & Tompsett, C. (2017). On the learning journey: What helps and hinders the development of social work students' core pre-placement skills? *Social Work Education, 36*(1), 6–25. https://doi.org/10.1080/02615479.2016.1249836

Tonsing, K. N. (2018). Instructor immediacy and statistics anxiety in social work undergraduate students. *Social Work Education, 37*(2), 223–33. https://doi.org/10.1080/02615479.2017.1395009

Tosone, C., Lee, M., Bialkin, L., Martinez, A., Campbell, M., Martinez, M. M., Charters, M., Milich, J., Gieri, K., Riofrio, A., Gross, S., Rosenblatt, L., Grounds, C., Sandler, J., Johnson, K., Scali, M., Kitson, D., Spiro, M., Lanzo, S., & Stefan, A. (2003). Shared trauma. *Psychoanalytic Social Work, 10*(1), 57–77. https://doi.org/10.1300/j032v10n01_06

Wayne, J., Bogo, M., & Raskin, M. (2010). Field education as the signature pedagogy of social work education. *Journal of Social Work Education, 46*(3), 327–39. https://doi.org/10.5175/jswe.2010.200900043

Wilson, M., & Gerber, L. E. (2008). How generational theory can improve teaching: Strategies for working with the "Millennials." *Currents in Teaching and Learning, 1*(1), 29–44.

Wilson, W. C., & Rosenthal, B. (1993). Anxiety and performance in an MSW research and statistics course. *Journal of Teaching in Social Work, 6*(2), 75–85. https://doi.org/10.1300/j067v06n02_07

Wolfe, M. L. (1989). Correlates of adaptive and maladaptive musical performance anxiety. *Medical Problems of Performing Artists, 4*(1), 49–56.

Wong, S. S. (2008). The relations of cognitive triad, dysfunctional attitudes, automatic thoughts, and irrational beliefs with test anxiety. *Current Psychology, 27*(3), 177–91. https://doi.org/10.1007/s12144-008-9033-y

World Health Organization. (2017). *Intimate partner and sexual violence against women: Fact sheet.* http://www.who.int/mediacentre/factsheets/fs239/en/

18 Teaching from the Margins: No Good Deed Goes Unpunished

SUSAN HILLOCK

This chapter is a continuation of the themes examined in chapter 3 on femagogy. There, femagogy was defined as an approach to teaching and education that emphasizes feminist-centred teaching theory, knowledges, and methods. From this viewpoint, the social work classroom is viewed as a consciousness-raising and social change laboratory where educators can choose to either perpetuate or disrupt cultural norms. Some have referred to this as teaching "from the margins" (Brown & Strega, 2005; Kirby & McKenna, 1989). As Brown and Strega (2005) explain:

> Teaching and learning from the margins is, on the one hand, self-explanatory in a generation of teachers and learners familiar with the influences of civil rights, "waves" of women's movements, critical race theories, queer theory, theories of disability and equity rights and so on. On the other hand, an awareness of these contemporary social movements is only a beginning in understanding how these theories are reflected and engaged within our classroom spaces, either intentionally or unexpectedly. (p. 3)

Others have described this as teaching "difficult knowledge" (Britzman, 1998, p. 13). At times, this "collision, then, of radical questions and liberal solutions, ... and a world naturally resistant to its critique" (Jeffery, 2007, p. 128) have been difficult for me, and my academic colleagues and students, especially as my resistance enterprise has been housed inside traditional liberal patriarchal universities.

This chapter further examines femagogy by taking up Razack's (1999) invitation to discuss major challenges social work educators face when they teach from the margins. Razack (1999) argues, "many articles tell us what to teach but tend not to deal with the major challenges the teacher and students face in the classroom" (p. 234). To more deeply examine this topic, I share personal academic experiences to illustrate some of the challenges inherent in applying alternative perspectives to social work education. Even though I make a point of using teaching methodologies consistent with feminist, and social work, values and principles, my efforts are often met with backlash. Backlash manifests itself in many ways, including hostile student/colleague reactions, harassment, complaints, lower course evaluations, classroom disruption, and resistance to critical ideas. These negative responses to individuals, methods, and knowledges outside the mainstream create and perpetuate an unequal and "chilly climate" for faculty who teach from the margins, as well as for students who learn from that location (The Chilly Collective, 1995). This chapter concludes with an exploration of the challenges inherent in applying femagogy to social work education and provides recommendations regarding how to better support educators and students who may experience backlash, how to transform/disrupt social work education to more effectively include voices and knowledges from the margins, and how to warm up campus climates by increasing inclusion, solidarity, and social action.

Teaching from the Margins: A Ton of Feathers

Some people may be familiar with the term *a ton of feathers* used to describe women's, and other marginalized groups, experiences of discrimination in academia (Caplan, 1993; The Chilly Collective, 1995). Others describe this as "death by a thousand papercuts." These experiences are consistent with much of the literature about the micro-aggressions that marginalized peoples encounter in their personal and professional lives (Pierce, 1995). An illuminating story about my academic experiences will help elucidate the above themes.

I started working as a full-time faculty member almost 20 years ago. I arrived on campus, a new faculty member, full of excitement and energy, expecting to work in an environment that would be personally, professionally, and intellectually stimulating and rewarding. Instead, I found myself in a conservative bastion of White, straight, male over-advantage that perpetuated discriminatory attitudes and practices. The combination of me being female and propounding alternative social work paradigms often resulted in my theoretical approaches and expertise being invalidated and minimized by colleagues. One time, while I was presenting feminist analysis in a faculty meeting, a male colleague exclaimed that "all feminist theory is crap." Disrespect for women is not unusual; indeed, Keller and Moglen (1987) found that "many women faculty experience ... patronizing judgements made by scornful male teachers and colleagues" (p. 26). Other micro-aggressions that I have experienced include being publicly told by a male faculty to "shut the fuck up," having a male director scream at me and wag his finger in my face like I was a small child, having another male colleague grab my ass, fighting off another male who tried to stick his hand down the front of my skirt, and once, when I refused to support a male colleague's proposal, having him come up to me and physically shake me. When I complained about the treatment I was receiving to the individuals involved, to directors and deans, even to my union, my experience was minimized, invalidated, denied, and brushed off as personality conflicts and misunderstandings. Indeed, the universities and their administrators refused to ever define or frame my experiences the way that I see them: as directly related to systemic gender and heterosexist discrimination within educational institutions.

Not only did I receive backlash for naming my gendered reality and demanding change but, in hindsight, I now see that one of my biggest sins was my refusal to perform the female gender adequately enough to meet my colleagues' sexist expectations. For instance, I was once asked in a faculty meeting to bake cookies for a student fundraiser. When I laughed and refused to do this, and pointed out the fact that no one expected or asked our male colleagues to bake, the female chair at the time responded, "Well, not all of us are as altruistic as others." Similar statements were made to me, and about me, when I refused to volunteer for unpaid weekend work at high school career fairs, despite being a lone-parent mother with two small children. Consistent with Williams et al.'s (2006) findings, the realities of managing lone-parent mothering and high academic workload demands are rarely acknowledged in university settings.

Moreover, although equality, respect, and anti-oppressive rhetoric abounds in the social work profession (Hillock, 2011), what I have found to be most painful are the colleagues who collude with the powers that be and stand by watching while those identified as "other" are being harmed. To survive, and succeed, they learn to side with power rather than speak to it or challenge it. Their silence, denial, refusal to act, and collusion underpin and support the gendered, racist, and cisgender/heterosexist dominant-subordinate relations that perpetuate oppression. These experiences can also lead to already marginalized faculty members experiencing loneliness, ostracism, and isolation at their workplace (Overall, 1998; Williams et al., 2006).

These academic experiences have been extremely painful for me. When I discuss this with others outside our profession, they are shocked that this happens within the social work profession, a profession where we claim to hold values like respect, caring, and human dignity. Rebick (2009) cites anti-racist teacher Shakil Choudhury:

> We have these fantastic theories, anti-racist theories, post-colonial theories. If our theories are so good, then shouldn't progressive organizations be the example of how to live in healthy relationship with one another … But often there is more dysfunction in these organizations than anywhere else. (p. 109)

Of course, we could mistakenly make the assumption that these concerns and personal experiences are more about organizational dynamics, personality conflicts, and individual hurts and inconveniences rather than oppression. However, this narrow view misses the point that work, how it is constructed, and our individual experiences within these social and cultural institutions are also influenced, mediated, and constrained by the same dominant-subordinate social relations that underlie all oppressions. Indeed, an individual experience of oppression or discrimination may seem as inconsequential and light as a feather, particularly when viewed from someone else's standpoint, often from a place of privilege, but over time from the view of oppressed persons, a "ton of feathers" can be overwhelming, exhausting, and debilitating (Caplan, 1993).

Being a Cisgender Female in Academia

Significantly, the reality of my lived experience is congruent with the research about women's experiences of discrimination in academia. Indeed, Overall (1998) discusses the common sexist experiences and consequences for women in the academy:

> There is much evidence – ranging from the dangers of sexual assault and harassment and the contempt for feminist scholarship, to women's higher workload in student counselling and committees and the paucity of women who are full professors or hold significant administrative positions. (p. 38)

As previously discussed in chapter 1, greater demands are also placed upon female professors. Female faculty "are expected to be 'restrained and endlessly supportive' of colleagues while picking up extra secretarial work and to be 'softer' and more available to students than male colleagues" (Williams et al., 2006, p. 82). Similarly, I received backlash when I refused to mother or counsel students on personal issues, thus breaking the existing "female" patterns and traditions in my particular faculty. This is something male colleagues do not experience or, at least, not to the same extent (El-Alayli et al., 2017; Williams et al., 2006). This gendered expectation that women do what has been called *emotional labour* results in more of our work hours being spent dealing with students' academic and personal issues than for our male colleagues (El-Alayli et al., 2017). The time and energy spent on these tasks can also negatively impact female faculty members' research and their tenure and promotion processes (Rinfrette et al., 2015). As well, in a classic double bind, if we are indeed "supporting and nurturing, female instructors risk being perceived as less authoritative and knowledgeable than their male counterparts" (Mulhere, 2014, p. 2).

Pay inequity is another example of a long line of discriminatory and exclusionary practices at universities. In agreement, Maranto and Griffin (2010) found that "procedural fairness and gender equity are powerful factors that foster inclusion and warm the climate for both men and women" (p. 139). However, the primary difference is that most cisgender, white, straight men generally do not have to worry about gender equity or fairness. Research clearly demonstrates that men are over-rewarded compared to their female counterparts (Acker & Armenti, 2004; Corrice, 2009; Maranto & Griffin, 2010; Overall, 1998). Correspondingly, while women continue to be treated unfairly, there is little appetite on campuses to talk about the simultaneous privileging and over-advantaging of cisgender, white, heterosexual, and able-bodied male faculty.

Backlash

Teaching from the margins is not easy or simple. Institutions of higher education are not immune from inequality, discriminatory practices, and oppressive forces. In fact, one might argue that it is not surprising that traditional institutions and their employees reflect the oppressive structures and dynamics of racist, classist, and patriarchal capitalist societies (Superson & Cudd, 2002). In addition, many students and faculty, who often come from privileged backgrounds, do not necessarily agree with progressive approaches or desire transformational teaching and learning experiences; therefore, backlash is likely to occur (El-Alayli et al., Hillock, 2011; Jeffery, 2007; Lund, 2010: Overall, 1998; Rebick, 2009; The Chilly Collective, 1995). One explanation for this might be that alternative teaching models are perceived as intrusions into social and cultural norms and institutional spaces. As Schick (2005) explains:

> When this intrusion happens – when an issue becomes too personal for comfort – participants use their indignation to re-establish the dominant identities and central positions. The space must be maintained; the

> identities – those who are in control and those who are not – cannot be confused. (p. 214)

Jeyapal and Grigg, in chapter 6, come to similar conclusions in their exploration of the phenomenon of the crying white woman.

In direct contradiction to the emancipatory and social justice rhetoric that abounds on university websites and in policy statements, Caplan (1993) and The Chilly Collective (1995) found that the educators who actively and consciously try to identify their bias, name their social locations and identities, disrupt traditional educational practices, and centre knowledge from the margins are more likely to experience backlash. In my opinion, little has changed over the last 20 years. In agreement, Redmond (2010) and Schick (2005) argue that resistance to alternative paradigms that attempt to interrogate and disrupt traditional knowledges is really about the privileging and entitlement of whiteness, racism, sexism, and classism, and how they are entrenched and maintained in classrooms and academic institutions. Furthermore, Schick suggests that

> cross-cultural, multicultural initiatives – also called anti-racist or oppositional – frequently meet with resistance. Difficulty in implementing and teaching such courses suggest that they pose some kind of threat in the spaces where they are introduced. (p. 210)

Intersectional Analysis

Student reactions to chilly campuses and alternative teaching perspectives vary greatly depending on the multiple identities and subjectivities of differentially located students (Muhtaseb, 2007). In their research into traditional male- and female-dominated academic disciplines, Morris and Daniel (2008) found that

> women found the climate chillier than men, non-white students found the climate chillier than white students, younger students perceived the climate chillier than older students, and students in traditionally female-dominated majors perceived the climate chillier than students in traditionally male-dominated majors. (p. 256)

Of course, some students always flourish when exposed to feminist ideas and methods. In my experience, they tend to be students who already occupy marginalized social locations/identities. Like female, racialized, and queer faculty, they too pay the price for being "othered" in traditional systems. For example, many female and queer students experience violence and sexual harassment on university and college campuses (Carey et al., 2015). Likewise, many racialized students and those living with disability feel unsupported and are pushed out of traditional educational systems (Schick, 2005).

In contrast, some students also have extremely negative reactions to feminist ideas, teaching, and learning. These reactions can include aggressively challenging the teacher's expertise and authority; refusing to cooperate with classroom activities; demanding special favours, extensions, and rewrites; being disrespectful in class; complaining to chairs and deans; and giving female faculty lower course evaluation scores (Coffey & Delamont, 2000; Redmond, 2010; Williams et al., 2006). Research clearly demonstrates that course evaluations are gender biased and "disadvantage female instructors" (Flaherty, 2016, p. 2). In fact, they are "biased against female instructors by an amount that is large and statistically significant" (Boring, Ottoboni, & Stark, 2016, p. 1), are "highly correlated with students' grade expectations" (Stark & Freishtat, 2014, p. 13), and measure gender, race, and physical attractiveness bias more than teaching effectiveness (Stark & Freishtat, 2014).

Ironically, the students who have been most upset or resistant in my classes have tended to be cisgender, straight, middle class, white women, which is congruent with what Jeyapal and Grigg also found. One would think female social work students, who tend to experience the feminization of poverty and high rates of sexual and physical abuse, would welcome feminist analysis and methods. That is often not the case. Bartky (2014) speculates that a feminism that genuinely challenges patriarchy actually "threatens women with a certain de-skilling ... it calls into question that aspect of personal identity that is tied to the development of a sense of competence" (p. 79). If done well, it also calls into question white, ableist, class, cisgender, and heterosexist privilege. The feminist instructor, who purposefully and actively disrupts these social norms, must then be punished for making the classroom feel "unsafe," especially for those with privilege.

The Challenges

Educators need to be aware that teaching from the margins is likely to increase the backlash they receive, as well as the discomfort and anxiety of some students, particularly those who have been taught to accept traditional pedagogical methods as the norm. It seems difficult for these students to resolve cognitive dissonance related to consciousness-raising about their privilege, over-advantage, social locations/identities, social/ethical responsibility and accountability, as well as to having their conventional worldviews challenged. According to Jeffery (2007), this may be because teaching from critical frameworks necessitates, for students, an "identity crisis, then offers partiality and incompleteness by way of assisting students to explore professional selves without settling on a stable solution" (p. 135). Teaching from the margins requires a delicate balancing act that invites teachers to critically deconstruct most of what their students have previously been taught and how, while simultaneously managing increased student anxiety and confusion.

Not every student has the maturity or self-awareness to handle these tasks. Nor does every social work program provide adequate support for these struggling students. Similarly, not every educator has the skills, knowledge, or aptitude to manage the classroom unease and disruption necessary for transformational teaching. It is also likely that as educators, we even perpetuate the very things that we are trying to dismantle, for example, racism, sexism, ableism, and classism (Breunig, 2005). To be fair, students' criticisms have some validity in terms of the contradictions they see between social work educators' professed beliefs in egalitarianism and democracy, our role as gatekeepers, and the institution's insistence that we evaluate and grade their efforts. As Davies and Leonard (2004) point out, there can be "a contradiction between the liberatory goals of the critical tradition and the actual oppressive practices that we, as educators and social workers, find ourselves engaging in" (p. xiii). Indeed, many social work educators interested in social justice struggle to balance these competing interests.

Although the challenges can be difficult and some of the criticisms from students are valid, the intensity and viciousness of some students' and colleagues' negative reactions still lead me to suspect that they are less upset about my challenging their ideas and worldviews from the margins, or how I do it, than they are about me being a woman and *daring* to do so. Consequently, although these experiences are painful, I have come to the hopeful conclusion that negative reactions are actually a strong indicator that we are successfully disrupting traditional educational systems and methods (Neverson et al., 2013; Rinfrette et al., 2015).

Femagogy and Social Work Education: Application

Application Challenges

Before instructors attempt to apply femagogy to social work education, they need to first consider their institutional processes and teaching methods. Table 19.1 highlights key application challenges that instructors need to anticipate.

Table 19.1. Femagogy and Social Work Education: Application Challenges

Institutional	Teaching
Managing a large number of students, with a variety of needs, interests, motivation, and capacity	Integrating progressive theory and practice in both the classroom and the field
Increasing demands and needs of the larger university including policies, service work, and grading	Managing cognitive dissonance; exploring identity, social location, and privilege emotionally difficult but rewarding
Teaching critical thinking, adult learning, feminism, social justice, and social work subject area content in short periods of time	Dealing with resistance of students/faculty/systems to innovative and relevant adult-based teaching/learning philosophies and modalities
Negotiating the traditional norms of university that tend to diminish the effectiveness of experiential educational methodologies and negate egalitarian relationships	Handling negative student reactions, including anxiety, complaints about workload, triggers, substance use and mental health issues, gendered demands for emotional labour, and gender-biased course evaluations
Expanding traditional education and its emphasis on content memorization, product, knowledge building, and sharing to critically exploring self as therapeutic tool for future practice	Dispelling myths that simply "being nice" and being aware of privilege, power differentials, and relational dynamics will lead to equality and empowerment of students/service users and effective social work practice; good intentions and consciousness are not always enough
Changing how backlash is received/perceived and creating supports for faculty and students who occupy the margins	Navigating the social work gatekeeping role to protect future at risk vulnerable service user groups by ensuring that students are aware of their privilege, suitable and prepared for practice, and comply with professional ethical standards
Mobilizing collectively across disciplines to research, support, and implement alternative teaching theory, curriculum, and methods	Assessing student and faculty' levels of stress, openness to alternative theory and methods, trust, and past histories
Advocating for progressive policies that target discriminatory and unequal oppressive practices, processes, and behaviours, such as pay, merit, tenure, and promotion equity policies	Not relying solely on compassion but teaching effective praxis (action on the world to make change) such as collective mobilization and social action strategies

Sources: Adapted from Anderson-Nathe et al., 2013; Breunig, 2005; Campbell, 1999, 2002; Coffey & Delamont, 2000; De Freitas & McAuley, 2008; Freire, 1970; Hillock, 2011; Hillock & Profitt, 2007; Penny Light et al., 2015; Razack, 1999; Williams et al., 2006.

Recommendations

Following are a series of recommendations related to how we can (1) better support educators and students who may experience backlash, (2) transform/disrupt social work education to more effectively include voices and knowledges from the margins, and (3) warm up campus climates by increasing inclusion, solidarity, and collective social action.

1. IMPROVING STUDENT AND FACULTY SUPPORTS

For those of us experiencing the highs, lows, and challenges of teaching alternative approaches, we need to create dialogues about, and research into, how to facilitate student learning through classroom and field instruction moments of identity awareness and deconstruction, as well as "stress and uncertainty" (Jeffery, 2007, p. 130). This entails finding more meaningful ways of supporting students as they work through transitional states and moments of intense classroom dynamics and emotional disruption related to learning and applying alternative discourses.

Additionally, Razack (1999) recommends organizing student and faculty coalitions dedicated to discussing, exploring, and resolving particular social justice issues. The aims of these coalitions are to use readings, experiential formats, exercises, dyad, journal work, small-group discussion, and role-plays to provide "a space where students can learn to talk respectfully about experiences of oppression and oppressive forces and can take this discussion outside of the classroom to disrupt and begin to challenge their world" (Jeffery, 2007, p. 243). The challenge then for us becomes one of creating space, within the classroom, field practicum, university, and social service agency, to dialogue respectfully about difference, power, and privilege, identify and explore unequal social and power relations in society, and act together to dismantle oppression. However, this recommendation also assumes that the well-intended critically conscious (Ellsworth, 1989) social work educator "can somehow minimize/dismantle the power imbalances and systemic oppressions that permeate the classroom" (Hillock & Profitt, 2007, p. 39). Research and scholarship are necessary to determine what strategies are most useful to identify, dismantle, and/or creatively use the substantial power differences that exist between various individuals and groups within classrooms and field practicum settings to act collectively inside and outside these "safe" (a contested term itself) sites to make social change.

2. DISRUPTING/TRANSFORMING SOCIAL WORK EDUCATION

Interrogating Intersectional Privilege and Power. Social work educators are strongly urged to examine whiteness, Western, ableist, heterosexist, and cisgender standpoints (De Freitas & McAuley, 2008). Whiteness as a location of structural advantage, as a standpoint from which white people judge themselves and others, and as a set of unnamed and unconscious cultural practices must be analysed and considered in terms of its impact on everyday practices, social work theory, education, therapeutic relationships, field instruction, and research (Lund, 2010; Yee, 2005). As well, men need to become cognizant of how their gender privileges them within their clinical, collegial, personal, and academic relationships. As potential anti-sexist leaders and role models, men are urged to challenge men's violence, harassment, and sexist behaviours; acknowledge their systemic over-advantage; reject pornography and negative stereotypes of women; and support female colleagues, feminist scholarship, and queer rights (Overall, 1998). Social work as a profession needs to consider what factors make it possible for members of dominant groups, who hold various types of privilege, to become more successful allies to equity-seeking groups. It is also essential to determine what barriers exist to transformational education and practice and what more can be done to support allied social workers/colleagues to overcome these barriers.

Teaching Feminist Analysis and Skills. Chapter 3 provides specific suggestions on how to apply femagogy specifically to social work education. In addition, Hillock's (2011) research participants identified specific feminist skills that they believed were essential to their social justice work. These include normalization, validation, reframing, consciousness-raising, and the building of strengths. It is important, then, that these skills are taught in all social work programs as they link the personal to the political and have the potential of motivating people to action (Breunig, 2005). Furthermore, intersectional analysis and understanding the implications of our own sites of oppression, privilege, and resistance are important (Fook, 1993). Carniol (2005) suggests that this intersectional awareness increases our capacity to build social empathy, which can be described as the recognition and understanding of the commonalities that we may share with others who are similarly oppressed.

Increasing Feminist Curriculum Content and Courses. There is an urgent need to foster and develop more feminist content and courses in social work curriculum and programs. Wilkin and Hillock (2015) in their review of the websites of the 23 accredited schools of social work in Canada, found only eight programs offering courses related to issues of abuse in families, violence against women, or feminist practice. This is ironic as most social workers, students, and service users are female. Within the schools that do offer feminist coursework, these courses are mainly offered as sessional electives. This sends the message that issues of oppression, gender-based violence, and stratified inequality are superfluous and unnecessary material compared to the vital and important conventional content being explored in core courses. The paucity of feminist analysis and content, coupled with the fact that most Canadian schools of social work tend to primarily teach dominant clinical models such as cognitive-behavioural, psychodynamic, and systems theories, results in a significant percentage of Canadian social work students graduating with little education on gender inequality, the root causes of gender-based violence, and feminist analyses of social issues (Wilkin & Hillock, 2015).

3. WARMING UP CAMPUS CLIMATES

Improving Working Conditions for Marginalized Groups in Academia. As highlighted in Table 19.1, advocating for progressive policies that target discriminatory and unequal oppressive practices, processes, and behaviours is an essential part of transforming educational institutions. Additionally, trans-disciplinarian networking and research across universities, disciplines, unions, student organizations, and social service/community organizations are helpful in terms of building alliances with others who share progressive philosophies. One model of effective community and academic collaboration is the Metropolitan Action Committee on Public Violence Against Women and Children and its work to raise public awareness; change laws, policies, attitudes, and behaviours; improve legislative, court, and service responses to survivors; develop new training for professionals; encourage increased reporting on college and university campuses; and implement safety audit plans (Ross-Marquette & Komiotis, 2016). In March 2015, the Ontario provincial government launched the It's Never Okay; An Action Plan to Stop Sexual Violence and Harassment, and in September 2017, a new law was enacted in Ontario, Bill 132, called the Sexual Violence and Harassment Action Plan Act (Ross-Marquette & Komiotis, 2016).

In terms of faculty response, Godderis (2016) recommends that we take a "collective responsibility to end violence" (p. 16) by learning more about the violence and harassment that is happening on our campuses; examining how violence and our work may be connected; taking concrete action to make local and global change; developing connections with community partners, university student associations, and equity-seeking groups to decrease violence and harassment on campuses; and showing our support for policy, legislative, attitudinal, and behavioural change.

Promoting Solidarity. We also need to promote solidarity and dialogue among, across, and between academics, students, and field instructors who are attempting feminist approaches within social work. Regular feminist academic and practice conferences, support groups for resistance workers, feminist integrative field seminars, and an interactive website dedicated to feminist practitioners that allows them opportunities to discuss issues related to their theory, practice, field instruction, and research would help support feminist practitioners and educators. Furthermore, a Canadian association of feminist social workers, educators, and programs and community and academic coalitions for interested feminist professionals would be helpful and decrease the isolation and stress that many feminist educators experience.

Providing Hope and Optimism. In my doctoral thesis work with social workers, respondents acknowledged that, at times, they felt hopeless. As a result, they identified the need for hope, optimism, and patience on the part of resistance workers (Hillock, 2011). Correspondingly, I am always surprised to find that many social work students seem more embittered, cynical, and hopeless going into the profession than I am after 30 years of practice and teaching. As social work educators, we need to demonstrate that the global situation is not hopeless. In fact, Rebick (2009) optimistically forecasts that "the combination of the environmental crisis, globalization and new technologies is producing profound new ideas about social and political change" (p. 9). Social work educators and field instructors, then, need to do a better job of finding, teaching, and modelling successful examples of social movements, resistance strategies, and social action.[1]

Conclusion: #MeToo and #TimesUp

In this chapter, I shared some of my personal experiences in academia, explored chilly campus climates, discussed backlash, and explored the challenges of applying femagogy to social work education. I also presented recommendations to better support educators and students who may experience backlash, transform social work education to more effectively include voices and knowledges from the margins, and warm up campus climates. Finally, from underneath the feathers, like the survivors and supporters of the current #MeToo (https://metoomvmt.org) and #TimesUp (https://www.timesupnow.com) movements, I speak and write to quench my rage but I am still left to ponder. How many more studies and statistics

1 For more on this topic, please read Anderson-Nathe et al. (2013), who offer further suggestions on how to nurture hope.

about harassment, discrimination, violence, and sexism do we need before we finally act to make change? From a broader perspective, how many hours, tears, energy, creativity, productivity, and people are wasted in workplaces in this struggle? How many women, and marginalized "others," are pushed out or choose to leave university life and careers rather than continue the daily struggle for respect and equality? How many people end up being forced to take "sick/stress" leaves, settle for teaching stream positions instead of tenure track jobs, or drop out of tenure track positions because of the expectations placed upon them to cope with the unfair demands? Systemic inequality must be stopped, and to do this, we must first work together to improve campus climates for everyone.

REFERENCES

Acker, S., & Armenti, C. (2004). Sleepless in academia. *Gender and Education, 16*(1), 3–24. https://doi.org/10.1080/0954025032000170309

Anderson-Nathe, B., Gringeri, C., & Wahab, S. (2013). Nurturing "critical hope" in teaching feminist social work research. *Journal of Social Work Education, 49*(2), 277–91. https://doi.org/10.1080/10437797.2013.768477

Bartky, S. L. (2014). Foucault, femininity, and the modernization of patriarchal power. In R. Weitz & S. Kwan (Eds.), *The politics of women's bodies* (pp. 64–85). Oxford University Press.

Boring, A., Ottoboni, K., & Stark, P. (2016). Student evaluations of teaching (mostly) do not measure teaching effectiveness. *Science Open Research.* https://doi.org/10.14293/s2199-1006.1.sor-edu.aetbzc.v1

Breunig, M. (2005). Turning experiential education and critical pedagogy theory into praxis. *Journal of Experiential Education, 28*(2), 106–22. https://doi.org/10.1177/105382590502800205

Britzman, D. (1998). *Lost subjects, contested objects: Toward a psychoanalytic inquiry of learning.* State University of New York Press.

Brown, L., & Strega, S. (2005). *Research as resistance: Critical, Indigenous and anti-oppressive approaches.* Canadian Scholars Press.

Campbell, C. (1999). Empowering pedagogy: Experiential education in the social work classroom. *Canadian Social Work Review, 16*(1), 35–48.

Campbell, C. (2002). The search for congruency: Developing strategies for anti-oppressive social work pedagogy. *Canadian Social Work Review, 19*(1), 25–42.

Caplan, P. J. (1993). *Lifting a ton of feathers: A woman's guide to surviving in the academic world.* University of Toronto Press.

Carey, K. B., Dunny, S. E., Shepardson, R. L., & Carey, M. P. (2015). Incapacitated and forcible rape of college women: Prevalence across the first year. *Journal of Adolescent Health, 56*(6), 678–80. https://doi.org/10.1016/j.jadohealth.2015.02.018

Carniol, B. (2005). Analysis of social location and change: Practice implications. In S. Hick, J. Fook, & R. Pozzuto (Eds.), *Social work: A critical turn* (pp. 153–66). Thompson Educational Publishing.

The Chilly Collective. (1995). *Breaking anonymity: The chilly climate for women.* Wilfrid Laurier University Press.

Coffey, A., & Delamont, S. (2000). *Feminism and the classroom teacher: Research, praxis, and pedagogy.* Routledge.

Corrice, A. (2009). Unconscious bias in faculty and leadership recruitment: A literature review. *Analysis in Brief – Association of American Medical Colleges, 9*(2), 1–4.

Davies, L., & Leonard, P. (Eds.). (2004). *Social work in a corporate era: Practices of power and resistance.* Ashgate Publishing.

De Freitas, E., & McAuley, A. (2008). Teaching for diversity by troubling whiteness: strategies for classrooms in isolated white communities. *Race, Ethnicity & Education, 11*(4), 429–42. https://doi.org/10.1080/13613320802479018

El-Alayli, A., Hansen-Brown, A., & Ceynar, M. (2017). Dancing backwards in high heels: Female professors experience more work demands and special favor requests, particularly from academically entitled students. *Sex Roles.* https://doi.org/10.1007/s11199-017-0872-6

Ellsworth, E. (1989). Why doesn't this feel empowering? Working through the repressive myths of critical pedagogy. *Harvard Educational Review, 59*(3), 297–324. https://doi.org/10.17763/haer.59.3.058342114k266250

Flaherty, C. (2016, January 11). *Bias against female instructors.* Inside Higher Education. https://www.insidehighered.com/news/2016/01/11/new-analysis-oers-more-evidence-againststudent-evaluationsteaching

Fook, J. (1993). *Radical casework: A theory of practice.* Allen and Unwin.

Freire, P. (1970). *Pedagogy of the oppressed.* Continuum.

Godderis, R. (2016). Supporting each other on the frontlines: How faculty can help end sexual violence on campus. *Academic Matters – OCUFA's Journal of Higher Education,* (Winter), 13–16. https://academicmatters.ca/2016/12/faculty-can-help-end-sexual-violence-campus/

Hillock, S. (2011). *Conceptualizing oppression: Resistance narratives for social work* (Paper No. 9528) [Doctoral dissertation, Memorial University]. Memorial University Research Repository. http://research.library.mun.ca/id/eprint/9528

Hillock, S., & Profitt, N. J. (2007). Developing a practice and andragogy of resistance: Praxis inside and outside the classroom. *Canadian Social Work Review, 24*(1), 39–54.

Jeffery, D. (2007). Radical problems and liberal selves: Professional subjectivity in the anti-oppressive social work classroom. *Canadian Social Work Review, 24*(2), 125–39.

Keller, E., & Moglen, H. (1987). Competition: A problem for academic women. In V. Miner & H. Longino (Eds.), *Competition: A feminist taboo?* (pp. 21–37). Feminist Press.

Kirby, S., & McKenna, K. (1989). *Experience, research, social change: Methods from the margins.* Garamond Press.
Lund, C. L. (2010). The nature of white privilege in the teaching and training of adults. *New Directions for Adult & Continuing Education,* (125), 15–25. https://doi.org/10.1002/ace.359
Maranto, C. L., & Griffin, A. (2010). The antecedents of a "chilly climate" for women faculty in higher education. *Human Relations – The Tavistock Institute, 64*(2), 139–59. https://doi.org/10.1177/0018726710377932
Morris, L. K., & Daniel, L. G. (2008). Perceptions of a chilly climate: Differences in traditional and non-traditional majors for women. *Research in Higher Education, 49*(3), 256–73. https://doi.org/10.1007/s11162-007-9078-z
Muhtaseb, A. (2007). From behind the veil: Students' resistance from different directions. *New Directions for Teaching & Learning,* (110), 25–33. https://doi.org/10.1002/tl.271
Mulhere, K. (2014, December 10). *Students praise male professors.* Inside Higher Education. https://www.insidehighered.com/news/2014/12/10/study-finds-gender-perception-affects-evaluations
Neverson, N., Fumia, D., Hernández-Ramdwar, C., Jamal, A., & Knight, M. (2013). *Inhabiting critical spaces: Teaching and learning from the margins at Ryerson University.* Ryerson University.
Overall, C. (1998). *A feminist 1: Reflections from academia.* Broadview Press.
Penny Light, T., Nicholas, J., & Bondy, R. (Eds.). (2015). *Feminist pedagogy in higher education.* Wilfrid Laurier University Press.
Pierce, C. (1995). Stress analogs of racism and sexism: Terrorism, torture, and disaster. In C. Willie, P. Rieker, B. Kramer, & B. Brown (Eds.), *Mental health, racism, and sexism* (pp. 277–93). University of Pittsburgh Press.
Razack, N. (1999). Anti-discriminatory practice: Pedagogical struggles and challenges. *British Journal of Social Work, 29*(2), 231–50. https://doi.org/10.1093/oxfordjournals.bjsw.a011444
Rebick, J. (2009). *Transforming power from the personal to the political.* Penguin.
Redmond, M. (2010). Safe space oddity: Revisiting critical pedagogy. *Journal of Teaching in Social Work, 30*(1), 1–14. https://doi.org/10.1080/08841230903249729
Rinfrette, E., Maccio, E., Coyle, J., Jackson, K., Hartinger-Saunders, R., Rine, C., & Shulman, L. (2015). Content and process in a teaching workshop for faculty and doctoral students. *Journal of Teaching in Social Work, 35*(1–2), 65–81. https://doi.org/10.1080/08841233.2014.990077
Ross-Marquette, G., & Komiotis, W. (2016). Community involvement and government leadership in challenging sexual violence on campus. *Academic Matters – OCUFA's Journal of Higher Education,* (Winter), 7–11.
Schick, C. (2005). Keeping the ivory tower white: Discourses of racial discrimination. In V. Zawilski & C. Levine-Rasky (Eds.), *Inequality in Canada* (pp. 208–20). Oxford University Press.

Stark, P. B., & Freishtat, R. (2014). An evaluation of course evaluations. *Science Open Research*, 1–26. https://doi.org/10.14293/s2199-1006.1.sor-edu.aofrqa.v1

Superson, A. M., & Ann E., Cudd (Eds.). (2002). *Theorizing backlash: Philosophical reflections on the resistance to feminism*. Rowman & Littlefield.

Wilkin, L., & Hillock, S. (2015). Enhancing MSW students' efficacy in working with trauma, violence, and oppression: An integrated feminist-trauma framework for social work education. *Feminist Teacher, 24*(3), 184–206. https://doi.org/10.5406/femteacher.24.3.0184

Williams, J. C., Alon, T., & Bornstein, S. (2006). Beyond the chilly climate: eliminating bias against women and fathers in academe. *Thought in Action – The NEA Higher Education Journal*, 79–96.

Yee, J. Y. (2005). Critical anti-racism practice: The concept of whiteness implicated. In S. Hick, J. Fook, & R. Pozzuto (Eds.), *Social work: A critical turn* (pp. 87–104). Thompson Educational Publishing.

19 Incivility or Bullying?: Challenges in the Social Work Classroom

JAN YORKE AND TANYA SHUTE

The instructional role of faculty in higher education is to assign students relevant and challenging tasks, guide them in their learning of new knowledge and skills, evaluate the quality of their performance, and assign grades in a manner that reflects appropriate evaluation criteria.

(Benton, 2007 as cited in Barrett et al., 2010, p. 144)

Amid the challenges and upheaval of the twenty-first century, forces from within and without colleges and universities have been working to shift scholarly institutions of higher learning away from the principles of collegial governance and academic freedom, as enshrined in the historical Oxford model, to become competitive educational corporations. As a consequence, many students have shifted from concerned, critically thinking citizens experiencing broad transformational learning to academic customers viewed no longer through an academic lens but rather, in economic terms, as revenue-producing units. In the current age of information, postsecondary education is valued as a credible commodity, providing the promise of higher socio-economic status and increased chances of success (McEldowney Jensen et al., 2014; Organisation for Economic Co-operation and Development, 2015). As valuable commodities, academic consumers pay premium tuition costs, and business, science, technology, and engineering departments in colleges and universities are often well supported by external corporate contributions. In some cases, this has resulted in accusations of a conflict of interest, where university administration and local business interests appear to be meshed (Canadian Association of University Teachers [CAUT], 2018). In contrast, social science and humanities departments appear to lag behind, with fewer philanthropic or research dollars contributed to their work. Well-designed marketing campaigns prevail in this competitive environment, fronting efforts to attract academic consumers with the greatest grade point averages (GPA). This in turn creates additional competition and pressure among those who vie for the "best" opportunity or the most scholarship money. This environment impacts faculty members who are then pressured to become the purveyors of the educational "product."

The labour market has shifted in past decades towards more precarious work overall. Academic corporations are hiring increasing numbers of precarious faculty members with no benefits, sick days, security of income, or rights; a situation that makes them vulnerable to external pressures, particularly when up against the academic customer. Recent research indicates that students taught by sessional faculty in the United States and Canada have doubled since 2001, making up an average of 30 to 80 per cent of faculty in Ontario university and community college departments, depending on the reporting body (Field et al., 2014; Hoeller, 2014). They thus compose an expendable, often female, LGBTQ+, or ethnically diverse set of scholars that is adjustable semester to semester. Sessional faculty at universities and full-time and sessional faculty at community colleges are encouraged to have graduate and doctoral degrees but often are not afforded the opportunity to do research as part of their workload. In addition, they do not feel that they have academic freedom or access to collegial governance given their current precarious circumstances, including being more vulnerable as a result of student appeals and evaluations, increasing hierarchical and regimented administration models, and strictly negotiated union contracts.

Many faculty members are reluctant to speak out regarding universities that prioritize economics over rigour, fearing consequences. Research dollars within and without the academic corporation become the primary commodity for advancement; increasingly, mechanisms for developing, prioritizing, approving, and submitting proposals are controlled, ranked, and co-opted by micromanaging administrative entities, such as appointed review committees, which replace or usurp traditional bodies of collegial academic governance, such as academically driven, faculty-dominated senates or faculty-driven funding organizations external to the university.

The low-cost approach these academic corporations use is to staff programs with part-time faculty or establish satellite campuses. They emphasize "chalk and talk" approaches, without the basic amenities found on main campuses, such as space for student-faculty collaboration or student life, athletic services, and support services. Entire undergraduate, graduate, and doctoral programs are now offered online. Meaningful interactions with professors or other students are being replaced with virtual experiences. This minimalist approach persists despite the growing demand by academic customers for more hands-on, interactive educational experiences, paid placements, mental health services, and guaranteed jobs tied to the completion of their degrees. In this competitive environment, academic outcomes become both secondary to and synonymous with corporate interests. Administrative priorities appear to rest on avoidance of litigiousness. Offers of certain employment for students upon graduation are dangled, as well as fast completion of customized credentialing, including competitive value for prior educational credits; signing bonuses, lavish residential housing, and free meal plans also entice students. These tactics are designed to enhance the pleasing aspect of the customer experience, not necessarily the rigour of the learning experience. Ironically, corporate entities, in turn, are making competition for full-time employment harder to realize and decry the lack of soft skills in communication among current graduates (McKinsey & Company, 2015).

The consequences of these changes are significant for the social work classroom. Students are becoming increasingly immersed in the world of technology, often distracting them from one-on-one interactions with peers and professors, in-class lectures, and discussions engaging them in the self-awareness processes necessary for development as a beginning social work practitioner. This shifting landscape has contributed to increasing student incivility, bullying, and positional violence in the social work classroom (Ausbrooks et al., 2011; Barrett et al., 2010). Teaching in the social work classroom involves developing the ability to relate anti-oppressive practice, feminist, LGBTQ, and anti-racist social justice theory with practice, which requires mentoring, raising students' self-awareness, doing group work, and demonstrating competency skills. Communication with others is essential for meaningful social work, and therapeutic communication is the specific skill required (Yorke et al., 2016).

Incivility in Education

Faculty-student interaction is a fundamental element of campus life and pedagogical/andragogical practice, both in and out of the classroom. Indeed, faculty-student interaction is associated and to some degree predictive of student GPA success and retention in both community colleges and universities (Deil-Amen, 2011; Kim & Sax, 2009; Mertes, 2015; Wirt & Jaeger, 2014). The scholarly and popular literatures have identified the emergence of incivility in faculty-student interaction across institutions (Clarke et al., 2012; Morrissette, 2001; White, 2013). Scholars have documented these phenomena in the postsecondary education system, citing generational problems, mental health issues, gender, ethnicity, and consumerism as contributing factors (Ausbrooks et al., 2011; Lampman, 2012; Lampman et al., 2016; Lampman et al., 2009; Vogl-Bauer, 2014). Civility in education has more recently become enshrined in respect and harassment policies and protocols in Canadian universities. Unfortunately, some of these policies have proliferated as administrative tactics to limit academic freedom and discourse, effecting the nature of faculty and student interaction in a number of significant ways (CAUT, 2018; McDonald et al., 2018). Incivility poses a threat to student success in a number of ways. Alberts et al. (2010) found that faculty who are female, younger, non-white, or perceived by some students to have lower status, such as sessional faculty, teaching assistants, and international or persons of colour, were more likely to be bullied or treated in an uncivilized manner by both students and other faculty.

In defining incivility in education, Feldmann (2001) has proposed a hierarchical spectrum of severity beginning with annoyances, followed by classroom terrorism, intimidation, and, finally, physical violence. He describes *annoyances* as minimal interruptions, such as talking while professors are lecturing or while other students are interacting with the professor; arriving late to interrupt class; obviously texting or responding to Facebook, Twitter, or Instagram, or other kinds of social media; talking on the phone; and carrying out other disengaging behaviours. He defines *classroom terrorism* as intolerant, disruptive, bullying, or interruptive behaviour designed to exert power over the professor or peers in class. *Intimidation* is described as students threatening professors with censure or bias through appeals or complaints to administrative authorities or committees in the university's governmental structure or giving "undeserved negative feedback on a course evaluation" (p. 138). Finally, classroom *violence* is defined as a serious threat against the professor or peers in the class or the school.

Knepp (2012) surveyed faculty regarding contributing factors that have arisen over the past two decades related to incivility. Surveyed faculty pointed to students being unprepared and unchallenged academically before entering college, having experienced lenient parenting, having a need to be entertained and for immediate gratification, having an expectation of grade inflation for attending, and having demonstrable substance use, fatigue, overextension (work and school), stress, emotional immaturity/lack of problem-solving skills, and redirected aggression (Kuhlenschmidt & Layne, 1999, as cited in Knepp, 2012). The role systemic or individual bias plays in this behaviour may provide some insight.

Kim and Sax (2009) reviewed 30 years of literature examining student-faculty interactions, both formal and informal, inside and outside the classroom. Their review found that positive outcomes of student-faculty interactions were "conditional" on race and gender, with students who are women, white, and/or from higher levels of social class benefiting more than racialized, low socio-economic males. Their study revealed that participating in faculty research and course-related faculty-student interactions led to increased GPAs and higher degree aspirations, critical thinking, and communication for most groups. Kim and Sax's (2009) two-tiered survey of 31,000 students focused on how faculty-student interactions are linked to positive student outcomes, including subject matter competence, cognitive skills and intellectual growth, attitudes and values, further educational attainment, and career choice and development. Their study also reinforced findings from their literature review indicating that student satisfaction with faculty interaction rises along with social class, race, gender, and size of educational institution. How marginalized students and their classmates interpreted these experiences could contribute to anger, resulting in direct or indirect belligerence and disrespectful or bullying behaviour. The extent to which incivility is related to inclusion versus exclusion of students' relationships with faculty with respect to class size, the relevance of course literature, and student and faculty individual characteristics may also be relevant and does not appear to be addressed in the current research.

Mental Health Issues

The growing frequency, complexity, and acuity of mental health needs and challenges among postsecondary students also must be considered as contributing factors to incivility. According to the National College Health Assessment (American College Health Association, 2016), one-fifth of Canadian postsecondary students experience depression, anxiety, and other serious mental health problems. Wait times and access to services are barriers both in the community and on campus. Colleges and universities are the lived context for the age cohort in which most first episodes of serious mental illness arise, as 75 per cent of mental disorders first appear when people are between 18 and 24 years old (American College Health Association, 2016). For students, the stress and uncertainty of first experiences of mental health and addiction symptoms, combined with the social and academic adjustment pressures of postsecondary programs, in addition to the distractions and outlets provided by social media in the classroom, are fertile ground for uncivil behaviour.

Studies of bullying in postsecondary settings have typically focused on instructor bullying of students, not on students as the aggressors. As bullying and similar aggressive behaviours are typically associated with young students in school settings, it seems logical to consider that they are carried into postsecondary settings as these behaviours can be maintained across the lifespan (Marraccini et al., 2015). Campus efforts at addressing the growing problem of postsecondary student mental health challenges rarely consider faculty needs and experiences as part of the campus community (Canadian Association of College and University Student Services & Canadian Mental Health Association, 2013). Given that the campus and the classroom constitute the workplace of faculty, this is a serious omission that can leave faculty quite vulnerable and feeling unsupported: "Educators are often overlooked as victims" (Espelage et al., 2013, p. 76). Faculty have indicated abuse from students provokes survival responses, dread, avoidance of some course material, and burnout (Morrissette, 2001).

Role of Technology

Ever-shifting social communication patterns and norms are ushered in by social media and its ubiquitous presence in our lives and classrooms. Students sometimes appear frustrated if faculty are not as technologically savvy as they are. Technology use, however, is a source of distraction for classmates and for the faculty trying to engage these students (Csiernik et al., 2006; Sana et al., 2013). The internet also provides a source of products to address the time-consuming demands of writing essays or reading literature to demonstrate learning prowess. This demand may increase frustration and anger in students looking for a quicker, less onerous, and more efficient result. Consumers feel entitled to satisfaction in the academic experience to get what they pay for, and online sources for purchasing essays grow in popularity. Fake degrees purchased online are on the rise also, underpinning the perceived value of the end product, not necessarily the process. Students may react with anger if accused of plagiarism, and universities may not encourage the use of software to catch plagiarism, such as Turn-it-In, as students have sued universities successfully for copyright infringement (Horovitz, 2008; Park, 2004).

Not all is bleak when we consider the technological shifts in education, such as access to a wealth of resources, online coursework, the software enhancements for students and faculty alike who can now use adaptations to overcome accessibility barriers, and other benefits. However, disruptive engagement with these tools is increasingly likely in the classroom and can be a source of angst for faculty as they try to engage large numbers of students in the classroom.

The Role of Administration

Current university administrative strategies are driven by for-profit assumptions (i.e., corporate for-profit tactics are more efficient or superior to not-for-profit methods). These assumptions are based upon early-twentieth-century Taylorian micromanaging methodology (Taylor, 1911) that asserts that postsecondary education is responsible for producing workers, not critically thinking citizens. Austerity initiatives instituted by governments at all levels has increased the academic consumers' share of the financial burden of postsecondary education. Corporate vendors use funds they might otherwise spend on personnel development as gifts to universities. Unspoken strings are often attached, along with the assumption that they can have input into curricula, faculty choices, endowments, and research funding. University administrations court private sector funders, encouraged by neo-liberal ideologies that promote public-private funding initiatives. This skews students' perceptions, and they confuse the purchase of a commodity with learning in the classroom. This shift in worldview promotes incivility when students experience hardship and challenges, don't get the marks they pay for, or suffer exposure to new ideas in the pursuit of learning.

Over-credentialing in a shifting economy contributes to a sense that postsecondary education is necessary to enter every labour market. Students without adequate economic means may feel at a disadvantage. The unspoken assumption may be that successful completion is owed as a right to academic customers who pay high tuition rates, whether or not they do the work or pass courses, based not on rigour but rather on efficiency and the pleasantness of the experience. This belief contributes to frustration and ultimately incivility.

Policy and protocol do not always support faculty and lean to the side of the adage *the customer is always right*, discouraging faculty from addressing threats, bullying, or incivility. A recent report on education in Canada indicated that the number of universities has increased from 65 in the 1980s to 246 today (McKinsey & Company, 2015). Academic departments are pressured to admit increased numbers of undergraduate, graduate, and PhD students, particularly international students, to fill the coffers. Faculty are forced to work against these internal and external pressures to engage academic customers as students, maintain quality of graduates, and preserve rigour in their disciplines. Unfortunately, as a consequence, a certain amount of grade inflation occurs at the secondary school or college level so students can compete for a limited number of university spaces in top institutions (Loffredo & Harrington, 2012; Schroeder, 2016). This inflation rewards some prospective academic customers over others, with some institutions generating higher marks for students, making them more competitive for admission than students coming from more rigorous secondary/postsecondary educational programs. Faculty become wary of administratively driven appeals processes that inevitably reward demanding students with passing grades for fear of litigation. This has the potential to impact competency levels in professional schools such as health and medicine and social work, where licensing assumes a gatekeeping function to protect the public. In educational corporations, academic customers are patronized the way any source of income in the retail market would be; they are guaranteed satisfaction through inviting websites; the advertising corporations compete to provide credits for previous educational paperwork (diplomas, degrees); and policy and protocol reinforce the academic customers' positional status. All these tactics subvert civility.

This culture of incivility results in a combative classroom and a focus on safety that confuses political correctness and anti-oppression with freedom of speech/academic freedom (McDonald et al., 2018). This shift has resulted in a hierarchical, hegemonic, and micromanaging approach that is demoralizing for faculty and emboldens those who commit harassing, bullying, or other kinds of uncivil behaviours (CAUT, 2018; Fox & Stallworth, 2010; Lutgen-Sandvik, 2006; Lutgen-Sandvik & Tracy, 2012; Namie & Lutgen-Sandvik, 2010; Namie et al., 2010; Vogl-Bauer, 2014).

Transactional Violence: Exploring Power in the Social Work Classroom Context

Undoubtedly, the faculty-student interaction in the classroom environment is not egalitarian, by merit or position. Workplace violence or harassment in university is traditionally conceived as lateral (peer to peer) or hierarchical (manager to employee). Changing expectations of what the purpose of higher education is has made the classroom and teacher-student interaction different from what many faculty experienced in their own undergraduate and graduate education. In the context of professional schools, faculty own and exert a great deal of power and gatekeeping authority over students and their academic fate. The behaviour of students who resort to bullying and harassment of faculty members can be conceived of as contra power harassment (Benson, 1984; Lampman et al., 2016). Benson (1984) first used the term *contra power harassment* to denote a situation in which a "person with lesser power within an institution harasses an individual with greater power" (as cited in Lampman et al., 2009). The transactional phenomenon ushered in by the student-as-consumer orientation disrupts the traditional professor-as-revered authority of the past. Contra power harassment's direction is upward in response to perceived classroom power and authority stemming from a more commodified understanding of the postsecondary experience, and students feel justified in behaving in such ways to discredit or delegitimize the person they perceive as responsible for them not getting what they want or think they deserve out of their educational transaction. The emphasis on safety for students shadows the impact of incivility on faculty. Positional classroom violence involves the physical or verbal harassment or intimidation of faculty either in class or online; it involves overt attempts to delegitimize the authority of and respect for the faculty member and alter the character of the pedagogical/andragogical relationship to one in which the faculty member is expected to comply with student demands, however inappropriate.

Incivility as Sanitized Discrimination and Prejudice

Faculty whose social identities are racialized, impacted by gender or sexual minority status, or marginalized as faith community members are possibly at a higher risk of harassment and bullying (Alberts et al., 2010) than faculty members who represent dominant identities, such as whiteness. Colleagues or administration commonly expect that moments of incivility or harassment be constructed as "learning opportunities" for the student. This is most problematic. For example, unique to social work curriculum are anti-oppression theory courses that have a critical self-reflexivity dimension in line with social work practice principles, values, and ethics. Students are often asked to take note of their own social location across many dimensions, such as racialized status, income, age, ability, gender, or sexual minority status, and demonstrate appropriate professional values of respect and non-discrimination. Invariably, in every stack of papers, students can be found defending their homophobic beliefs or experiences of "reverse racism" in ways that are not critical self-reflection but at students' nascent stage of un-learning read more as micro-aggressions in the form of homework.

Reading and hearing such content semester after semester about themselves can be vicariously traumatic for faculty. Where faculty are "out" or visibly identifiable, their vulnerability can be exploited by students who use the opportunities to marginalize, for example, noting that they do not agree with homosexuality but will tolerate it under professional circumstances. The response to "use" this behaviour to "help the student learn" ignores the effect on the faculty whose identities are being contested with such impunity and how it manifests on a public platform, with the class as the audience. Codes of conduct that regulate postsecondary classrooms to some degree do not provide inoculation from the bias, discrimination, and hate that follow students into our classrooms. The lack of recognition of these events as micro-aggressions or workplace harassment or bullying means that faculty are working without the safety net of student accountability.

Workplace Environment and Social Work Faculty

In social work specifically, Barrett and colleagues (2010) describe a spectrum of incivility that escalates from rudeness to violence, across classrooms, both in person and on social media, in contrast to the expectation that classrooms are a safe place. Ausbrooks and colleagues (2011) suggest that the lack of consequences for incivility in social work classrooms increases the likelihood of its occurrence; if faculty do not clearly address it, they can lose the respect of other students in the class who expect them to control it. This presents unique challenges for social work faculty in their identities as professional practitioners-turned-vocational educators.

Barrett et al. (2010) state that safety is identified as a mainstay of education or classroom interaction despite the

> dearth of empirical evidence documenting that safe classrooms are more effective at achieving these goals than other types of classroom environments. The commonplace, and uncritical, acceptance of safety as a bedrock of quality education is curious, given not only the lack of empirical data to support the effectiveness of the safe classroom in enhancing learning outcomes but also the absence of a precise definition of what exactly safety entails. (p. 1)

Bandow and Hunter (2008) assert that safety in the classroom requires conditions that allow individuals the capacity for psychological risk-taking. This is echoed in the social work literature (Ellsworth et al., 1993; Holley & Steiner, 2005). Holley and Steiner's (2005) research with 243 social work graduate students indicates that students place responsibility for safety on the professor (59.8 per cent), despite the fact that they assigned student self-characteristics as the reason for their lack of participation (shyness, 43.4 per cent; lack of preparation for the class, 39.7 per cent; or too personal, 36.8 per cent). Safety includes freedom from bullying as an expression of hate and from fear about social differences. Disturbingly, heterosexism and homophobia are more prevalent in first-year BSW students and in all male BSW students than their female counterparts (Brownlee et al., 2005). Ellsworth and colleagues (1993) indicate that creating safe classrooms is not always the purview of the faculty. If they can't create safety for themselves, it is difficult to create it for others (students). Finally, students who experienced more LGBTQ+ content in their courses were more likely to experience heterosexism, although some of the research indicates that specific experiential and multi-modes of teaching can address this propensity better than others (Hillock, 2017). Safety and civility go hand in hand, and faculty require tangible tools to address the consequences or universities risk losing talented scholars through burnout.

How Can the Social Work Professor Respond?

In social work programs, as mentioned previously, researchers indicate that if faculty do not respond to incivility or bullying, it gets worse, leading to disrespect from other students (Feldmann, 2001; Hogan, 2007; Kuhlenschmidt & Layne, 1999; Schneider, 1998; Sorcinelli, 2002; Young, 2003, as cited in Ausbrooks et al., 2011). Some of the literature suggests that reluctance by faculty to respond may be based on a lack of confidence that administrators will support their actions. Additionally, faculty may not know how to address such annoyances or, as discussed earlier, may attempt to avoid negative evaluations or bad tenure reviews by ignoring it. Having some useful techniques at hand can help.

To begin with, well-written syllabi, including rationales for specific expectations, and the development of opportunities for meaningful interaction across diverse groups, are essential to satisfactory experiences for students (Bjorklund & Rehling, 2009; Kim & Sax, 2009). Miller-Fox (2014) uses common notions about the consumer perspective to explore how this applies to education in the classroom at the beginning of her courses, assessing the value of education as a product. She asks students to identify what appears useful for preparing them for their future job, the nature of the student-professor relationship, and what currency is being exchanged in education – money or time and attention. It is helpful to discuss incivility and bullying in the first class of a course, including the collaborative, mutual development by faculty and students of a set of expectations and perhaps classroom civility rules; how do we debate and disagree while remaining respectful? It is also useful to applying consequences and/or consistent reinforcement of the rules throughout the academic year. Teaching assistants, for example, can reinforce these expectations by providing a matrix of support for students across social work programs. They can assist with one-on-one support, tutorials, and mentoring. These more experienced students can be used to lessen anxiety about assignments, especially in first-year students. Faculty or student class group leaders can develop contracts based on the rules for students to agree on and sign, which will be enforced by faculty and student leaders. Although these rules are not strictly speaking enforceable, they provide an overt benchmark and spoken expectation of behaviour based on institutional policy. It is also worthwhile to have open discussions with the class about the research into the impact social media and laptops have on learning for other students. Conversely, employing technology in a useful way, such as virtual group discussions and posting of course material, can further contribute to positive interaction.

Dealing with classroom violence and intimidation may require different tactics. Approaches that can be useful include identifying and addressing inappropriate behaviour with the student individually, if safe, as soon as possible. Violent or threatening situations may require intervention by security or law enforcement. Engaging students with campus counselling or support services can help flag mental health and addiction problems. Students need ways to safely provide feedback about issues of intimidation, plagiarism, cyberbullying, or fear of reprisal. This can occur at class, department, university committee, and senate levels through in-class discussions, evaluations, and the development of policy and protocol. Faculty need to feel confident they can address behaviour safely and be supported by the administration.

Universities have been accused of developing respectful workplace or civility policies that undermine faculty capacity to address bullying behaviour by students and administration, thwarting academic freedom or limiting faculty to grieve or appeal when accused. In addition to confidentiality, faculty should have access to "due process in investigations; including timeliness, openness, transparency, prohibition of the use of anonymous materials, access of the respondent to all material upon which an investigator relied to come to a decision, and the requirement that the respondent be provided with the identity of all complainants" (CAUT, 2018, p. 6). Consequences for unaddressed annoying behaviours should be clearly laid out in administrative policy and protocol, for example, and faculty should have the opportunity to remove a student or group of students from the classroom if they are seen by the professor or other students to bully, verbally abuse, or otherwise be uncivil with others. Incident reports can track the number and severity of incidents both students and faculty experience. Protocol should include mechanisms for re-entry to the classroom or online behaviour that clearly outline expectations and possibly include a contract. Faculty also need to be trained to make a routine practice of documenting difficult or uncivil interactions with students in case it escalates or to provide a foundation for future institutional action with the student. Social work departments can incorporate suitability policies into their protocol for accreditation (Canadian Association for Social Work Education – l'Association canadienne pour la formation en travail social, 2018).

As well, unions and faculty associations should regularly survey members to identify rates of perceived incivility or bullying between administration and faculty, between faculty and other faculty, and between faculty and students. Evaluation and appeal policies in particular should not be used to instigate or perpetuate student classroom annoyances, terrorism, intimidation, or violence.

Finally, violence by students includes serious threats towards faculty or students or the institution. This can occur in person; can be verbal, emotional, or psychological; can include physical altercations, sexual innuendoes, suggestions, or abuse; and can be threats to the building, a department, or personal possessions. Violence can also include a range of behaviours, from damage to cars, institutional property, computers, or assignments, to extremes such as threats against faculty family members. These actions could cause professors to fear for the safety of other students or themselves or result in a complaint or refusal to attend class by the student's peers or the faculty, requiring the involvement of campus security, police, or other outside resources. As faculty, we, the authors, have experienced being screamed at in class, being followed into restrooms, receiving physical threats, needing security escorts to the institutional parking lot, being blocked by students from leaving our offices, being physically threatened in our staff offices, and having students attending classes who were not registered eight weeks after the term's commencement. These examples of incivility or faculty bullying are important to track. They could be associated with severe mental health or other kinds of personal crises that lead to distressed behaviour in a student. They could be red flags that represent a need for counselling or assistance. They are certainly opportunities for university faculty and student advocate professionals to intervene and offer help. Administrators need to establish an incident report policy that allows faculty, staff, and students to report any incident that constitutes violence, or the potential for it, supported by clear protocol for responding, including immediate involvement with security and possibly the police, if required, the pressing of charges, or institutional sanctions/consequences that are identified in a bill of human rights for the campus.

Conclusion

Several identifiable yet difficult-to-control factors have shifted the social relations in our classroom to the extent that most faculty members have had or will experience some form of student incivility, positional violence, or harassment. The authors attribute this to the transactional social relations that result from a corporatist approach to higher education that positions the student as consumer and faculty as instruments in the pursuit of completion rates and credentialing, instead of professionals and academics. Several recommendations are provided to address these new realities, but faculty also need to respond to the larger forces at play, including the corporatization of the university, the deskilling and exploitation of faculty by their institutions, and the pervasive forces of systemic and institutionalized identity marginalization and oppression that many faculty experience in their classrooms as their workplaces.

REFERENCES

Alberts, H. C., Hazen, H. D., & Theobald, R. B. (2010). Classroom incivilities: The challenge of interactions between college students and instructors in the US. *Journal of Geography in Higher Education, 34*(3), 439–62. https://doi.org/10.1080/03098260903502679

American College Health Association. (2016). *American College Health Association-National College Health Assessment II: Canadian reference group executive summary.* https://www.acha.org/documents/ncha/NCHA-II%20SPRING%202016%20CANADIAN%20REFERENCE%20GROUP%20EXECUTIVE%20SUMMARY.pdf

Ausbrooks, A. R., Jones, S. H., & Tijerina, M. S. (2011). Now you see it, now you don't: Faculty and student perceptions of classroom incivility in a social work program. *Advances in Social Work, 12*(2), 255–75. https://doi.org/10.18060/1932

Bandow, D., & Hunter, D. (2008). Developing policies about uncivil workplace behavior. *Business Communication Quarterly, 71*(1), 103–6. https://doi.org/10.1177/1080569907313380

Barrett, S., Rubaii-Barrett, N., & Pelowski, J. (2010). Preparing for and responding to student incivilities: Starting the dialogue in public affairs education. *Journal of Public Affairs Education,* 143–59. https://doi.org/10.1080/15236803.2010.12001591

Benson, K. A. (1984). Comment on Crocker's "An analysis of university definitions of sexual harassment." *Signs: Journal of Women in Culture and Society, 9*(3), 516–19. https://doi.org/10.1086/494083

Benton, T. H. (2007). Remedial civility training. *Chronicle of Higher Education, 53*(36), C2.

Bjorklund, W. L., & Rehling, D. L. (2009). Student perceptions of classroom incivility. *College Teaching, 58*(1), 15–18. https://doi.org/10.1080/87567550903252801

Brownlee, K., Sprakes, A., Saini, M., O'Hare, R., Kortes-Miller, K., & Graham, J. (2005). Heterosexism among social work students. *Social Work Education, 24*(5), 485–94. https://doi.org/10.1080/02615470500132756

Canadian Association of College and University Student Services & Canadian Mental Health Association. (2013). *Post-secondary student mental health: Guide to a systemic approach.*

Canadian Association for Social Work Education – Association canadienne pour la formation en travail social. (2018). *Commission on accreditation resources.* https://caswe-acfts.ca/commission-on-accreditation/coa-resources/

Canadian Association of University Teachers. (2018, February). *Discussion paper: Respectful workplace policies.* https://www.wlufa.ca/2018/02/22/caut-discussion-paper-respectful-workplace-policies-document-de-travail-de-lacppu-politiques-de-respect-en-milieu-de-travail/

Clarke, C. M., Kane, D. J., Rajacich, D. L., & Lafreniere, K. D. (2012). Bullying in undergraduate clinical nursing education. *Journal of Nursing Education, 51*(5), 269–76. https://doi.org/10.3928/01484834-20120409-01

Csiernik, R., Furze, P., Dromgole, L., & Rishchynski, G. (2006). Information technology and social work: The dark side or light side? *Journal of Evidence-Based Social Work, 3*(3/4), 9–25. https://doi.org/10.1300/j394v03n03_02

Deil-Amen, R. (2011). Socio-academic integrative moments: Rethinking academic and social integration among two-year college students in career-related programs. *Journal of Higher Education, 82*(1), 54–91. https://doi.org/10.1353/jhe.2011.0006

Ellsworth, C., Muir, D., & Hains, S. (1993). Social competence and person-object differentiation: An analysis of the still-face effect. *Developmental psychology, 29*(1), 63–73. https://doi.org/10.1037/0012-1649.29.1.63

Espelage, D., Anderman, E. M., Brown, V. E., Jones, A., Lane, K. L., McMahon, S. D., & Reynolds, C. R. (2013). Understanding and preventing violence directed against teachers: Recommendations for a national research, practice, and policy agenda. *American Psychologist, 68*, 75–87. https://doi.org/10.1037/a0031307

Feldmann, L. J. (2001). Classroom civility is another of our instructor responsibilities. *College Teaching, 49*(4), 137–40. https://doi.org/10.1080/87567555.2001.10844595

Field, C. C., Jones, G. A., Stephenson, G. K., & Khoyetsyan, A. (2014). *The "other" university teachers: Non-full-time instructors at Ontario universities.* Higher Education Quality Council of Ontario.

Fox, S., & Stallworth, L. E. (2010). The battered apple: An application of stressor-emotion-control/support theory to teachers' experience of violence and bullying. *Human Relations, 63*(7), 927–54. https://doi.org/10.1177/0018726709349518

Hillock, S. (2017). Social work, the academy, and queer communities: Heteronormativity and exclusion. In S. Hillock & N. Mulé (Eds.), *Queering social work education* (pp. 73–92). UBC Press.

Hoeller, K. (2014). *Equality for contingent faculty: Overcoming the two-tier system.* Vanderbilt University Press.

Hogan, M. (2007). *The effects of perceived disruptive behavior on classroom civility.* University Ombuds Office, University of Arkansas.

Holley, L. C., & Steiner, S. (2005). Safe space: Student perspectives on classroom environment. *Journal of Social Work Education, 41*(1), 49–64. https://doi.org/10.5175/jswe.2005.200300343

Horovitz, S. J. (2008). Two wrongs don't negate a copyright: Don't make students Turnitin if you won't give it back. *Florida Law Review, 60*(1), 229. http://scholarship.law.ufl.edu/flr/vol60/iss1/5

Kim, Y. K., & Sax, L. J. (2009). Student–faculty interaction in research universities: Differences by student gender, race, social class, and first generation status. *Research in Higher Education, 50*, 437–59. https://doi.org/10.1007/s11162-009-9127-x

Knepp, K. A. F. (2012). Understanding student and faculty incivility in higher education. *Journal of Effective Teaching, 12*(1), 33–46. https://doi.org/10.1080/13562510701192073

Kuhlenschmidt, S. L., & Layne, L. E. (1999). Strategies for dealing with difficult behavior. *New Directions for Teaching and Learning, 1999*(77), 45–57. https://doi.org/10.1002/tl.7705

Lampman, C. (2012). Women faculty at risk: US professors report on their experiences with student incivility, bullying, aggression, and sexual attention. *NASPA Journal About Women in Higher Education, 5*(2), 184–208.

Lampman, C., Crew, E. C., Lowery, S. D., & Tompkins, K. (2016). Women faculty distressed: Descriptions and consequences of academic contrapower harassment. *NASPA Journal About Women in Higher Education, 9*(2), 169–89. https://doi.org/10.1080/19407882.2016.1199385

Lampman, C., Phelps, A., Bancroft, S., & Beneke, M. (2009). Contrapower harassment in academia: A survey of faculty experience with student incivility, bullying, and sexual attention. *Sex Roles, 60*(5–6), 331–46.

Loffredo, D. A., & Harrington, R. (2012). Age-related grade inflation expectancies in a university environment. *Education Research International,* 789470. https://doi.org/10.1155/2012/789470

Lutgen-Sandvik, P. (2006). Take this job and …: Quitting and other forms of resistance to workplace bullying. *Communication Monographs, 73*(4), 406–33. https://doi.org/10.1080/03637750601024156

Lutgen-Sandvik, P., & Tracy, S. J. (2012). Answering five key questions about workplace bullying: How communication scholarship provides thought leadership for transforming abuse at work. *Management Communication Quarterly, 26*(1), 3–47. https://doi.org/10.1177/0893318911414400

Marraccini, M. E., Weyandt, L. L., & Rossi, J. S. (2015). College students' perceptions of instructor/student bullying: Questionnaire development and psychometric properties. *Journal of American College Health, 63*(8), 563–72. https://doi.org/10.1080/07448481.2015.1060596

McDonald, T. W., Stockton, J. D., & Landrum, R. E. (2018). Civility and academic freedom: Who defines the former (and how) may imperil rights to the latter. *College Quarterly, 21*(1), EJ1169339.

McEldowney Jensen, J., & Worth, B. (2014). Valuable knowledge: Students as consumers of critical thinking in the community college classroom. *The Journal of General Education, 63*(4), 287–308. https://doi.org/10.1353/jge.2014.0025

McKinsey & Company. (2015). *Youth in transition: Bridging Canada's path from education to employment.* https://www.cacee.com/_Library/docs/Youth_in_transition_Bridging_Canadas_path_from_education_to_employment_2_.pdf

Mertes, S. J. (2015). Social integration in a community college environment. *Community College Journal of Research and Practice, 39*(11), 1052–64. https://doi.org/10.1080/10668926.2014.934973

Miller-Fox, D. (2014, May 19). *Education and consumerism: Using students' assumptions to challenge their thinking.* Faculty Focus. https://www.facultyfocus.com/articles/effective-teaching-strategies/education-consumerism-using-students-assumptions-challenge-thinking/

Morrissette, P. J. (2001). Reducing incivility in the university/college classroom, 5(4). *IEJLL: International Electronic Journal for Leadership in Learning.* https://cetl.olemiss.edu/wp-content/uploads/sites/83/2016/03/ClassroomIncivility.pdf

Namie, G., & Lutgen-Sandvik, P. (2010). Active and passive accomplices: The communal character of workplace bullying. *International Journal of Communication, 4*(31), 343–73.

Namie, G., Namie, R., & Lutgen-Sandvik, P. (2010). Challenging workplace bullying in the United States: An activist and public communication approach. In S. Einarsen, H. Hoel, D. Zapf, & C. L. Cooper (Eds.), *Bullying and harassment in the workplace: Developments in theory, research, and practice* (pp. 447–67). CRC Press.

Organisation for Economic Co-operation and Development. (2015). *Education policy outlook 2015: Making reforms happen.*

Park, C. (2004). Rebels without a clause: Towards an institutional framework for dealing with plagiarism by students. *Journal of Further and Higher Education, 28*(3), 291–306. https://doi.org/10.1080/0309877042000241760

Sana, F., Weston, T., & Cepeda, N. J. (2013). Laptop multitasking hinders classroom learning for both users and nearby peers. *Computers and Education, 62*(1), 24–31. https://doi.org/10.1016/j.compedu.2012.10.003

Schneider, A. (1998, March 27). Insubordination and intimidation signal the end of decorum in many classrooms. *The Chronicle of Higher Education,* A12–A14.

Schroeder, N. (2016). *Grade inflation: Faculty lived-experiences and perceptions* (Publication No. ED566476) [Doctoral dissertation, Northcentral University]. ProQuest Dissertations & Theses Global.

Sorcinelli, M. D. (2002). Promoting civility in large classes. *Essays on Teaching Excellence Toward the Best in the Academy, 15*(8), 1–4.

Taylor, F. W. (1911). *Principles of scientific management.* Harper Brothers; McGraw-Hill.

Vogl-Bauer, S. (2014). When disgruntled students go to extremes: The cyberbullying of instructors. *Communication Education, 63*(4), 429–48. https://doi.org/10.1080/03634523.2014.942331

White, S. J. (2013). Student nurses harassing academics. *Nurse Education Today, 33*(1), 41–5. https://doi.org/10.1016/j.nedt.2011.11.004

Wirt, L. G., & Jaeger, A. J. (2014). Seeking to understand faculty-student interaction at community colleges. *Community College Journal of Research and Practice, 38*(11), 980–94. https://doi.org/10.1080/10668926.2012.725388

Yorke, J., Grant, S., & Csiernik, R. (2016). Horses and baseball: Social work's cultivation of one's "third eye." *Social Work Education, 35*(7), 845–55. https://doi.org/10.1080/02615479.2016.1189526

Contributors

Gail Baikie is an assistant professor at the School of Social Work at Dalhousie University in Nova Scotia. She has an MSW and is completing a PhD in Indigenous and decolonizing research methodologies and social work practices. Her recent areas of research include critical reflection methods, cross-worldview praxes, and the implications of natural resource development on marginalized women in northern communities. Before joining academia in 2002, Gail had a lengthy professional career focused on the healing and social development of Indigenous communities.

Stephanie L. Baird, MSW, PhD, RSW, is an assistant professor at the School of Social Work at King's University College at Western University in Ontario. Stephanie's research interests focus on trauma, intimate partner violence, and social work education. Her research is informed by her clinical and community social work practice.

Cyndy Baskin, PhD, is of Mi'kmaq and Celtic descent. Her clan is the fish and her spirit name translates as "The Woman Who Passes on the Teachings." She is an associate professor in the School of Social Work at Ryerson University in Ontario. Her teaching, research, and writing interests involve how Indigenous worldviews can inform education, spirituality, violence towards Indigenous women, and healing from trauma. Cyndy is the chair of Ryerson University's Aboriginal Education Council and the academic coordinator of the certificate in Aboriginal knowledges and experiences. She is the author of two novels; a textbook, which is now in its second edition; and numerous journal articles and book chapters. Cyndy also acts as a consultant in the area of Indigenous programming and services.

Laura Béres, MSW, RSW, PhD, is an associate professor in the School of Social Work at King's University College in Ontario. She writes in the areas of narrative therapy, spirituality, and critical reflection. Recent publications include *The Narrative Practitioner* (2014); an edited book, *Practising Spirituality: Reflections on Meaning-Making in Personal and Professional Contexts* (2016); and *Learning Critical Reflection: Experiences of the Transformative Learning Process* (2020), edited with Jan Fook. In addition, she recently completed a thesis for an MA in Christian spirituality on Teresa of Avila and Edith Stein, examining their conceptions of the soul and how those conceptions may contribute to ongoing discussions in postmodern therapeutic practices.

Rachel Birnbaum, MSW, LLM, PhD, is a professor, cross-appointed in childhood and social institutions (interdisciplinary programs) and social work at King's University College at Western University in Ontario. Rachel has over 25 years of clinical practice experience working with children and families of separation and/or divorce. Her research projects and publications involve interdisciplinary scholarship with colleagues in law, social work, medicine, and psychology. Rachel is a member of the Royal Society of Canada, College of New Scholars, Artists and Scientists; was the 2016 recipient of the Hugh Mellon Distinguished Research Award; and was the 2014 recipient of the Stanley Cohen Distinguished Research Award, given by an international interdisciplinary organization involved in family justice. She was the president of the Ontario College of Social Workers and Social Service Workers for four years, the president of the Canadian Council of Social Work Regulators for two years, and the president of the Association of Family and Conciliation Courts – Ontario, 2014–2015.

Marion Bogo is a professor at the Factor-Inwentash Faculty of Social Work, University of Toronto in Ontario. Her research focuses on social work education, including field education and the conceptualization and assessment of professional competence. She has published over 125 journal articles and book chapters and seven books, and was associate editor North America for *Social Work Education: The International Journal*. In 2013, the Council of Social Work Education, USA, awarded her the Significant Lifetime Achievement in Social Work Education Award. In 2014, she was appointed as an Officer of the Order of Canada for her achievements in social work as a scholar and teacher, and for advancing the practice in Canada and abroad. In May 2018, she received an honorary doctor of laws (*honoris causa*) from Memorial University in Newfoundland and Labrador.

Carolyn Campbell, PhD, was a faculty member for 25 years at the School of Social Work, Dalhousie University in Nova Scotia. She was awarded the Faculty of Health Professions Teaching Excellence Award (2012) and the Award for Excellence in Teaching from Dalhousie University (2015). Her scholarly work focuses on the scholarship of teaching and explores teaching theories and processes that are consistent with critical social work content. Carolyn co-chaired the CASWE-ACFTS Women's caucus for four years, and sat on several CASWE-ACFTS working groups. She served as a member of the board of directors for six years, three of those as president, and is currently leading a project under the auspices of the Educational Policy Committee to revise the educational policies and accreditation standards of the association.

Diana Coholic, PhD, RSW, is a clinical social worker and an associate professor in social work at Laurentian University in Ontario. She is an experienced qualitative researcher with a current focus on investigating the effectiveness of arts-based mindfulness methods for the improvement of resilience and self-concept in marginalized populations, especially youth. Her current SSHRC-funded project has her team working with youth 11–17 years old who are experiencing challenges with schooling. Further information on Diana's research can be found on her research website: https://www.dianacoholic.com.

Cassandra Cornacchia is the client services coordinator at the Centre for Mindfulness Studies, located in downtown Toronto. The central focus of her work there is to connect adults experiencing anxiety, depression, stress, and other mental health concerns to mindfulness-based mental health programs. Cassandra is in the process of becoming a certified facilitator of mindful self-compassion (MSC), a therapeutic modality rooted in learning how to treat yourself the way you would treat a close friend during times of suffering. Before her time at the Centre for Mindfulness Studies, Cassandra completed a bachelor and a master of social work at Ryerson University in Ontario. With the guidance of Dr. Cyndy Baskin and Joanne Dallaire, Elder and traditional counsellor, Cassandra completed a master's research project advocating and reflecting upon the necessity of integrating Indigenous women's voices on land protection into the field of social work from a European settler perspective. She aspires to continue to learn from and be deeply impacted by Indigenous worldviews, perspectives, and teachings so she can support the healing of relations.

Rick Csiernik, BSc, BSW, MSW, PhD, CCAC, RSW, professor, School of Social Work, King's University College at Western University in Ontario, has written and edited 14 books, including *Practising Social Work Research* for University of Toronto Press. He has authored over 200 peer-reviewed articles and book chapters and has presented at over 200 national and international conferences, workshops, and seminars. He has been part of research teams that have received over $4.5 million in funding and has been the recipient of both the King's University College and McMaster University Continuing Education Teaching Excellence Awards. Rick serves on the editorial boards of the *Journal of Teaching in Social Work*, *Social Work Practice in the Addictions*, and the *Journal of Workplace Behavioural Health* and was the 2019 recipient of the Hugh Mellon Excellence in Research Award.

Gissele Damiani-Taraba is the director of administration and quality assurance at Brant Family and Children's Services in Brantford, Ontario. She holds a master's degree in health research methods and an MSW from Wilfrid Laurier University in Ontario.

Nancy Freymond, PhD, is an associate professor and associate dean (MSW program) in the Faculty of Social Work of Wilfrid Laurier University in Ontario. She is interested in collaborative forms of child welfare research and pedagogies that honour lived experiences.

Scott Grant works as a social worker in mental health in Kitchener, Ontario. He engages in individual and group therapy with participants based upon his formal training from Wilfrid Laurier University and Laurentian University and through his lived experience as a consumer of mental health services. Scott has also taught micro-oriented social work classes at the college level.

Liz Grigg has worked as a teacher's assistant in both social work and labour studies at McMaster University in Ontario. Her social work practice has ranged from working in shelters for women to research and to systemic advocacy. Most recently, she has been engaged with research work concerning knowledge and the coloniality of power in international social work and resettlement in Canada. She lives in Treaty 6 Territory and works on the traditional lands of the Haudenosaunee and Anishnaabeg. This territory is covered by the Upper Canada Treaties, is within the lands protected by the "Dish With One Spoon" wampum agreement, and is directly adjacent to Haldiman Treaty territory.

Susan Hillock, BA, BSW, MEd, PhD, is an associate professor of social work at Trent University in Ontario. She teaches anti-oppressive theory and practice, as well as queer theory, social justice/change, intimate partner violence, trauma practice, feminism, structural social work, human rights, anti-racism, community development/organization, family practice, and diversability. From 2014 to 2016, as Trent's Department of Social Work director, she led the development and implementation of all aspects of a new four-year BSW program at Trent University and achieved CASWE-ACFTS pre-accreditation for the program. As well, she is the co-editor, with Nick J. Mulé, of the first North American book on *Queering Social Work Education* (2016). In 2018, Susan was also nominated for Trent University's Symons Award for Excellence in Teaching in recognition of outstanding teaching and exemplary concern for students. In 2019, Susan received the Ontario Confederation of University Faculty Association's Status of Women and Equity Award of Distinction, which recognizes outstanding OCUFA members whose work has contributed meaningfully to the advancement of professors, academic librarians, and/or academic staff who are Indigenous, women, racialized, LGBTQ2S+, living with disabilities, and/or belong to other historically marginalized groups.

Kathy Hogarth, PhD, is an associate professor in the School of Social Work at Renison University College, University of Waterloo, in Ontario. She is actively involved in teaching students at the undergraduate and graduate levels about the pedagogy of social change. She is well known for course designs that challenge students to become critical thinkers and to position themselves as agents of social change for the greater good of humanity. Beyond teaching in social work, Kathy is fully engaged in the practice of social change in her local community and also at national and international levels.

Daphne Jeyapal teaches in the School of Social Work and Human Service at Thompson Rivers University in British Columbia. Her research centres on challenging racial discrimination in social work, social activism, and Canadian social policy. She is the principal investigator for a SSHRC-funded study, "Anti-terrorism or Anti-activism?" that examines public and policy discourses on the criminalization of diasporic resistance in Canada. She is the co-editor, with Robert Harding, of *Canadian Social Policy for Social Workers* (Oxford University Press, 2019). She lives and works on the Tk'emlups te Secwepemc territory, the unceded traditional lands of the Secwepemc Nation.

Andrew Koster has 45 years of continual experience with various child welfare agencies in Ontario. He is presently the executive director of Brant Family and Children's Services in Ontario and past president of the

Child Welfare League of Canada. He has completed provincial reviews, authored reports, and testified in the cases of children who have died while under the care of child welfare agencies in a number of regions of Canada. He has also participated in projects and research that emphasize collaboration and engagement. Andrew has taught numerous social work courses at McMaster School of Social Work and is currently teaching for the MSW program at Renison College in Ontario while completing his PhD at Wilfrid Laurier University.

Sherri-Lynn Manto (Drinkwater) is a financial adviser, wife, mother, friend, and former "kid in care" who is trying to find her way. She studied business at Fanshawe College in Ontario and is a mentor with Brant Family and Children's Services in Ontario in their Youth LEAD (Learning, Experiencing, Advocating, Doing) program. She is a member of a youth advisory committee that aims to bring youth voices to child welfare governance. Sherri has a passion for helping people, and in her spare time, you may find her reading, gardening, or hosting family and friends for gatherings.

Claude Olivier, PhD, RSW, is an associate professor with the School of Social Work at King's University College in Ontario. His teaching and research interests include diversity, oppression and social inclusion, attachment and adoption, anti-oppressive and structural social work, and social work with groups and communities. His current research and practice centres around the use of theatre as a means of empowerment and bringing about social change. Claude has over a decade of experience working with community-based HIV/AIDS organizations in the delivery of front-line services and administration.

Sarah Robertson is the manager of learning and development, equity, and special projects with Brant Family and Children's Services in Ontario. She has been in the child welfare field for more than 20 years and has worked at various agencies in many different roles, including after-hour emergency services, intake, children services, family services, and screening, and as the manager of a community-based child protection team. Sarah has made several presentations on community-based child protection and has taught the Child Welfare Foundations training for new workers.

Leigh Savage, MSW, has been working at Brant Family and Children's Services in Ontario for 13 years in a variety of positions. She has been working as a community development coordinator for the past seven years within the Child Development Unit.

Bharati Sethi, PhD, is an assistant professor at King's University College, School of Social Work, Western University in Ontario, where she teaches policy and community practice to undergraduate and graduate students. Her research interests are fuelled by her lived experiences as an immigrant to Canada from India. She engages in community-based participatory research with immigrant communities. Bharati uses arts-based methodology to translate academic knowledge to community stakeholders. She is currently a co-investigator in three SSHRC-funded multi-site research projects ($450,000) on the impact of immigrant/refugee integration in Canada. She is also a co-investigator in a SSHRC/CIHR Partnership Project ($1.5 million) to mobilize and scale up the Canadian Standards Association Carer-Inclusive and Accommodating Organizations Standard. Her research has earned her several prestigious community and academic awards.

Marilee Sherry, MSW, RSW, has been employed by Brant Family and Children's Services in Brantford in Ontario since 1998. Before becoming the family group conferencing/family group decision making (FGC/FGDM) coordinator and manager for the family group decision making team in 2005, she was a front-line child protection worker and manager primarily in community-based settings. She is a FGC/FGDM trainer and mentor for new coordinators in Ontario and has provided training for coordinators in New Brunswick and the United States. Her passion is transforming child welfare through the leadership of the children and their families who are receiving child welfare services, particularly through FGC/FGDM. She has been focused on embedding these values and principles in the child welfare system locally and provincially. Marilee has her BA from St. Francis Xavier University in Nova Scotia and her MSW from Wilfrid Laurier University in Ontario.

Tanya Shute is a lecturer at Laurentian University's School of Social Work in Ontario. Before her post at Laurentian, Tanya worked front-line in shelter and drop-in services for women escaping violence, homelessness community development, and community mental health and addictions services for 20 years. She also taught full-time in community studies and social services programs for Seneca College in Ontario for several years after leaving the service field. Tanya's research interests are in community-based research projects and collaborations that serve local and grassroots organization and community development needs and priorities, specifically around community health, poverty, housing and homelessness, and consumer/survivor initiatives and movements. She also studies social work pedagogy and transformative vocational education.

Tracy Smith Carrier, BA(Hon), BEd, MSW, PhD, is an associate professor and the graduate program coordinator in the School of Social Work at King's University College at Western University in Ontario. Tracy's program of research touches upon a number of different fields in the social policy arena, including access to social welfare benefits, social assistance receipt, food in/security, basic income, and poverty. Tracy is a contributing researcher with the London Poverty Research Centre at King's, chair of the Basic Income Guarantee London Chapter, and co-director of the Multidisciplinary Applied Research Centre at King's.

Akin Taiwo was born in Nigeria. He earned degrees in political science and philosophy before becoming a social worker and obtaining his PhD from the University of Windsor in Ontario. Akin has worked as a therapist and an administrator in a variety of clinical settings in Canada. He has also taught social work courses at both the graduate and the undergraduate levels at King's University College in Ontario, the University of Windsor in Ontario, and the University of Detroit Mercy in the United States. His research interests include political social work, social justice and social change, multicultural practice with diverse populations, and social work poetics.

Anne E. Wagner, PhD, is an associate professor at Nipissing University in Ontario in the Department of Social Work. Her research interests include anti-oppressive social work practice, critical approaches to higher education, neo-liberalism in academia, and critical pedagogies.

June Ying Yee is an associate professor at Ryerson University's School of Social Work in Ontario, as well as the academic coordinator of the Internationally Educated Social Work Professionals Bridging Program. Her professional and scholarly research interests are in the areas of health, education, child welfare, and organizational change processes in social services.

Jan Yorke, BA, MSW, PhD, is an associate professor in the School of Social Work at Laurentian University in Ontario. Since 1973, she has worked as a front-line mental health/substance use crisis worker, a withdrawal management/hospital department director, and a tenured faculty member. Her current areas of interest are therapeutic communication (simulation in social work education, human animal interaction, and bio-behavioural interaction), ecological social work, substance use and abuse (crisis intervention and at-risk populations), and LGBTQ advocacy. The environment and its impact on healing and change are factors that figure prominently in her work. She has explored the impact equine-human interaction has on bio-behavioural responses of children suffering from PTSD. She facilitated the consultation process for HIV/AIDS strategies for the Province of Nova Scotia (2000), emphasizing rural, First Nations, and Afro-Nova Scotian community recommendations. Along with community stakeholders, she has recently completed a study on the health needs of rural men who have sex with men.